THE
NEW
AGE

THE NEW AGE

Notes of a Fringe Watcher

Martin Gardner

PROMETHEUS BOOKS
Buffalo, New York

Published 1991 by Prometheus Books

95 94 93 92 91   5 4 3 2 1

Library of Congress Cataloging-in-Publication Data

Gardner, Martin, 1914–
    The new age: notes of a fringe watcher/by
Martin Gardner
    p.   cm.
    Includes index.
    ISBN 0-87975-644-6
    1. Psychical research—Controversial literature. 2. Occultism—
Controversial literature. 3. New Age movement—Controversial
literature. 4. Science—Miscellanea. 5. Impostors and imposture—
Miscellanea. I. Title.
BF1042.G22   1988
133—dc19   87-35967
                                                                CIP

Printed in the United States of America on acid-free paper

To Paul Kurtz,
a friend whose vision,
courage, and integrity
began it all

Contents

Preface

My first column in the *Skeptical Inquirer,* a lively, fast-growing quarterly devoted to reporting and debunking fringe science, was in the Summer 1983 issue. I have been writing the column ever since. At first it was headed "Notes of a Psi-Watcher." This was later changed to "Notes of a Fringe-Watcher" so that I could discuss topics outside the narrow range of psi (psychic) research.

Part 1 of this anthology is a reprinting in chronological order of my first nineteen columns. At the end of most of them I have added an Afterword to update the material and take advantage of welcome feedback from readers. Part 2 consists of fourteen articles and book reviews about pseudoscience that appeared in various magazines.

Readers interested in my other writings about fringe science will find them in *Fads and Fallacies in the Name of Science* (Dover), *Science: Good, Bad and Bogus,* and, a few chapters of *Order and Surprise.* The last two books are published by Prometheus Books and have Oxford University Press softcover editions in the United Kingdom.

For information about how to subscribe to the *Skeptical Inquirer,* write to Post Office Box 229, Buffalo, NY 14215-0229.

THE NEW AGE

PART 1

1 | Project Alpha

Foreword

This, the first of my columns in the *Skeptical Inquirer,* requires considerable background to be understood. In 1979, a year before his death, James McDonnell, chairman of the board of McDonnell Douglas Corporation, gave half a million dollars to Washington University, in St. Louis. The grant was for establishing a laboratory to study psychic phenomena. Peter Phillips, a physicist at the university, was put in charge.

As all magicians know, physicists are among the easiest people in the world to be fooled by magic tricks. They are so used to working with Mother Nature, who never cheats, that when confronted with the task of testing a psychic charlatan they have no comprehension of how to set up adequate controls. To prove this, magician James Randi, long a foe of psychic flimflam, prepared an elaborate hoax. He arranged for two teen-age magicians, Steven Shaw and Michael Edwards, to separately visit the McDonnell Laboratory for Psychic Research, or "McLab," as it became known. For almost two years Phillips and his associates were convinced that the boys possessed amazing psi powers.

At an annual convention of parapsychologists at Syracuse University in 1981, Phillips delivered a research report in which he described how the boys had bent metal objects, produced streaks of light on film, caused a clock to slide off a table, turned a motor under a glass dome, made fuses blow, and similar wonders. In 1983 Randi exposed the hoax at a large press conference in Manhattan.

How did Shaw move the clock? He told laboratory scientists that he did it by imagining he had an invisible thread stretched between his hands. What he didn't tell them was that he actually *did* have an invisible thread stretched between his hands! How did the boys move the motor? They secretly raised an edge of the glass dome by an imperceptible amount, then blew through the opening!

Before the hoax was exposed, the *National Enquirer* gave the lads marvelous publicity. Berthold Schwartz, a parapsychologist who served as a McLab consultant, told the tabloid (December 22, 1981): "It is an understatement to say that he [Shaw] is one of the best psychics in the world. There is just nobody like him in the field. He is a prodigy." Another parapsychologist, Walter Uphoff, declared (January 19, 1981) that Edwards "is certainly one of the strongest, most exciting psychics in the world. . . . He has passed all kinds of stringent tests before 18 people, including metallurgists, physicists, and psychiatrists."

Uphoff detailed many cases of spontaneous metal distortions that occurred when Edwards visited his laboratory in Oregon, Wisconsin: A fingernail file bent, one prong of a pair of tweezers twisted, a paperclip on the floor bent into an M shape, a wire coat-hanger wrapped itself around the bar of a closet. "I am convinced," said the gullible Uphoff, "that the experiences we had with him were genuine."

Randi's revelation that Shaw and Edwards were magicians received widespread media coverage. I will cite only the more outstanding articles: "Magicians Score a Hit on Scientific Researchers" (*Washington Post,* March 1, 1983), "Psychic Abscam" (*Discover,* March 1983), "Magician's Effort to Foil Scientists Raises Questions" (*New York Times,* February 15, 1983), "The Amazing Randi Hoodwinks the Spoon-benders" (*New Scientist,* February 3, 1983), and Randi's two-part article "The Project Alpha Experiment" (*Skeptical Inquirer,* Summer and Fall, 1983).

The McDonnell Foundation closed down McLab in 1985. "Psyched Out" was the headline of a long obituary in the *St. Louis Post-Dispatch* (August 18, 1985). Uphoff, who never gives up, told the paper that even though the boys admitted cheating it didn't prove they have no psychic powers. Phillips was reported to be studying Chinese so he could visit China to check out reports of children who, after being blindfolded, read the writing on papers that are folded and stuck in their ears or under their armpits.

It should be said that no leading parapsychologists, so far as I know, went on record as saying they thought Shaw and Edwards were genuine psychics, or even that they thought competent research was under way at McLab. Perhaps their early enthusiasm for Uri Geller had taught them something.

In 1986 Randi was given a MacArthur Foundation grant of $272,000 to continue his admirable work in debunking bunkum.

My column follows.

Was Randi's Alpha Project unethical? I think not, but before explaining why, let's consider a few past instances in which deception was used to demonstrate the incompetence of researchers.

Early this century René Blondlot, a respected French physicist, announced his discovery of a new type of radiation, which he called "N-rays," after the University of Nancy where he worked. Dozens of papers on N-rays were soon being published in France, but American physicists were dubious. One skeptic, a physicist at Johns Hopkins University, Robert W. Wood, enjoyed playing practical jokes, especially jokes on spirit mediums. His humorous book *How to Tell the Birds from the Flowers* is still in print. Perhaps you have seen on television a little pinheaded, bald creature with a huge flexible mouth that is produced by painting eyes and a nose on someone's chin, then viewing the chin upside-down. It was Wood who invented this whimsical illusion.

In 1904 Wood made a trip to Nancy to observe N-ray research first-hand. In one experiment he secretly removed from the apparatus an essential prism. This had no effect on what the experimenters said they were observing. In another test Wood surreptitiously substituted a piece of wood for a steel file that was supposed to be giving off N-rays. The imagined radiation continued to be reported by the Nancy scientists. Wood told his hosts nothing about either prank. Instead, he went home and wrote a devastating account of his visit for the British magazine *Nature*. It was a knockout blow to N-rays everywhere except at Nancy.

The reaction of the Nancy group to Wood's disclosures was well summed up by Irving Klotz in his fine article "The N-ray Affair," *Scientific American,* May 1980:

> According to Blondlot and his disciples, then, it was the sensitivity of the observer rather than the validity of the phenomena that was called into question by criticisms such as Wood's, a point of view that will not be unfamiliar to those who have followed more recent controversies concerning extrasensory perception. By 1905, when only French scientists remained in the N-ray camp, the argument began to acquire a somewhat chauvinistic aspect. Some proponents of N-rays maintained that only the Latin races possessed the sensitivities (intellectual as well as sensory) necessary to detect manifestations of the rays. It was alleged that Anglo-Saxon powers of perception were dulled by continual exposure to fog and Teutonic ones blunted by constant ingestion of beer.

When N-rays became a huge embarrassment to French science, the journal *Revue Scientifique* proposed a definitive test that would settle the matter. "Permit me to decline totally," Blondlot responded, ". . . to cooperate in this simplistic experiment. The phenomena are much too delicate for that. Let each one form his own personal opinion about N-rays, either from his own experiments or from those of others in whom he has confidence." Like Percival Lowell, the American astronomer who drew elaborate maps of Martian canals, Blondlot could not prevent his strong desires from strongly biasing his observations. He lived another quarter-century. If he had any doubts about N-rays, so far as I know he never expressed them.

Move ahead to 1974. J. B. Rhine had appointed Walter J. Levy, 26, his successor as director of his laboratory. Levy was already famous in psi circles for his "carefully controlled" investigations of animal-psi. (One of them suggested that embryos in chicken eggs had psychokinetic [PK] powers.) Three members of Rhine's staff were suspicious of Levy's string of successes. What did they do? They set a cruel trap. While Levy was testing the PK ability of rats to alter a randomizer, they watched through a peephole and saw Levy repeatedly beef up the scores by pulling a plug. Better yet, they installed another set of instruments, without Levy's knowledge, that kept an accurate score. The untampered record showed no evidence of PK. Levy confessed, and vanished from the psi scene.

To me the saddest aspect of this scandal was not Levy's deserved disgrace but the fact that it had never occurred to Rhine to check on Levy's honesty. Rhine himself was deeply shaken by the revelations. If the trap had not been set, Levy's papers would still be cited as strong evidence for animal-psi.

There are two reasons why traps to detect fraud are more essential in PK research than anywhere else. First, the claims are far more extra-ordinary and therefore require much stronger evidence. Second, the field has always been soaked with fraud. In the days when eminent physicists were convinced of the reality of floating tables and glowing ectoplasm, an enormous service to science was performed by Houdini and others who were capable of setting traps for the mediums and willing to do so.

This brings us to the main moral of Randi's hilarious hoax. Paranormal metal-bending is so fantastic a violation of natural laws that the first task of any competent experimenter is to determine whether a psychic who bends spoons is cheating or not. In England, when physicists John Taylor and John Hasted were convinced that scads of children could twist cutlery by PK, one would have expected the two scientists to devise some elementary traps, but they did not. The only good trap was set by two scientists at the University of Bath who did not even mean to set it. Puzzled by the fact that no one ever *sees* metal bend—Taylor called it the "shyness effect"— they put some spoon-bending youngsters in a room, then filmed them through a one-way mirror. The purpose was not to embarrass the children, but to record the shyness effect. To their amazement, they saw the children cheating. Taylor soon became disenchanted, but such revelations had no effect on Hasted's mind-set. Some spoon-benders cheat, so what? Not in *his* laboratory. You can read all about his naive experiments in his recently published book, *The Metal Benders.*

Hasted and Phillips typify psychic research at its shabbiest. In spite of many letters from Randi telling him that his two young subjects were frauds, Phillips made no effort to check on their backgrounds. Not until the very end, after Randi had severely criticized Phillips's videotapes, did he start to tighten controls. Of course the wonders ceased. On many occasions when controls were unbelievably lax, the two "psychics" suspected a trap. It was never sprung. They overestimated the acumen of their monitors.

Peter Phillips

Think what the results might have been had the boys decided to become professional psychics. They would have left Phillips's lab complaining that excessive controls were inhibiting their powers. Soon they would be appearing on television documentaries as wonder workers whose powers had been validated by respected scientists. Uri Geller never tires of talking about how the Stanford Research Institute (now SRI International) validated his psychic abilities. Phillips's two young subjects are even better than Geller. One of them invented a way to make one tine of a fork visibly and unshyly bend that is superior to any of Geller's crude methods. When Steven Shaw demonstrated this lovely illusion at Randi's Manhattan press conference, the entire audience gasped. "Can you tell us how you did that?" a startled reporter asked. Shaw walked to the mike and said, "I cheat." It brought down the house.

It is to Phillips's credit that he had the courage to say (*Washington Post,* March 1, 1983), "I should have taken Randi's advice." It is to the credit of parapsychologist Stanley Krippner, a true believer in PK if ever there was one, that he called Randi's project "a much-needed" experiment. It remained for sociologist Marcello Truzzi to start a hue and cry about how Randi had engaged in unethical sabotage of a legitimate research program. "Randi is hurting the field with his gross exaggeration," Truzzi told the *New York Times* (February 15, 1983). "In no way will his project teach psychic researchers a lesson and make them more likely to trust magicians' advice. Quite the contrary. This outside policeman thing sets up magicians as the enemy."

On this point Truzzi may be right. I, too, would be surprised if psychic researchers suddenly decided to study conjuring or to seek the active help of knowledgeable magicians. Conjurors are indeed the enemy. Their bad vibes alone are enough to kill any PK powers just by their being there as observers; perhaps (as has actually been suggested) even their *reading* about the experiments afterward influences the outcome by backward causality! But perhaps Randi's scam will have a salutary effect on funding. After all, the half-million bucks the McDonnell Foundation gave to Washington University could have gone to worthwhile research instead of down the drain to a group unqualified to investigate metal bending.

Am I saying that all psychic researchers should be trained in magic, or seek the aid of magicians, before they test miracle workers? That is exactly what I am saying. The most eminent scientist, untrained in magic, is putty in the hands of a clever charlatan. Without the help of professional deceivers—the conjurors—no testing of a superpsychic is worth ten cents of funding. That is the big lesson of Randi's hoax. That is why it is likely to become a landmark in the history of PK research.

2 | Margaret Mead

Margaret Mead, who died in 1978, was an intelligent, energetic anthropologist of strong convictions. No one can question the sincerity and dedication of her work or that her influence on public opinion in many fields was as refreshing as it was admirable. This year (1983), as a result of Derek Freeman's book *Margaret Mead and Samoa*, grave doubts have been cast on the soundness of her earlier field studies. Freeman marshals compelling evidence that when Mead investigated Samoan culture she had little comprehension of the need for stern measures to suppress what is now called the "experimenter effect"—the unconscious tendency of researchers to bias data in the direction of intensely held beliefs.

In the publicity surrounding Freeman's attack, surprisingly little has been said about Mead's lifelong interest in the paranormal. I have made no attempt to research this aspect of her life, so what follows is based only on books, notes, and clippings at hand.

In an interview published in this country's leading occult magazine, *New Realities* (vol. 2, no. 2, 1978), Mead spoke of a great-great aunt (Louisiana Priscilla Ramsay) who was said to have the ability to float about rooms, diagnose ills, and read minds. Her family, said Mead, accepted these phenomena as genuine. In her autobiography, *Blackberry Winter*, Mead refers to her aunt as "one who could read people's minds."

As a young anthropologist, Mead's field studies persuaded her that "special gifts" of this sort were common in primitive cultures. Do some cultures have a larger percentage of psychics than others? No, Mead told *New Realities*, cultures differ mainly in how they treat their psychics. Some encourage them, some repress them. "But I didn't find in them any more cases of what you'd call great sensitives than what you'd find here." In Appalachia, she added, children with psychic gifts are taught to conceal them. "It's a great protection, for there's nobody who's more of a nuisance than a psychic child."

In 1942 the American Society for Psychical Research recognized Mead's interest in psi by electing her a trustee (see the society's journal, April 1942),

and in 1946 she was appointed to its research committee (ibid., April 1946). In 1969 the American Association for the Advancement of Science, largely because of Mead's passionate advocacy, voted to allow the Parapsychological Association (founded by J. B. Rhine) to become a member organization.

For sixteen years (1963 to 1979) Mead wrote a monthly column for *Redbook* magazine. In the October 1967 issue she spoke of field work in cultures where "trance behavior is an everyday occurrence" and said it was her impression "that when individuals are specially chosen, they have extraordinary capacities for exercising the special supernatural powers exhibited under trance." In a later column (March 1977) she described the fantastic upsurge of interest among young people in such practices as astrology and numerology. Although she deplores these obsessions, she thinks they signal a healthy dissolving of barriers that have too long isolated the scientific community from serious investigations of psi:

And on this growing edge of knowledge, scientists are devising experiments that may—almost certainly *will*—give us, in time, new insight into the powers attributed to seers and clairvoyants, to those who have the power to "see" auras, to communicate with plants, to dream or visualize events outside the bounds of time. . . . Here the most open-minded scientists and the most open-minded believers in occultism can meet and carry out experiments in the atmosphere of expectant, skeptical but also meticulous, careful exploration. We are living on the edge of the unknown. . . .

Interviewed by the *New Yorker's* "Talk of the Town" (March 7, 1977), Mead declared: "Dowsing is a fact, you know." When her interviewer expressed doubts, she added: "Oh, yes. There are people who can dowse, because they have a greater sensitivity to the changes within the physical world. Some people can do it and some people can't."

At the 1974 meeting of the American Anthropological Association, Joseph K. Long organized a symposium on psi research and later edited the papers for a collection titled *Extrasensory Ecology: Parapsycholgy and Anthropology* (Scarecrow Press, 1977). Speaking on "An Anthropological Approach to Different Types of Communication" Mead argued that belief and disbelief should be irrelevant in investigating psi. She strongly objected to such terms as *extrasensory* and *paranormal* because they suggest forces beyond the reach of science. *Other-sensory* would be a better term. She recommended that psi research be part of normal anthropology, not a separate discipline.

One of the great difficulties of such research, Mead said, is that if psi is a normal aspect of a culture's rituals and belief system it is almost impossible to distinguish genuine psi from the counterfeit. Shamans, for example, constantly resort to trickery. Mead startled her audience by revealing that in all her studies of Bali and of the Manus of New Guinea, she had never encountered a single instance she could positively classify as telepathy, clairvoyance, precognition, or psychokinesis. The only possible exception was an instance of precognition "by a drop of oil on a fingernail" that a collaborator had reported. It is much easier, she said, to recognize genuine sensitives in a modern culture where disbelief is prevalent.

"How much intensive research may be needed to find a sensitive when a whole village goes into a trance, or when a whole cult group becomes healers, is a matter for further exploration. But exploration should not be hampered by claims that involve belief or disbelief." Such claims, said Mead, only muddle research. "The point is whether we can find ways of studying these phenomena which will make them as accessible as the stars or chromosomes."

In her introduction to *Mind-Reach* (1977), a now largely discredited book by Harold Puthoff and Russell Targ in which they describe their amateurish testing of Uri Geller and other self-proclaimed psychics, Mead has no reservations about the significance of their work. It demonstrates, she writes, the existence of a "hitherto unvalidated capacity." Their controls, she says, "far outstrip the normal procedures to guarantee scientific credibility." Their investigations are as sound as "the study of communication among bees." Experiments in which psychics describe a "target area" *before* the area has been randomly selected are taken by Mead as strong evidence for precognition. Suppose one precognizes a train wreck. Does this mean that death can be avoided by not taking the train? As Mead correctly perceives, this raises deep questions about determinism and free will. "This issue is not yet faced," she writes, "by the experimenters, but will, I understand, be on their future agenda."

The most embarrassing of Mead's *Redbook* columns was surely the one she wrote for the September 1974 issue in answer to the question, "Do you believe in UFOs?" Her answer is an unqualified yes. That there are waves of "visits" by UFOs, she writes, "seems incontestable." Of course many sightings are hoaxes, but this no more proves that all are hoaxes than similar arguments "demolish the evidence of psychic phenomena. Just because fake mediums sitting in darkened rooms can induce gullible dupes to shake hands with cold, sand-filled rubber gloves, there is no reason to deny the reality of psychic phenomena we cannot yet explain."

Assuming that UFOs are from outer space, she continues, fascinating questions arise: "What are they doing?" and "Why don't they declare themselves?" There is, she adds, "some possible evidence of occasional landings. There is a giant crater in the Soviet Union that cannot be explained by any existing meteorological or geological knowledge. And there are unexplained accounts of brief landings."

What purpose "lies behind the activities of these quiet, harmlessly cruising objects that time and again approach the earth? The most likely explanation, it seems to me, is that they are simply watching what we are up to—that a responsible society outside our solar system is keeping an eye on us to see that we don't set in motion a chain reaction that might have repercussions far outside our solar system." However, Mead cautions, we cannot be certain there is intelligent life aboard the UFOs. "They may well be unmanned vehicles controlled from elsewhere in space." An editor's note adds that Dr. Mead recommends to *Redbook* readers two "helpful" books: *Man's Contact with UFOs,* by Ralph and Judy Blum, and *Challenge to Science: The UFO Enigma,* by Jacques and Janine Vallee.

Mead could not have picked two more worthless volumes. The Blums said in their introduction: "We predict that by 1975 the government will release definite proof that extraterrestrials are watching us." Philip Klass at once wrote to Ralph Blum proposing a $10,000 wager on this, even extending the time to the end of 1976. Blum never replied.

I have given only sketchy hints of Mead's beliefs about the paranormal. How did she integrate them with her Christian beliefs? In the lengthy article on Mead in the *Biographical Supplement* of the *International Encyclopedia of the Social Sciences,* she is described as "a devout, practicing Episcopalian . . . not only an active laywoman in the Episcopal Church, but also in many ecumenical committees, conferences, and activities of both the National Council and the World Council of Churches." When Mead was asked in *Redbook* (May 1963) if she believed in God, she answered with one word: "Yes." Perhaps someone who knew Mead well will someday tell us in detail about these little-publicized facets in the philosophy of one of this century's most colorful and influential anthropologists.

Afterword

"It may come as a surprise," writes Robert Cassidy, opening a chapter on religion in *Margaret Mead* (1982), "that Margaret Mead was a deeply religious person." Just what Cassidy meant by the word *religious,* however, remains obscure. Reacting against the agnosticism of her parents, Margaret joined the Episcopal church when she was 11. Throughout her life she was active in church affairs, but in what sense was she a believing Episcopalian?

It is characteristic of today's Laodicean Christian culture (with the exception, of course, of fundamentalist and evangelical groups) that one can profess a faith in any Protestant denomination, or even Roman Catholicism, and such a declaration will convey no information about one's doctrinal beliefs. When Mead said she believed in God, did she mean the personal God of Jesus, the pantheistic God of Spinoza, Hegel, and Paul Tillich, or the "God" of atheist John Dewey?

Cassidy's biography, and two later biographies—*Margaret Mead* by Jane Howard and *With a Daughter's Eye* by Mead's daughter Mary Bateson—fail to answer this simple question. We learn a great deal about Margaret's secular passions—for a world state, for helping the poor, for combating injustice, for limiting population growth, for cleaning up the environment, and so on—admirable goals that any secular humanist could applaud. We learn of her fondness for gays and that she herself was bisexual. Thrice married, she had numerous affairs with both men and women, the most intense and lasting with her mentor Ruth Benedict.

I confess I am less interested in who Margaret slept with than in who or what she worshipped. My guess is that, like George Santayana, she managed to combine her secular humanism with a lifelong fondness for high church ritual. According to her daughter, she kept a Saint Christopher medal on her key ring. Maybe she thought it would protect her even if she didn't believe in it.

"When I say I am a Christian," Mead once declared, "it doesn't mean I am not a Moslem, not a Buddhist, not a Jew." In what sense, then, was she a Christian? A collection of 16 of her papers on religious topics was published by Harper & Row in 1972 under the title *Twentieth Century Faith.* You will not find anywhere in this book what Mead believed with respect to any Christian doctrine. In the final chapter, "The Immortality of Man," she discusses three views of the afterlife: Christian, Eastern reincarnation, and the secular view that one lives on only in the influence one has on history. There is no hint as to which view she favored.

In 1978, knowing she was dying of cancer, Mead began seeing daily a Chilean psychic healer in New York who called herself the "Reverend Carmen diBarazza." *The Star*, a sleazy competitor of the *National Enquirer*, headlined an October 31, 1978, story: "Famed Scientist Calls Faith Healer to Bedside in Bid to Beat Cancer."

Mead had been introduced to Carmen by her good friends Robert L. Schwartz and Jean Houston. Schwartz heads the Tarrytown Group, in Tarrytown, New York, a forum that sponsors workshops and a newsletter stressing all aspects of the "New Age" movement—holistic medicine, parapsychology, psychic phenomena, and so on. Schwartz and Mead cofounded the group. A promotional leaflet sent to me a few years ago begins: "This is your invitation to join a worldwide bunch of cranks and crazies. . . . It is your opportunity to network with some of the most irreverent thinkers on earth. . . . "

Jean Houston, a glamorous former actress and author of many New Age books on consciousness-expanding, is cofounder and codirector with her husband of the Foundation for Mind Research, in Pomona, New York. Margaret was president of the foundation's board of directors. The foundation's laboratory contains a variety of devices for altering consciousness, but none more innovative than a modernized version of what in the Middle Ages was called a "witches' cradle," reportedly used by witches for inducing visions. The subject is strapped into a swing and blindfolded with sleep goggles. As the body sways, the mind is said to go on strange trips. Houston and Masters call it their ASCID (Altered State of Consciousness Induction Device).

Jean is reported to be writing a book about her close mother-daughter-like relationship with Margaret. Perhaps she will address, as Mead's biographers have not, the interesting question of what experiences and metaphysical underpinnings made it possible for Mead to combine her Episcopalianism with occultism, and with her conviction that benevolent aliens are visiting the Earth from outer space.

3 | Magicians in the Psi Lab

Harry Collins, a University of Bath sociologist, is best known for his extreme relativistic philosophy of science (see my review of *Frames of Meaning,* which he coauthored, in the Fall 1983 issue of *Free Inquiry*), and for having caught a group of spoon-bending children at cheating. The *New Scientist* (June 30, 1983) printed his "Magicians in the Laboratory: A New Role to Play," in which he discusses what he calls the "vexed relationship" between magicians and psi researchers. His article contains many misconceptions about magic; but, before detailing them, first a sketch of his views.

Randi's recent Project Alpha, Collins writes, has reminded us again of how easily psi researchers can be hoodwinked. Because the history of paranormal research has been riddled with fraud, Collins wisely recommends that, no matter how innocent a subject may appear, experiments must be designed on the assumption that the subject is "a notorious cheat." Unfortunately, he adds, completely fraud-proof tests are impossible because there is no way to anticipate new methods of cheating. Since magicians know standard ways, they can be enormously useful as advisors. But because they are not much better than nonmagicians in spotting new methods they are of little value as observers.

He feels that magicians should not be allowed to monitor experiments because they are usually unfriendly toward psi research and have a vested interest in seeing psychics discredited. Collins doesn't mention the belief of most parapsychologists that hostile observers inhibit psi phenomena, but even aside from this he thinks magicians would have a damaging effect on experiments if they were allowed to monitor them.

How, then, can conjurors help? One way, Collins says, is by breaking their code of secrecy and explaining to researchers how cheating can be done. If magicians are unwilling to do this, they should serve as "protocol breakers," by demonstrating the same paranormal phenomena under the same controls applied to the psychic. If they fail to break the protocol, this "would act as a certificate of competence in experimental design."

Misconception 1: Collins fails to distinguish stage performers from magicians who specialize in close-up magic. Throughout his article he repeatedly refers to "stage magicians" and "illusionists." The distinction is vital, because the methods used by psychic charlatans have almost nothing in common with stage magic. Although psychics like Uri Geller and Nina Kulagina may use a few concealed "gimmicks" (magnets, "invisible" thread, nail writers, palmed mirrors, and so on), for the most part they perform close-up magic that requires no apparatus.

Some stage magicians are knowledgeable about close-up magic, but not all are. A stage performer is essentially an actor playing the role of a magician, relying for his miracles on costly equipment designed by others. Any good actor could easily take over Doug Henning's role in the Broadway musical *Merlin,* for example, and the stage illusions would work just as well. It is important for psi researchers to know this. Otherwise they might seek the help of a prominent stage performer who has less knowledge of close-up magic than thousands of amateurs.

Misconception 2: Collins is persuaded that magicians are not much better than scientists in spotting new ways to cheat. He concedes that "skilled practitioners of deception" may be better than scientists at seeing loopholes develop in an experiment, but he adds, "I think it would be hard to demonstrate this."

On the contrary, it is easy to demonstrate. Collins could convince himself of this simply by accompanying someone like Randi to a magic convention at which dealers demonstrate new tricks for the first time and see how he compares with Randi in figuring them out. It is true that magicians sometimes fool other magicians, but not often and not for long. The "magicians's magician" who enjoys inventing tricks to fool his colleagues bears no resemblance to the psychic charlatan. The charlatan is usually a mediocre performer who has hit on some crude methods of deception all his own—methods that are transparent almost at once to any knowledgeable close-up magician who sees the charlatan perform.

When new tricks come on the market, dealers like to advertise them in magic periodicals with glowing descriptions that seem to rule out all standard methods. Magicians are often extremely good in guessing the modus operandi from the ad, without even seeing the trick performed. Of course, if they actually *saw* the trick demonstrated, it would be enormously easier. And if they saw it more than once, it would be a rare trick indeed that would resist unraveling.

A few years ago my friend Persi Diaconis, a statistician who is also a skilled card magician, telephoned to say that a certain Oriental conjuror was appearing that night on television and would be performing a sensational new trick with a silk. The silk is twisted like a rope, cut in half, the halves rolled into a ball, and when unrolled, the silk is restored. Persi had not yet seen the trick, but had heard it described by puzzled magicians. After discussing several methods, we finally agreed on what we thought was the most probable technique. When we watched the show that night, our hypothesis was verified. The point is that we guessed the method before we even saw the trick.

Sometimes it is impossible to guess from a description. When I was a young man in Chicago, Joe Berg's magic shop advertised a miracle called the "none-such ribbon effect." A ribbon, the ad said, is cleanly cut in half and the ends widely separated. After the restoration, the ribbon is the same length as before. No ribbon is added or taken away, and no adhesives, magnets, or other secret aids are needed. I was unable to guess the method. A few days later, in Joe's shop, I asked him to demonstrate the trick. As soon as he did, I understood. I am free to give away the secret because this clinker of a trick has never been performed by a magician, and never will be. The "ribbon" proved to be crepe paper. It was genuinely cut, the halves folded into a parcel, one half palmed away, then the other half was pulled out of the fist in such a manner that it stretched to twice it's original length!

New methods of deception are invariably based on ancient general principles that any experienced conjuror knows in his bones. No magician could have witnessed the none-such ribbon effect without seeing at once how it worked, even though no one had ever before thought of restoring a ribbon in this peculiar way. Scientists are helpless at the hands of a clever charlatan, whether he uses old or new methods, but knowledgeable magicians are far from helpless regardless of how unorthodox the new methods may be. Their ability to detect fraud by novel techniques is vastly superior to that of any investigator without a magic background, even if he has a high I.Q. and a Nobel Prize.

Misconception 3: The suggestion that magicians should advise but not observe is naive. Until a magician actually sees a clever psychic perform, he is in a poor position to know what controls should be adopted. It is no good to rely on a scientist's memory of what he saw, because such memories are notoriously faulty. Good magic is carefully designed to conceal a trick's most essential aspects, and even what a magician says is planned to make a spectator forget crucial details. The medium Henry Slade, for example, was once tested by a group of scientists. No one recalled afterward that a slate had "accidentally" slipped out of Slade's hands and dropped on the rug. Yet it was at just this instant that Slade switched slates. Magicians are alert to such misdirection. Nonmagicians are not. Incidentally, in Slade's day many scientists were totally convinced that his slate writing was genuine.

Is it not curious that chalked messages appearing on slates have disappeared from the repertoire of modern psychics?

Conjurors obviously can be of great help in designing protocols, but if a charlatan is using new methods, or performing a feat never before performed (such as "thoughtographer" Ted Serios's trick with Polaroid cameras), it is almost essential that he be observed initially by a magician. True, in many cases a committee of magicians may, on the basis of a careful, accurate description of a psychic's performance, figure out how the psychic could be cheating and suggest adequate controls. In some cases, however, the memories of psi researchers are too vague and flawed to permit such reconstruction. Only by seeing the psychic do his or her thing can the magician make intelligent guesses and not waste the researcher's time by suggesting 20 different ways the psychic could have cheated. Of course it is essential that a psychic not know a magician is present. Psi powers have a way of evaporating even if the psychic only suspects a magician may be present. The reason D. D. Home was seldom caught cheating was that Home took extreme precautions to perform miracles only in the presence of persons he knew to be untrained in magic.

Suppose a club suspects a member of cheating at card games. How should members go about catching him? It is folly to ask an expert on card-swindling to design precautions, because there are thousands of ways to cheat. I can show you 50 ways to false-shuffle a deck, and as many ways of getting secret peeks of top and bottom cards. Persi can demonstrate twenty different ways to deal the second card instead of the top one, some by using only one hand. There are dozens of subtle ways to mark certain cards in the course of a game. Nor is it feasible for a card "mechanic" to give club members an adequate course in cheating. It would require many months. Obviously nothing is gained by having the mechanic sit in on games if the hustler knows who he is. And how can club members be sure that the hustler doesn't know?

The fact is that there is only one good way to settle the matter. A trap must be set. Let the expert observe a game secretly, either through a peephole or a carefully constructed one-way mirror. This is such a simple way to trap a cheat that one of the great marvels of modern psi research is that the only researchers of recent decades who have used it seem to be Collins and the parapsychologists in Dr. Rhine's laboratory who set a peephole trap for the director, Walter Levy.

Consider the sad case of John Hasted, a Birkbeck College physicist who firmly believes that children can paranormally bend paperclips inside a glass sphere, provided the sphere has a hole in it and the children are allowed to take it into another room and do their psychic bending unobserved.

A ridiculously easy way to settle this hypothesis would be to videotape the youngsters secretly, the way Collins did. If Hasted ever tried this, I haven't heard of it. It is passing strange that parapsychologists who become convinced that psychics can bend metal seem absolutely incapable of devising a simple trap. This augurs ill for the hope that they will ever seek the aid of magicians in any significant way.

Misconception 4: It is naive to suppose that most researchers are capable of setting up controls for a magician that are identical to those imposed on a psychic in a past experiment. If a videotape of an entire experiment is made, without breaks, it might be possible; but even here there are major difficulties. Take the case of Ted Serios. Suppose a tape had been made that showed Ted holding his "gizmo" (a rolled piece of paper) in front of the camera lens and a picture of the Eiffel Tower appearing on the film. A magician asked to break protocols would ask: Was the gizmo examined immediately before the event was recorded? The researcher may honestly say yes; but unless a magician had been there, there is no way to rule out the possibility that Ted palmed an optical device into the gizmo *after* it had been examined. Even if the tape showed the gizmo being examined, if Ted were careful of camera angles nothing on the film would reveal palming. Similarly, an adequate tape would have to show the gizmo examined immediately after the camera snapped, and in such a way that it ruled out Ted palming a device out of the gizmo.

Jule Eisenbud, who wrote an entire book about Ted, has repeatedly challenged Randi to break his protocols. Why has Randi refused? Because Eisenbud, having learned from magicians how Ted could have cheated, now wants to impose on Randi controls that were never imposed on Ted. Magicians think Randi has already broken Eisenbud's protocols; but Eisenbud does not think so, and neither do many top parapsychologists. Researchers typically demand of magicians that they repeat past miracles under conditions radically unlike those that prevailed when the "psychic" produced them. The fact is that there is no way to make sure controls are identical unless a magician has been there to see the psychic perform. Memories of researchers untrained in magic are far too unreliable. Of course one could ask that a magician and a psychic produce a paranormal event under identical controls, supervised by outsiders, but what psychic charlatan would ever agree to such a test?

Misconception 5: Collins makes much of his belief that magicians refuse to give away methods used by psychics. They do indeed refuse to give away secrets of tricks by which professional magicians earn a legitimate living, including entertainers like Kreskin who pose as psychics; but at the low level of prestidigitation on which psychics operate, magicians have never hesitated to give away secrets.

As Collins knows, Houdini constantly exposed the methods of fraudulent mediums. Randi has tirelessly explained the methods of Uri Geller
and other mountebanks. The three magicians who investigated Serios for
Popular Photography (October 1967) explained in detail how to produce
all of Ted's effects with an optical gimmick. One of the three, Charles
Reynolds (who designs illusions for Doug Henning and other stage
performers) is certainly not going to tell Collins how Doug dematerialized
an elephant or how David Copperfield made the Statue of Liberty disappear,
but he minds not at all telling any parapsychologist willing to listen how
Geller bends keys. Surely Collins knows about my *Science* article (reprinted
in *Science: Good, Bad and Bogus*) that exposes the secrets of eyeless vision,
except for Kuda Bux's method—and that was because Kuda made his
living with it. Surely Collins knows of the two books by Uriah Fuller,
on sale in magic stores, that give away all of Geller's basic techniques.
Randi and I will happily tell anyone how Nina Kulagina uses invisible
threads to move matches and float table-tennis balls, and how Felicia Parise
could have moved a pill bottle for Charles Honorton. How Collins got
the impression that magicians are reluctant to explain secrets of psychic
fraud is beyond me. Even the secrets of legitimate magic are readily available
to any psi researcher who cares to buy a few dozen modern books on
the subject.

Misconception 6: Collins actually thinks that if magicians were routinely
asked to observe psychic wonders it would wreck science. It is not just
that fraud is possible in all experiments and there aren't enough magicians
to go around; but psi research, like all research, is a vast social enterprise
extending over long periods of time. It simply would not work, says Collins,
if hostile magicians were perpetually underfoot.

What Collins ignores here are two all-important distinctions. One is
between the operations of nature and human nature; the other is between
ordinary and extraordinary phenomena. As I like to say, electrons and
gerbils don't cheat. Even among psychics, very few claim such fantastic
powers as the ability to bend metal by PK, translocate objects, and levitate
tables. It is only when exceedingly rare miracles like these are seriously
investigated that it is essential to call in an expert on the art of close-
up cheating. And it is essential in many cases that the expert be there
to watch, not just give advice at some later date to researchers who, more
often than not, in the past have paid not the slightest attention to such
advice.

Some of the most widely heralded miracles are one-time events that
the psychic never does again, such as the time Geller translocated a dog

through the walls of Puharich's house, or Felicia moved a pill bottle, or Charles Tart's sleeping subject guessed the number on a card that Tart had put on a shelf above her line of vision. Since no expert on fraud was there as an observer, no one should take seriously the claims of Andrija Puharich, Charles Honorton, and Charles Tart that those events were genuine. Who can take seriously today J. B. Rhine's claim that Hubert Pearce correctly guessed 25 ESP cards in a row? Only Rhine observed this miracle, and there are 20 ways Pearce could have cheated. When a psychic produces events this extraordinary, it is impossible to imagine that he or she would ever submit to retesting under controls recommended by a magician, let alone being observed by a magician during the retesting.

In sum: If parapsychologists seeking the aid of magicians were to try to follow Collins's naive guidelines, it is easy to predict what the outcome would be. In a word—zilch.

4 | Shirley MacLaine

Personally, I used to believe in reincarnation, but that was in a previous lifetime.
—Paul Krassner

John McTaggart Ellis McTaggart, who died in 1925, was one of Cambridge University's great eccentrics. He claimed to be a follower of Hegel, though other Hegelians considered him a renegade. In his peculiar philosophy, space, time, and matter are all illusions arising from our "misperception" of reality. The only real world is a community of selves, each undergoing endless reincarnations. Although time is unreal, history had a beginning and will end when all souls are united by love in a timeless perfect state.

For McTaggart, Hegel's Absolute is the totality of all selves, but with no more selfhood of its own than London has. McTaggart was almost alone among Western philosophers in combining atheism with a belief in the survival and preexistence of the soul. Bertrand Russell wrote that, during his student days at Cambridge, he and McTaggart were "intimate friends" until Russell, in a "rash moment," read Hegel and discovered that his works were "little better than puns." The breakfasts at McTaggart's bachelor lodgings, to which his favorite students were invited, were famous, Russell recalled, for their "lack of food." Students took to bringing their own eggs. When Russell decided that stars really existed even when no one was aware of them, McTaggart "asked me no longer to come and see him because he could not bear my opinions. He followed this up by taking a leading part in having me turned out of my lectureship."

In H. G. Wells's novel *The New Machiavelli,* McTaggart appears as "dear old Codger . . . as curious and adorable as a good Netsuké . . . his round innocent eyes, his absurdly nonprehensile fat hand carrying his cap, his grey trousers braced up much too high, his feet a trifle inturned, and going across the great court with a queer tripping pace . . . it was a wonderful web he spun out of that queer big active childish brain that had never loved nor hated nor grieved nor feared nor passionately loved— a web of iridescent threads . . . as flimsy and irrelevant and clever and beautiful . . . as a dew-wet spider's web slung in the morning sunshine across the black mouth of a gun."

Here are J. B. Priestley's memories:

> While listening to him I could not find a flaw in his lucid and highly ingenious arguments, but never believed anything he had told me once I was out of his presence. . . . He had a curious high voice, a large moon-baby face with spectacles on the end of its nose. . . . Some odd disability gave him a crablike walk, and one met him coming sideways around buildings, like a sheriff about to shoot it out with the bad men in a Western. . . . He believed in human immortality, was a staunch supporter of the Church of England, and having cheerfully argued God out of the universe, he was an atheist.

Although McTaggart has been totally forgotten by today's thinkers, his views were once so influential that the Cambridge philosopher C. D. Broad devoted two volumes (1,250 pages!) to refuting McTaggart's metaphysics. McTaggart, said Broad, had not a single disciple. That is—until 1983.

My mind did a double-take when I encountered his name on page 219 of Shirley MacLaine's third best-seller, *Out on a Limb.* (Her first book, *Don't Fall Off the Mountain,* told of her travels abroad and her early life in Hollywood; her second book, *You Can Get There from Here,* was mainly about her work for George McGovern in the presidential race of 1972, and the making of her documentary film on Maoist China.) Somehow, in her voracious reading about reincarnation, Shirley discovered McTaggart. She quotes a long passage from his book *Human Immortality and Preexistence* and calls

John McTaggart Ellis McTaggart

him the greatest of this century's philosophers who believed in reincarnation.

Miss MacLaine's citations of other famous believers are curious. They include names of many who had no interest in reincarnation in the sense of cycles of lives on earth—Aristotle, Kant, Carlyle, Milton, Benjamin Franklin, to name a few. Conspicuously absent are such philosophers as F. C. S. Schiller and C. J. Ducasse, and the poet William Butler Yeats, who really did believe. (In his poem "A Bronze Head," Yeats refers to "profound McTaggart.") John Dewey, a hard-nosed secular humanist and foe of all metaphysics, would have been dumbfounded to find himself listed among those great minds who "deeply believed in metaphysical dimensions that would ultimately explain the mystery of life."

Shirley is impressed by spiritualist mediums of the past, and by such contemporary miracle workers as Sai Baba, an Indian conjuror who specializes in "materializing" jewelry and ash in his closed fist. She saw a lama in the lotus position levitate three feet. Her far-out American guru—she calls him David—persuaded her that Jesus, like Moses and Buddha, was a superpsychic and that he actually rose from the dead. The Shroud of Turin was produced, Shirley is convinced, by the fantastic spiritual energy of his corpse. Before Jesus began his ministry he studied yoga in India and Tibet—an old occult claim that Shirley takes with great seriousness. Why are there no references in the Bible to Jesus' teachings about reincarnation? Because, we are informed, all such passages were expunged by the Council of Nicaea to protect the power of the Roman church. Jesus' rejection of the notion that a man born blind was being punished for a previous sin (John 9:1-3) is never mentioned. McTaggart, by the way, had a low opinion of Jesus. "If one was a Christian," he wrote, "one would have to worship Jesus and I don't like him very much. . . . Would you like a man or a girl who really imitated Christ?"

Flying saucers, according to Miss MacLaine, are from outer space, perhaps propelled by "thought energy," which is much faster than light. Shirley believes the aliens are anxious to help us and have visited the earth many times in the past, as recorded in the works of Erich von Däniken. In Peru, David told her how he learned all his secret wisdom from Mayan, a beautiful young woman who came here from a planet in the Pleiades. She asked David to pass this wisdom on to Shirley. When Johnny Carson, on his "Tonight Show" (September 7, 1983), wondered why the aliens have never contacted our government, Shirley responded like a true UFO buff. The aliens probably have, she said, but our government is concealing this to prevent panic.

Miss MacLaine's budding interest in reincarnation came to full flower when she began to converse with discarnates on the "astral plane," a theosophical term for the place where souls live between incarnations. These entities—one was a former Irish pickpocket named Tom McPherson—spoke to Shirley through the mouths of trance mediums. She learned many surprising things. At the moment of the Big Bang, she and David had been created "soul mates." In a more recent incarnation, she had been married to Gerry.

Gerry is the name Shirley gives to an ambitious married member of

British Parliament with whom she, at the time of her visits to the mediums, was having a passionate and secret love affair. Shirley describes him as a socialist who wants to become prime minister. He has an unruly shock of hair, a tendency to stumble over furniture and confuse closet doors with exits, and a little finger with a missing upper joint. But Shirley admits she put in many false clues designed to conceal Gerry's identity. There have been numerous guesses in the British press: Olof Palme, the Swedish prime minister? Andrew Peacock, the Australian conservative? Shirley isn't blabbing. At one press conference she said, "I guarantee you Gerry is not Margaret Thatcher." According to *People* magazine (July 18, 1983), a voice from the rear shouted, "That's one down!" Shirley added: "If I'd balled as many politicians over the world as you guys say I have, I'd be inside a bottle in the U.N."

Shirley probably doesn't know it, but by one of those unusual coincidences that she likes to call "synchronicity," Wells's *The New Machiavelli* is the story of a British socialist leader who falls in love with a woman not his wife. Like Gerry, he cannot divorce his wife without wrecking his political career. Unlike Gerry, he finally chooses to wreck it. A spirit speaking through a California medium tells Shirley that her former marriage to Gerry, when they lived in Atlantis, had been even stormier. Why? Because of his excessive devotion to "important work involving cultural exchanges with extraterrestrials."

Miss MacLaine's book swarms with fashionable paranormal notions: energy vibrations (of which love is the highest), other dimensions, precognition, out-of-body travel, déjà vu (a proof of past lives), karma, ESP, the Aquarian Age, Atlantis, Lemuria, and the wonders of the Great Pyramid of Egypt, which she mistakenly thinks is on our dollar bills. David teaches her that the atom is a miniature solar system, apparently having never learned that this primitive model of the atom was long ago abandoned. She is a great admirer of Edgar Cayce, the American trance psychic whose name peppers her pages. Discarnates who through mediums reveal to Shirley the details of her past lives—she calls it "trance channeling"—get their information from the Akashik Records, another theosophical concept. These are archives on which are stored the vibrations of every event and thought that has occurred since the creation of the universe.

Shirley repeats all the ancient arguments for reincarnation: its vast sweep and beauty, its simple explanation of irrational evil, the fact that more people around the world believe in it than don't. Little is said about researchers who claim to have found persons who recall past lives under hypnosis, perhaps because Shirley knows how shaky this evidence is. She mentions none of the doctrine's negative aspects. When reincarnation is coupled with karma, for example, it is not easy to feel compassion for those who experience great suffering. Are they not being justly punished for sins in previous lives? This abominable view still strengthens the contempt that higher castes in India feel for the untouchables, and the great respect they pay the rich and powerful.

The Judeo-Christian-Muslim view of an afterlife at least offers escape from an endless round of lives on earth. "It is no more transcendental," wrote Gilbert Chesterton (in *Everlasting Man*), "for a man to remember what he did in Babylon before he was born than to remember what he did in Brixton before he had a knock on the head. . . . Reincarnation as such does not necessarily escape from the wheel of destiny; in some sense it *is* the wheel of destiny."

Today, when educated young people throughout the East are abandoning belief in reincarnation, it is astonishing how faddish it has become in certain circles of the West. Even more surprising is how the doctrine can cause an intelligent, beautiful, talented woman to write page after page of kindergarten metaphysics that read like reports in one of those shabby little spiritualist journals that flourished around the turn of the century when the upper classes amused themselves with table tipping.

Although Shirley never mentions a single book by a skeptic, she is honest enough to record conversations with three good friends who were profoundly shocked by her new faith. Bella Abzug was polite but dismayed. A New York City writer who for a time had been Shirley's lover ("his quirky brilliance had been a major factor in keeping me interested in him for quite a number of years") reminded her of how gullible she had once been about modern China. Her occult enthusiasms, he told her, were even more preposterous.

It was Shirley's burly labor leader, as down to earth as David is floating high, who said it all during a remarkable argument about reincarnation and trance mediums that they had in Stockholm before their relationship ended:

> He shook his head. "I don't know what to say," he muttered. "I mean, you just can't be serious about this."
>
> "Why not?"
>
> "Well, my God, isn't it obvious? These mediums are psychos, or weird, dragging stuff up out of their own unconscious. Or else they're taking you. You surely don't believe they're actually communicating with *spirits?*"
>
> "*They* aren't communicating. They're just channeling—they don't even remember what's been said."
>
> "Whatever they're doing, it's utter rubbish. They do it for money, exploiting gullible people who want to be told some sugary nonsense about dead relatives

or some other damned thing."

"Edgar Cayce took no money, the advice he gave was sound, and it didn't come from his unconscious because he had no medical training."

Gerry looked at me helplessly. "Why in the name of God do you have to get involved with this sort of thing?" he asked desperately.

Afterword

For more about Shirley MacLaine—her television miniseries based on *Out on a Limb,* and her fourth and fifth autobiographies—see Chapters 28 and 29. Some of the foregoing material is repeated in Chapter 28.

5 | Freud, Fliess, and Emma's Nose

Your manuscript is both good and original. But the part that is good is not original, and the part that is original is not good.
—Samuel Johnson

For several decades Freud's reputation has been steadily going downhill. One reason surely has been the realization by leading feminists that Freud never rose above Victorian male chauvinism, but the main reason is much stronger. It is the growing awareness that Freud had only the flimsiest understanding of how to test a conjecture. Over and over again he tossed out brilliant guesses; ingenious, yes, but with an absence of empirical underpinning exceeded only by his dogmatic claims of certitude.

On matters for which he is given the most credit, such as the influence of repressed memories on behavior, Freud took over a commonly accepted opinion. You'll find long discussions of unconscious causes of psychosomatic ills in William James's *Principles of Psychology*, published ten years before Freud began to invent his theories. It is where Freud departed from his colleagues that he should be judged, and it is precisely these departures that are coming to be seen, as Karl Popper and Peter Medawar have long insisted, as little more than colorful mythology projected by a neurotic genius. Even Freud's theory of dreams is now under fire, as recent research suggests that dreams may be mostly random by-products of the brain's process of clearing its circuits and that trying to recall dreams may actually harm a patient.

In a chapter of my *Mathematical Carnival* I tell of Freud's strange and passionate friendship with one of the giants of German crackpottery. He was a Berlin nose-and-throat doctor named Wilhelm Fliess—two years younger than Freud, handsome, charming, conceited, paranoid (he later thought Freud was trying to kill him), and utterly irresponsible. It is hard to believe, but for more than ten years he was Freud's most intimate confidant.

Fliess suffered from two major obsessions. He believed that all living processes conform to two cycles: a male cycle of 23 days, and a female cycle of 28 days. The theory became known as biorhythm, and later his disciples added a third cycle.

Fliess's second obsession was the unshakable conviction that all neuroses and sexual abnormalities are intimately related to the nose. He diagnosed such ills by examining a nose's interior and thought he could cure these ills by cauterizing or applying cocaine to the nose's "genital spots." Masturbation, for example, altered the left middle turbinate bone in its frontal third, and this in turn caused stomach pains. In cases of severe symptoms he removed a piece of nasal bone. Young Freud was enthusiastic about both of these great scientific discoveries. At one time he even feared he would die at 51 because 23 plus 28 equals 51. Several times he allowed Fliess to operate on his nose.

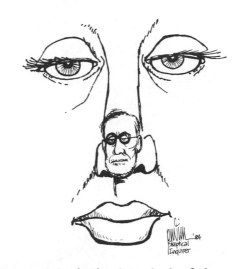

Freud apparently destroyed all of Fliess's letters, but much of Freud's side of the correspondence has survived. His daughter Anna edited a selection of these letters for a book, but she suppressed the letters and passages she considered damaging to her father. These censored writings have now come to light in Jeffrey Masson's explosive new book, *The Assault on Truth*. The book has generated an enormous controversy in newspapers and magazines, including two long articles in the *New Yorker* in December 1983, in which Janet Malcolm drew unflattering portraits of Masson and his chief rival in the debunking of Freud, Peter Swales. Swales's biography of Fliess, *Freud's Other*, will soon be available. Psychiatrists outside the Freudian tradition (they are the vast majority) are reacting with surprise and glee, but the elderly custodians of Freudian orthodoxy are doing their best to minimize the books' impact.

There were two whopping reversals in Freud's early speculations. He stopped using hypnosis when he found it unreliable for gaining access to a patient's real past; and he abandoned his strongly held theory—he once likened it to finding the source of the Nile—that large numbers of neurotic women suffer from suppressed memories of being violently raped by their fathers. Masson argues that Freud did not abandon the second view for scientific reasons but for a variety of unconscious personal motives, and that a horrendous event involving his idolized Fliess played a pivotal role in this decision.

Wilhelm Fliess (right) and Sigmund Freud in the 1890s.

Freud had a young woman patient, Emma Eckstein, of whom he was extremely fond but with whom he was making little progress. To cure her hysterical symptoms, mainly severe stomach pains, he brought Fliess to Vienna in 1895 to remove the offending bone from Emma's nose. As suppressed letters to Fliess revealed, Freud had full confidence in this crazy operation. When it was over, Fliess returned to Berlin but poor Emma's nose began to hemorrhage. The mysterious, massive bleeding refused to stop, and Masson prints stomach-turning reports that Freud sent Fliess, which read like passages in a horror-fantasy potboiler. Not until Emma was on the brink of death did Freud finally seek the help of a reputable surgeon—a doctor who had strongly opposed the original operation. He opened Emma's nose. Inside, wadded into the nasal cavity, he found half a meter of gauze that Fliess forgot to remove. Freud was so stricken that he had to leave the room and imbibe some booze.

"So we had done her an injustice," Freud wrote to Fliess. "[The bleeding] was not at all abnormal, rather a piece of iodoform gauze had gotten torn off as you were removing it, and stayed in for 14 days, preventing healing. . . . How wrong I was to urge you to operate in a foreign city where you could not follow through on the case."

Emma recovered, though disfigured for life because the loss of bone caused one side of her nose to cave in. Although Freud originally attributed the bleeding to Fliess's bungling, he made clear that he considered it one of those unfortunate mistakes that even the best of surgeons sometimes make. A year later, however, Freud had found a better way to absolve Fliess of guilt. He decided that the bleeding was entirely hysterical, springing from the young woman's desire to be loved. This had been Fliess's opinion, which he naturally related to critical days in her 23- and 28-day cycles.

In letters censored by Anna, Freud tells Fliess about his "completely surprising explanation of Eckstein's hemorrhages—which will give you much pleasure. . . . You were right, that her episodes of bleeding were hysterical, were occasioned by longing, and probably occurred at the sexually relevant times (the woman, out of resistance, has not yet supplied me with the dates)."

These "relevant dates" refer, of course, to Fliess's numerology. Emma almost bled to death because she wanted Freud at her bedside! He reports happily on his discovery that Emma had nosebleeds when she was a child. "As far as the blood is concerned," he assures Fliess, "you are completely without blame!" Masson believes that this attempt to exonerate Fliess, along with other personal matters involving Freud's relatives—not clinical data— led Freud to his new theory that sexual fantasies are more important causes of neurotic behavior than actual episodes (such as Emma's operation) in the past. He thinks this shift of emphasis was damaging to the analytic movement, and he sides with those modern researchers who are trying to move the emphasis back to traumatic events that really did occur.

It took Freud more than ten years to realize that his dear friend was a crank. Fliess was the first to break the bond, accusing Freud of abusing him and stealing his ideas. In my chapter on Fliess you'll find the details of how, many years later, Freud suddenly fainted during a lunch with Jung at a hotel in Munich. He told Ernest Jones (who devotes a chapter to Fliess in his classic biography of Freud) that he fainted because an argument with Jung had reminded him of a violent quarrel with Fliess at the same hotel.

Fliess's mad cycle-theory is still going great guns in the biorhythm movement, now unregrettably fading, but I know of no current boosters of his nasal theory. A quack doctor could make a fortune by reviving it. The background material is readily available, in monstrous detail, in Fliess's untranslated tomes and papers. A popular book titled *The Nose Knows* could outfleece any book on acupuncture. Illustrations showing how bones of the nose connect with the penis and vagina would provide marvelous erotic fare. Plastic surgeons could combine the nose therapy with remodeling the nose to improve the face. After it became a Hollywood fad, "NOVA" could produce a great documentary on it.

It is hard to know which deserves the stronger condemnation: Freud's childish credulity or the shameful way his daughter and other guardians of the orthodox analytic flame have done their best to prevent the lurid facts about Freud's early career from reaching the general public.

Afterword

Janet Malcolm's *New Yorker* hatchet job on Jeffrey Masson and Peter Swales has been published as a book: *In the Freud Archives* (Knopf, 1984). Needless to say, both her book and Masson's were widely reviewed— traditional Freudians attacking Masson and praising Malcolm, and anti-Freudians commenting from a reverse perspective.

The Complete Letters of Sigmund Freud to Wilhelm Fliess, translated and edited by Masson, was issued by Harvard University Press in 1985. It, too, received extensive critical attention, notably by Charles Rycroft (*New York Review of Books*, May 30, 1985) and by Daniel Goleman in his cover article for the *New York Times Magazine* (March 17, 1985; see also the Letters section of April 21).

The strongest, most thorough attack on psychoanalysis yet to appear is *Foundations of Psychoanalysis* (University of California Press, 1984), by the distinguished philospher of science Adolf Grünbaum. His book has two central themes. Karl Popper has long claimed that psychoanalysis is unfalsifiable and therefore empty of empirical content. Not so, says Grünbaum. Its claims *are* testable, and such testing has falsified them. Of the many reviews of this book I particularly recommend Frank Sulloway's, in *Free Inquiry* (Fall 1985) and the same magazine's interview with Grünbaum (Winter 1985/86).

Jonathan Lieberson, reviewing Grünbaum's book for the *New York Review of Books* (January 31, 1985) summed up the case against psychoanalysis this way:

> The profession has become increasingly isolated from organic medicine; it has found no new Freud; its theoretical development has been stagnant. It is arguable that what seems evidently true in Freud, such as his notion of repression or his emphasis on the unconscious and on the irrational springs of much of human behavior, has long been known and that Freud introduced an unnecessary technical language and a dubious metaphysical backdrop to describe these

phenomena. And it is possible that psychoanalytic therapy will be replaced in time by shorter therapies of various kinds and by psychopharmacology derived from new developments in the neurosciences.

6 | Koestler Money Down the Psi Drain?

In March 1983, after a long, dramatic career, Arthur Koestler ended his life dramatically by killing himself. He and his wife, Cynthia, were found dead in their home near London, both having taken overdoses of barbiturates. The Hungarian-born writer, age 77, had been suffering from terminal leukemia. His wife, in her fifties, was not ill. A suicide note expressed Koestler's "timid hopes for a depersonalized afterlife beyond due confines of space, time, and matter, and beyond the limits of our comprehension."

Koestler's intellectual pilgrimage falls into three parts: (1) active communist, (2) active anti-communist and author of the influential anti-Stalinist novel *Darkness at Noon,* which made him famous, and (3) active promoter of the paranormal. Koestler was firmly convinced that parapsychology is ushering in a new Copernican Revolution.

The Koestlers left a will in which about $750,000 was set aside for the endowment of a chair of parapsychology at a United Kingdom university. Oxford, Cambridge, and other leading universities declined the endowment on the grounds that it would cast doubt on their other research programs. Only two finally sought the funding: the University of Wales, at Cardiff, and the University of Edinburgh. Koestler's trustees finally gave it to Edinburgh. Earlier, retired businessman Instone Bloomfield, a friend of Koestler, had independently established a Koestler Foundation. He announced that he would increase Koestler's endowment by another $750,000 if the chairman of the new department planned a research program that his foundation approved.

At the time of this writing, the chairman has not yet been chosen. However, a psychologist at Edinburgh and one of the leading figures in British parapsychology, John Beloff, was a good friend of Koestler. Beloff's *New Directions in Parapsychology* (1974) has a postscript by Koestler. Although Beloff is noted for the negative results of his experiments, especially when he tried to replicate U.S. tests of psi, he is a firm believer in the paranormal, including the psi powers of the great mediums of the past, and in the powers of modern psychics like Uri Geller and Ted Serios.

Beloff has always been enormously impressed by the fact that the Scottish medium D. D. Home was never caught cheating, but he is not in the least dismayed that other famous mediums, such as Eusapia Palladino, were often caught in deception. In an article in *Encounter* (January 1980), he wrote: "Everyone knew that she [Palladino] would cheat if given half a chance to do so; but skeptics prefer to forget that the effects she could achieve in this way were quite feeble and that her most spectacular seances were conducted under the most stringent conditions. . . ." In our own times, he continues, we have Uri Geller, now generally considered a mere entertainer. "He, too, is probably a mixture of the genuine and fraudulent." This view of Uri was shared by Koestler. Koestler was described as "visibly shaken" when he once saw Uri produce bursts in a Geiger counter, though he conceded later that Geller also at times resorted to trickery.

In 1975, Beloff reviewed three books about Geller: Geller's autobiography, Andrija Puharich's biography, and John Taylor's *Superminds,* in which Uri is the hero. Beloff opens this lengthy review (*Journal of Parapsychology,* September 1975, pp. 242-50) by deploring the tendency of his colleagues to turn away from Uri because of his money-grubbing show-biz background. "This attitude, though understandable, is, I am convinced, profoundly misguided. It is just possible that Geller may prove to be the most gifted all-round psychic subject that there has ever been, not excluding D. D. Home!"

"The Geller case," he continues, "has long since passed the point where it is sensible to doubt that Geller possesses paranormal powers. . . ." To support this, Beloff cites Uri's die test at the Stanford Research Institute (now SRI International), which he considers impossible to explain by deception. (This was written before information about the die test leaked out that proved it to have been almost totally uncontrolled. See this book's chapter 20, and my *Science: Good, Bad and Bogus,* pp. 106-08.)

Beloff regards Uri's ESP and PK powers as so "indisputable" that he considers it a "waste of time" to debate their "basic authenticity." The most indisputable, he argues, are those feats that Geller performs on order: fork-bending, starting stopped watches, and clairvoyance. His less predictable miracles, such as dematerializations and teleportations, "so familiar to those who have had the good fortune to work closely with Geller," are not quite so indisputable. Geller just *might* have used trickery.

In the review, Beloff considers the notorious incident in 1973 when Geller, as he himself described it, was bodily teleported from the east side of Manhattan to Puharich's house 30 miles away in Ossining. Beloff concedes that Geller *could* have been playing a joke, but he adds: "I ask these questions because I want to emphasize that, where Geller is concerned, nothing should

be allowed to go by default and nothing is too fantastic to be worth probing." Earlier cases in which powerful mediums were similarly teleported are cited. The tales may sound like the *Arabian Nights,* he admits, but "the word *impossible* does not belong in the vocabulary of parapsychology."

"Some people," Beloff goes on, find Uri "exasperating, but many more quickly succumb to his boyish charm and striking good looks. But what should make him of interest to readers of this journal is that his life, by all accounts, has been one prolonged poltergeist episode with amazing things happening at every turn. While, in the usual case, the poltergeist focus loses his [*sic*] powers in childhood, in Geller's case they appear to go from strength to strength as he gets older. He may well have reached the peak of his powers and, if we neglect him now, posterity may not lightly forgive us. The fact that he lacks the docile temperament to make a good experimental subject should not deter us. Great psychics, like great geniuses in any field, are so rare and so precious we have to learn to accept them as we find them."

Puharich's crazy book, *Uri,* is criticized by Beloff on the grounds that Puharich was blind to the possibility that the tapes made by Geller, on which voices from UFOs were heard (before the cassettes mysteriously dematerialized or were erased), were not (as Puharich claimed) from extraterrestrials who were pumping psi power into Uri. More likely they were recordings made by Uri's PK. A photograph in Puharich's book purports to show three flying saucers. Beloff is of the opinion that this was a "typical Serios effect." He is here referring to Ted Serios, the Chicago bellhop who claimed the ability to project his thought pictures onto Polaroid film. Beloff has written elsewhere about Serios, who he thinks was a powerful psychic.

John Taylor is praised for his pioneer work with children who bend metal, and congratulated on having the privilege of being among the first to "witness some authentic bending phenomena with these subjects, whose powers usually seem to desert them when they are placed in a controlled situation." It never occurs to Beloff that this may be because the children previously cheated. Taylor, by the way, later repudiated his ridiculous book and concluded that Geller is a fraud and that paranormal metal-bending does not exist.

By 1981, when Beloff addressed the 24th Annual Convention of the Parapsychological Association, in Syracuse, he had become more skeptical of Geller, though not of the "Geller-effect." He expressed his continued belief in its reality and said it had been strongly confirmed by the metal-bending of the French magician-turned-psychic Jean-Pierre Girard. "Indeed," declared Beloff, "the tests carried out by Crussard on the French metal-bender Girard were about as conclusive as one could well imagine. . . ." (For details on these amateurishly designed tests see Randi's book *Flim-Flam!*) It does not bother Beloff in the least that Girard, like Geller, was once a stage magician or that the metallurgist Charles Crussard is as naive and ignorant of conjuring methods as himself. "If the effect is a real one . . . ," Beloff said, in the most sensible remark of his address, "it ought not be beyond the wit of man to prove it."

Here is how Beloff ended his rhapsodic 1975 review:

After reading these three volumes it occurs to me that what we need even more than another good experimental investigation of Geller is a really reliable, detailed, and documented biography. And this work should be started as soon as possible while those connected with Geller are still available for questioning. If any wealthy benefactors would care to finance such an enterprise, they may be assured that parapsychology would be permanently in their debt.

At the time I write, the question of whether Beloff will be in a position to carry out this great project remains in doubt. He has stated that he has no desire to chair the new department, but even if he is not appointed, his input into how the funds will be used will be formidable. An objective biography of Uri would be of great interest. It is just possible that we might learn how he managed to fly from Manhattan to Ossining, or how he was able to teleport Wellington, Puharich's dog, through the walls of Puharich's house.

There are hopeful signs that Beloff may be entertaining serious doubts about some of the phenomena he considered unassailable a few years ago. His office recently issued an official report of his investigation of a self-styled psychic identified only by the pseudonym "Tim." At Beloff's request, Randi supplied detailed protocols by which Tim could be caught cheating, and Beloff—with considerable misgivings, which are expressed in his report—did adopt Randi's simple procedures. The young man was caught blatantly cheating.

If the University of Edinburgh is capable of making sure that research conducted by the new department is in the hands of persons who know the meaning of "stringent controls" and who have the wisdom and courage to seek the help of the only experts on deception—the magicians—then perhaps the Koestler fortune will not flow down the usual psi drain.

Afterword

In 1985 the American parapsychologist Robert Morris was appointed chairman of the University of Edinburgh's new department of parapsychology. For my reactions, and more about John Beloff, see Chapter 11.

The following letter from Beloff appeared in *Skeptical Inquirer* (Spring 1985):

> There are some people who never learn from experience but stay all their lives stuck fast in their prejudices. The late Arthur Koestler was certainly not one of them, nor, I hope, am I. I am not ashamed, therefore, to admit that I sometimes change my mind. Martin Gardner quotes at length from a 1975 book review of mine in an effort to show that I am unfit to be allowed any say in how my university uses the Koestler bequest.
>
> No doubt a lot of wishful thinking went into the writing of that review. But, ten years ago, it did not seem so silly to suppose that Geller might yet prove to be the powerful psychic we need who, in the right hands, might transform the whole situation with respect to parapsychology. What we did not realize at the time was that—for whatever reason—Geller was simply not interested in cooperating in any serious research. In the event, we shall probably never know the whole truth about Uri Geller, although each of us is fully entitled to his own opinion. I would still maintain, however, that there has been enough evidence during the past ten years to suggest that the Geller-effect as such may well be real.
>
> I am an avid reader of the skeptical literature, including the writings of Martin Gardner, but I cannot help it if I do not always find this literature very convincing. Consequently, I have kept an open mind about the paranormal, and I sincerely hope that our new Koestler Professor, when he or she is appointed, will do likewise and will not be cowed by the more strident debunkers. On

the other hand, I am always ready to collaborate with Randi and others in exposing fake claims.

As regards our "Tim," after we circulated that report by my student, Deborah Delanoy, to which Martin Gardner alludes, he made a full confession. It transpired that he is a keen young magician and his admiration for Randi led him to think that it would be fun to try fooling the parapsychologists at Edinburgh. He is no longer sure that it was such a clever idea, and he has apologized for wasting our time.

I replied as follows:

When I read Professor Beloff's first paragraph I had high hopes that he would go on to demonstrate how his mind has changed by telling us that he now considers Uri Geller a fraud. But no. To my amazement he says no such thing. He is disappointed only because Geller will not cooperate on "serious research." There is nary a hint that Beloff comprehends why Geller so refuses. On the contrary, Beloff still maintains that metal-bending by the mind may be genuine! Because Beloff has not seen fit to disclose how his mind has altered—for example, does he still take Ted Serios seriously?—I see no reason to suppose that he has departed in any substantive way from the strong opinions I quoted from his 1975 paper.

7 | Targ: From Puthoff to Blue

Mind Race, by Russell Targ and (Stuart) Keith Harary, was published in 1984 by Villard Books, a division of Random House. Physicist Targ was formerly at SRI International, where he and his associate Harold Puthoff "validated" the clairvoyant powers of Uri Geller. *Mind-Reach,* an earlier book by Targ and Puthoff, concerned their work with Geller and their experiments in clairvoyance, or "remote viewing," as they prefer to call it.

Mind Race summarizes the SRI's remote-viewing research, but most of the book is devoted to the theme that psychic powers are perfectly normal, that anyone can develop these abilities by following the book's simple instructions. Geller has mysteriously vanished—there is not a word about him in the book. Puthoff, once an ardent Scientologist, remains at SRI, but Targ has left the big Menlo Park think-tank to join Harary in founding a psi-research organization they call Delphi Associates.

Keith Harary, better known by his nickname "Blue," is famous in psi circles for his OBEs (out-of-body experiences) at the Psychical Research Foundation, in Durham, North Carolina. His pet kitten, Spirit, was placed in a cage, and Blue, in another building, would project his astral body into the lab. The kitten reportedly calmed down whenever Blue's invisible body arrived. In one test, reported by the foundation's director, William Roll, Spirit meowed 37 times during the control period, but not once during the OBE period.

There are, say the authors, nine ways in which psi can be useful to the readers: it can help them to detect hidden defects in their cars, locate parking spots, advance in business by following correct hunches, win at racetracks and casinos, find lost children, tune in to the "feelings and emotions of distant friends, relatives, or sweethearts," be "in the right place and at the right time for worthwhile opportunities," use the psi content of dreams, and take along an "unlikely item that will later prove to be invaluable" when going somewhere.

The authors have not the slightest doubt that psi powers are useful in gambling. Targ won a lottery on a hunch, he tells us, while the book

Scientists believe this man can leave his body and 'travel' through walls

By PAUL DOUGHERTY

A YOUNG university graduate has stunned scientists with his apparent ability to leave his body and travel through solid walls.

The "mind traveler" is 23-year-old Stuart Harary, and now researchers at prestigious Duke University, N.C., are backing up his claims following a series of amazing tests.

Observed under strict testing conditions, Harary has reportedly:

• Left his body and traveled to distant rooms, reporting in great detail on what is happening there;

• Moved into the body of a cat in another room and performed several feats involving the animal with scientists watching;

• Made "mind trips" to the rooms of several research workers, who reported being awakened in the night by floating orbs of light.

Harary is still undergoing tests three times a week at Duke Medical Center, where he is wired up to seven electronic monitoring devices.

One of the most startling displays of Harary's mind powers involved his pet cat. Harary and the animal were placed in separate rooms, while scientists checked their reactions.

Harary described rising out of his body, gazing down at himself and talking about it without someone coming up with a similar experience," he said.

"We had an engineering student who came in here to see what we were doing.

"When we started talking about it, he recalled getting stuck in a hollow tree when he was young. Then he had the sensation of standing outside it looking at himself in there, with his leg bent a certain way.

"When he saw that, he made the appropriate movements, and freed himself.

"Then you hear cases of combat pilots suddenly getting the sensation of being above the battle, and seeing it whole, including their own aircraft.

"The point is, it happens to all kinds of people. We're hoping we'll be able to tell them just WHAT is happening to them."

Parapsychologist and author Dr. Scott Rogo told The Star: "There is no doubt in my mind, or in that of others who have worked with Harary that he does have the uncanny ability to liberate his mind from his body.

"One morning I awoke to see an odd red orb floating quickly through my room. I made a note of the incident at the time.

"Several hours later I found that Harary had had an OOB experience spontaneously at that same time and that he had tried to appear to me.

"Other workers at the P.R.F. have reported darting shadows and flashing lights which seemed to herald Harary's presence."

Harary is still shy of discussing his powers with strangers: "I'm always afraid girl-friends will think I'm crazy if I mention it," he said.

"And I don't advise anyone else to attempt it. It could be dangerous. On the other hand, people it does happen to should be reassured that it doesn't mean they are crazy, or they're dying.

"This is an experience that many people have, and it's appropriate that we should study it."

And so, three times a week, Harary settles back on a couch at Duke Medical Center, wired up to seven electronic monitoring devices, and does whatever it is that he does.

Fellow workers of this serious young researcher, who shies away from any suggestion that he exploit his talents, flatly rule out any suggestion that he is a fraud.

Stuart Harary, the "mind traveler" whose feats are amazing scientists, talks to The Star at Duke University last week.

Story about Harary's supposed abilities in a 1976 issue of *The Star*.

was being written. Blackjack is recommended as the best cardgame at which "you may reliably win." One of Targ's nameless remote viewers used psi successfully on slot machines at Lake Tahoe. "The scheme worked wonderfully, for more than an hour," then suddenly she had a strong feeling about a nearby machine. While she fumbled for a quarter, the woman next to her played the machine, winning the jackpot "that was waiting for the next coin."

The most sensational claims of Delphi Associates, loudly trumpeted by Targ and Harary in their appearances on the Phil Donahue and the Merv Griffin television shows, have been in predicting the silver futures market. Harary did the precognizing. One forecast was so accurate, the authors write, that the odds against its being chance are 250,000 to 1. With successes like this, why is Delphi seeking funding?

If psi can be used for good purposes, does it not follow that it can also serve evil ends? The authors have not overlooked this. In a section on "How to Defend Yourself Against Psychic Attack," they admit they are not certain that "black magic" (the term is not used in the book, though it appears in the index) is possible—but they add, "we would not be surprised to learn that it is."

To be safe, the authors recommended one of the funniest, most paranoid books ever written, *Psychic Defense*, by Dion Fortune. Who is Dion? Her real name was Violet Firth, a renowned British occultist who died in 1946 after making a fortune by writing crazy books under the Fortune pseudonym.

Violet firmly believed that evil psychics could conjure up vampires, werewolves, and other monster "thought-forms" capable of mangling and killing. She herself once managed to fabricate a wolf. The poor woman was constantly being attacked by these vicious thought-forms—in one case it was a cat twice the size of a tiger. You can read all about her in *Mysterious Powers* (a dreadful book published here by Grolier Enterprises in 1976), written by Colin Wilson with Uri Geller as his chief consultant. There is even a two-page spread in blazing color, showing Violet being threatened by the giant cat.

Targ and Harary have only contempt for such cult leaders as Jim Jones and Sun Myung Moon, but L. Ron Hubbard is never mentioned. They are down on occult movies, pyramid power, and communication with plants, but are even more hostile toward skeptics who try to expose fraud. Randi is branded "deceitful," and CSICOP is repeatedly called an organization of "psi-cops" whose goal is "to control your ability to access and interpret information and to walk a beat on your mind. In this respect they are not unlike cult leaders or Big Brother in George Orwell's *1984*."

An attack on me includes a charge so totally false that it deserves some background. In a 1975 *Scientific American* column (reprinted as Chapter 7 of my *Science: Good, Bad and Bogus*) I criticized an effort by Puthoff and Targ (hereafter called P and T) to evaluate an ESP teaching machine. The experiment had three parts. Phase one, a preliminary experiment, had almost no controls. Positive results encouraged P and T to proceed with the main test, phase two, in which rigid controls were imposed by having the data recorded by a computer. The results were negative. P and T blamed this mainly on tension created in the minds of subjects by knowing their guesses were being monitored by a machine. In the third phase, the computer was abandoned and positive results were obtained again, chiefly by their associate Duane Elgin. The experiment had been funded by NASA and supervised by the Jet Propulsion Laboratory.

The JPL considered the experiment a fiasco and, although P and T wanted to continue it with more NASA funds, a new grant was denied. One reason for the JPL's dim view of this work was a report by a person hired by the laboratory to check the original records. He told me that the paper tapes, which recorded the informal results of the first phase, were in poor shape. Of the 145 subjects, 100 were SRI employees or friends and relatives of the experimenters. They worked alone on machines in the lab and kept their own records. Forty-five were schoolchildren who used machines supervised by an experimenter or a teacher. I was told by the JPL investigator that occasionally a machine malfunctioned and then the tape records were kept by hand. He described the tapes as being in "bits and pieces," a phrase

I quoted. Of course he did not mean that anyone had torn the tapes into little pieces—I never used the word *torn*—but only that the tapes were not in the form of complete unbroken folds for every trial run.

After my column appeared, P and T wrote a strong letter (*Scientific American* published it in January 1976) insisting that all the tapes were intact for every trial run that entered into their statistics. To settle the matter, I was authorized by Gerard Piel, publisher of *Scientific American*, to write to Puthoff and propose that a statistician acceptable to both sides be permitted to examine the tapes at the magazine's expense. This letter was never answered.

Now back to *Mind Race*. On page 157, in a paragraph blasting me, the following incredible passage appears:

> He falsely alleged that the subjects in this experiment tore up their unsuccessful data tapes, and only handed in the successful ones. He said in his article, "I am not guessing when I say that the paper tape records from Phase I were handed in to Targ in bits and pieces." We now know the reason he could say that he "wasn't guessing." This is because he recently confided to a fellow reporter that he had just made it up, "because that's the way it must have happened." The reporter was so shocked at this disclosure, that even though he is not particularly sympathetic to our work, he felt compelled to call up the SRI researchers to pass on this remarkable piece of news.

Note that my alleged remark is inside quotes, as if the authors had had a tape recording. Of course I never made such a preposterous statement and couldn't possibly have done so. I wasn't "guessing" because I had talked to a man who had seen the tapes. The reporter referred to turned out to be Ron McRae. Here are excerpts from the letter he sent to *Fate* after the publisher of that moronic magazine quoted the passage above in full (July 1984) under the heading "Quote of the Month."

> I am the "fellow reporter" to whom Martin Gardner supposedly confided that he had deliberately lied about an ESP teaching machine experiment carried out by SRI in 1974. . . . In fact, I have never made any such claim to Mr. Targ or anyone else. What did happen is that, during an extensive interview for my own book, *Mind Wars,* with Hal Puthoff . . . I mentioned that I had heard another person make such a claim. I did not consider the claim reliable. I was not "shocked at this disclosure," and I did not feel "compelled to call up the SRI researchers to pass on this remarkable piece of news." Mr. Targ's use of fourth-hand, unreliable information is unfortunately typical of the often ill-founded claims in his book.

I considered the paragraph in *Mind Race* libelous because it implied that as a science writer I make up facts to score points. I at once wrote to the chief editor of Villard Books to say I was prepared to sue unless he assured me that the passage would be removed from all later printings and from all spinoffs, such as paperback and foreign editions. The editor apologized for the slander, and when he promised to do what I requested I decided not to take legal action. A similar letter to *Fate* produced an even quicker apology. The editor wrote back that "after conducting our own investigation" they concluded I was absolutely correct. *Fate*'s October 1984 issue published a strong apology to their readers for publishing this "baseless accusation," following it with a slightly edited version of McRae's letter. In a way, I am sorry the matter did not go to court. Even if I lost, it would have had the merit of forcing Targ to allow outsiders to examine the tapes in question. There is an important lesson here. When a scientist refuses to allow outsiders to see the raw data of a controversial experiment, one has good reason to suspect a coverup.

For Blue Harary, *Mind Race* is a big step up in his struggle for recognition as a powerful psychic, even though he can't bend spoons or animate pill bottles. For Targ, unquestionably a sincere believer but with a mind as naive and gullible as a child's, the book is a disaster.

Afterword

You can imagine my anger when I checked the paperback edition of *Mind Race,* published by Random House under the imprint of Ballantine Books, and found the libelous passage still there. Since I had promised not to sue if the passage were removed, and because Villard's top editor had agreed to remove it, I felt obliged to take legal action. It was my hope that the case would go to trial and the paper tapes could be subpoenaed, but Random House offered to settle out of court for $10,000 and I accepted.

A trenchant analysis of *Mind Race*, "Outracing the Evidence" by psychologist Ray Hyman, appeared in the *Skeptical Inquirer* (Winter 1984/85). For an amusing, informative front-page story on Delphi Associates, see "Did Psychic Powers Give Firm a Killing in the Silver Market?" by Erik Larson, in the *Wall Street Journal* (October 22, 1984).

According to the *WSJ*, the third partner in Delphi is Anthony R. White, identified as an "art investor and manager of a family fortune." After the firm's initial success in predicting silver futures, White is quoted as saying: "Our major client suffered from an attack of hubris and started pressing us for more predictions." Can you blame him? After Delphi failed on the next two tries, said White, "our client got apoplectic."

Philosopher Paul Kurtz commented to the *WSJ*: "In order to say anything, they'd have to have several hundred, several thousand, investments. It's a very small sample. My Aunt Martha could do better."

Delphi is reported by the *WSJ* to be working on many other projects: using RV (remote viewing) to search for oil, gold, and other minerals, to develop computer ESP games, to locate lost airplanes, and to find a publisher for a novel about a teenage psychic. The most intriguing project is a "psychic switch." This is a switch too stable to go off by itself, but sensitive enough to be triggered from a long distance by psi power. Targ told the *WSJ* that their prototype worked fairly well. "Keith turned it on from San Francisco," he said, and Harary added, "Twice." Clearly such a switch would be a technological breakthrough of mind-boggling applications, both good and evil.

Occult writer D. Scott Rogo, writing on "Psychics Beat the Stock Market" in *Fate* (July 1984), reports a long conversation with his friend Blue Harary. Here is how Delphi, at least at the outset, handled its market predictions. The technique is called ARV (associative remote viewing). Suppose that on Thursday Delphi wants to know whether a particular stock will go up more than .25, go down more than .25, or make no significant change. The numbers 1, 2, 3 are randomly assigned to the three possibilities. Targ phones White to ask him to assign the same numbers to three objects that are quite different.

Next, Targ phones Harary. Without telling him what the three objects are, he asks him to use his powers of precognition to "see" what object he (Targ) plans to give him on Monday. If Harary's vision matches one of the objects, Targ checks the object's number against the numbers assigned to the market futures and passes the prediction on to the client. Of course on Monday Targ must give the designated object to Harary, otherwise the backward causality wouldn't operate properly.

Rogo provides an actual case. On Delphi's second effort to predict silver futures the three objects were a cylindrical vial of perfume, a plastic bag of washers, and a pair of eyeglass frames. Harary's impression was of a "tubular ring of some kind—like a flourescent light fixture," or "a tube inside a paper towel." Moreover, it "had a funny smell." This was taken to mean the perfume bottle, which had the same number as the rise of silver. The market did in fact rise over the weekend, and the investor made a profit.

I have been told the following variation of the technique. Instead of objects, numbers are assigned to nearby areas. Harary is then asked to remote view the site to which Targ will travel on Monday. If he succeeds in describing one of the randomly selected sites, its number gives the market prediction. To make sure the procedure works, Targ has to make the required trip. Curious paradoxes would result if he failed to go there or went to the wrong spot.

Why did the technique later fail? Harary dismissed the widespread view among parapsychologists that precognition somehow doesn't operate whenever greed is involved. The failures were caused, he told Rogo, by his own "fatigue and boredom" in trying repeatedly to satisfy the demands of Delphi's greedy clients.

It has not been easy to keep up with the whereabouts and activities of Targ and Puthoff since they left SRI International. My latest information is that Puthoff is doing research, no doubt very hush-hush, at the Institute for Advanced Study, at Austin, Texas. In 1987 Targ was working on lasers at Lockheed and running what he called the National ESP Laboratory from his home in Portola Valley, California.

The laboratory is conducting the following experiment. For a fee of $35 you can enroll in a program designed to teach you how to develop your powers of remote viewing (clairvoyance) and precognition. The fee provides you with ten tests, evaluation of the results, a leatherette folder in which to keep records, descriptive material, a 24-page instruction booklet, and $10,000 of "simulated money." On certain days you are asked to remote view the future of the stock market, and send your investment for two weeks ahead. The emphasis is on silver futures because their values fluctuate so rapidly.

The experiment began in April 1987. Targ told *Fate* (October 1987) that by June the forecasts of his participants were 85 percent accurate.

"It is wonderful to work with a gifted psychic," Targ said, "but even more wonderful to work with people all across America. . . . We believe it is time that ESP abilities get used, not just talked about. Somewhere out there are the ESP geniuses—we hope to find them."

If Targ finds any such geniuses, then of course he should have ample funds for further research, and become one of the world's richest men to boot.

8 | The Relevance of Belief Systems

In the January 1984 issue of the *Journal of the American Society for Psychical Research,* my *Science: Good, Bad and Bogus* was reviewed at length by Douglas M. Stokes. Dr. Stokes (his Ph.D. is in experimental psychology at the University of Michigan) is chairman of the mathematics department at the Shipley School, a private preparatory school in Bryn Mawr, and an associate editor of the *Journal of Parapsychology.* Although he spent a year in Rhine's laboratory, he has since retired from experimental work in parapsychology. He is more skeptical than most parapsychologists; indeed, he stopped doing work in the field of psi phenomena because of frustration at his failure to obtain reliable evidence.

I must say that Stokes's nine-page review was much more tolerant of my opinions than I would have expected, and I am grateful for his many generous remarks. There is, however, a passage in his review on which I should like to comment because, although it expresses a notion common in the rhetoric of parapsychology, I consider it to be misguided. I refer to the belief that in evaluating psi research it is always irrelevant to mention the researcher's religious views.

If by "religious views" one means a metaphysical system nowhere in sharp conflict with firmly established science, then they are indeed irrelevant. But if the system demands adherence to eccentric science, the situation is quite different.

Stokes takes me to task for pointing out that Harold Puthoff was once a believer in Scientology and that one of Puthoff's assistants and some of his most successful subjects in remote viewing were and are Scientologists. "Gardner maintains," Stokes writes, "that this is relevant information, as the Church of Scientology adheres to a belief system which is, in Gardner's view, irrational." Stokes goes on to say that many "orthodox religions" are equally irrational. "Would it not be offensive," he asks, "to argue that, say, a cosmologist's research is suspect because he is a Catholic?"

Well, it all depends on the kind of research and the nature of the scientist's Catholic beliefs. In the days of Galileo, when all Catholics believed

the earth to be the immovable center of the universe, those convictions were strongly relevant to the research of Catholic astronomers. Today, I know of no Catholic beliefs that bear significantly on modern cosmology. The day is long past when Catholics were obliged to assume that the earth does not move and that the universe was created less than 10,000 years ago. Indeed, a Catholic may believe with Saint Augustine that the universe has an infinite past and still is the creation of God.

When we turn to present-day fundamentalism there is an inescapable conflict with science. Not only do most creationists deny the fact of evolution—but they insist that the earth and all living things on it did not exist before the six-day period of creation described in Genesis. The leading "geologist" of modern times who defended the flood theory of fossils—the theory that fossils are records of life destroyed by Noah's flood—was George McCready Price. I consider his 726-page work, *The New Geology* (1923), to be a masterpiece of modern crankery. Almost all creationist books now in print steal shamelessly from this ingenious volume, sometimes even reproducing its pictures without credit.

Now Price was a devout Seventh-Day Adventist, and Adventists are fundamentalists who take the "days" of Genesis to be 24-hour periods. It is almost impossible for Adventists to hold a contrary view because that would mean going against the revelations of their inspired prophetess, Ellen Gould White. When I discussed Price's geology in a chapter of my book *Fads and Fallacies* I spoke at length about Price's religious background.

I hope Stokes does not consider that irrelevant. As a Seventh-Day Adventist, Price had no choice except to regard fossils as relics of the flood, a fact that renders all his "research" suspect. Of course the same can be said of a book like *The Genesis Flood* (1961) by John Whitcomb, Jr., and Henry Morris. This 518-page volume is priceless Price. In evaluating its "research," surely it is not irrelevant to point out that the authors are fundamentalists. Can you imagine a secular university giving a doctorate in cosmology to a student who firmly believes that the cosmos did not exist before 10,000 years ago and that God created it with light already on its way from stars that are millions of light-years distant?

It is not offensive to point out that today's leaders of creationist science are Protestant fundamentalists; nor is it offensive to mention that a parapsychologist is a Scientologist. It is impossible to be a Scientologist without accepting the reality of all psi phenomena, as well as a variety of other paranormal powers. A Scientologist must believe in reincarnation and that an embryo, immediately after conception and long before it develops inner ears, starts to record all conversations in which its mother participates. One must also believe that an E-meter is capable of uncovering these "engrams" and that severe neuroses can be successfully treated by bringing engrams to light and erasing them. (The best reference I know on the pseudoscientific dogmas of Scientology is Christopher Evans's *Cults of Unreason*. On the roles of Scientologists in Puthoff's research, see the chapter on "World of Thetans" in John Wilhelm's *The Search for Superman*.)

The Church of Scientology is proud of a letter that Puthoff once wrote on the stationery of Stanford University. Here are some excerpts:

As part of my professional work in education and technology, I am continuously involved in assessing various forms of educational systems. In this capacity I have come in contact with and have studied extensively the system developed by L. Ron Hubbard known as Scientology.

Although critics viewing the system from outside may form the impression that Scientology is just another of many quasi-educational quasi-religious "schemes," it is in fact a highly sophisticated and highly technological system more characteristic of the best of modern corporate planning and applied technology. Examination of the system at close hand reveals that upwards of millions of manhours of carefully supervised research have gone into the development of the system, and the successes obtained in the rehabilitation of people's abilities and emotional stability is truly phenomenal. . . .

From a more technical viewpoint, the use of the "E-meter" to measure physiological variables which correlate with emotional responses can be viewed as representative of a large-scale innovation in medical analysis and computer education known as "physiological feedback." . . . In the technological community here at Stanford, we have projects underway employing the techniques developed in Scientology, which techniques have been found to be quite advanced and practical.

The philosophy and understanding of human nature which has arisen from these studies and is expounded in the Scientology literature I find to be an uplifting and workable system of concepts which blend the best of Eastern and Western religious traditions. After seeing these techniques in operation and experiencing them myself, I am certain that they will be incorporated eventually on a large scale in modern society as the readiness and awareness level develops.

My quotes are from a photocopy of the letter on page 31 of the appendix of *Scientology: A World Religion Emerges in the Space Age,* published by the Church of Scientology in 1974. I have no idea how much of this letter Puthoff would today defend because, as far as I know, he has not repudiated the letter or written about his present religious views. We do know he was married in a Scientology ceremony, that he was pronounced "clear" of engrams, and that he reached the church's rank of Class III Operational Thetan.

Stokes thinks that Puthoff's religious beliefs are irrelevant in discussing his research. Mentions of such opinions, writes Stokes, are ad hominem attacks that have no place in scientific discourse. It is as irrelevant, he insists, as calling attention to the fact that a scientist is a Christian or even a philosophical theist.

I find it hard to believe that Stokes cannot see the enormous difference between modern Christianity—which, except for Protestant fundamentalism, involves no dogmas that render any aspect of today's science impossible to accept—and the myriad wild scientific claims that cluster at the core of Scientology. It is indeed irrelevant in evaluating the research of, say, Arthur Holly Compton or Sir Arthur Stanley Eddington to consider their Protestant beliefs. It is indeed irrelevant in evaluating John von Neumann's contributions to quantum mechanics to call attention to his conversion to Catholicism. It is not irrelevant to call attention to a parapsychologist's belief in a cult as scientifically illiterate and as morally unscrupulous as Scientology. Can anyone who believes that experiments have shown that a week-old embryo records its mother's conversations have a sound understanding of the need for adequate controls in behavioral research? It is like expecting a doctor who thinks diseases can be diagnosed by spots on the iris to engage in sound ophthalmological research.

Come to think of it, why does Stokes consider Scientology a religion? Does he not know that L. Ron Hubbard moved from dianetics, a form of quick quack therapy, to reincarnation and Scientology only to get the word *church* into the name of his cult and thereby obtain tax-free status? Does Stokes really imagine that Hubbard was the charismatic founder of a new faith and not a con man out to make a fortune? If so, he has never bothered to inform himself about Hubbard's history. When I spoke of Puthoff's enthusiasm for Scientology, I was not even speaking of his "religion." I was speaking of his immersion in a system of bogus science. Nothing is learned about a scientist's competence if you discover he is a Lutheran. A great deal is learned about his competence if you discover he is a Scientologist.

It is possible, of course, that Puthoff has now matured to the point at which he sees Scientology as a tissue of moonshine. If so, it would be helpful if he would issue a statement of precisely where he stands with respect to Hubbard's dogmas. If he no longer believes them, it will no longer be important to call attention to them.

One more caveat. Stokes quotes a passage in which I say it is difficult for a skeptic to evaluate the work of parapsychologists like Helmut Schmidt who have not made their raw data available to outsiders. "Why is it," Stokes wonders, ". . . that such extreme measures are not needed in evaluating other areas of science?"

Has Stokes forgotten that cardinal rule, so crisply put by Marcello Truzzi, that extraordinary claims demand extraordinary evidence? Does he not see the vast gulf between the need for extraordinary controls in support of Schmidt's claim that psychics can alter, by time-reversed causality, a recording of random emissions from a radioactive substance and the need for such tight controls with respect to the mild claims of most research papers? If Schmidt's claim is true, it would revolutionize physics. No comparable revolution follows from the validity of 99 percent of published research papers.

"The more a statement of fact conflicts with previous experience," wrote Thomas Huxley in his book on Hume, "the more complete must be the evidence which is to justify us in believing it." We do not need extraordinary controls when a scientist reports that a cockroach can push a plastic pill bottle six inches. But if a scientist reports that a cockroach or a live chicken egg can influence a randomizer by PK, or that a psychic can push a pill bottle six inches without touching it, then extraordinary controls are called for. No one has made this elementary point more eloquently than Huxley. That is why the vast majority of experimental psychologists demand stronger confirmatory evidence for psi wonders than they demand for the mostly dull and humdrum claims of "other areas of science."

Afterword

Two readers commented on my column in letters that were published in the *Skeptical Inquirer* (Fall 1985):

> Martin Gardner is a national treasure. In a better world than this he would hold a cabinet post: Secretary of Sanity. But even Gardner has blind spots, one of which is his apparent conviction that a vast moral and intellectual chasm separates crude, upstart systems of superstition, which he calls cults, from sophisticated, entrenched systems of superstition, such as modern

Christianity. It is this conviction that underpins his arguments that modern Christianity, "except for Protestant fundamentalism, involves no dogmas that render any aspect of today's science impossible to accept," and hence that it is irrelevant to consider a scientist's (nonfundamentalist) Christian beliefs in evaluating his research.

In fact a number of evolutionary biologists and historians of science have argued persuasively that Judeo-Christian theology is profoundly at odds with Darwin's theory of evolution. As Stephen Jay Gould has pointed out, Darwin's 20-year delay in publishing his theory did not result from his fear of advocating evolution—evolutionary ideas had been commonplace since the late eighteenth century—but rather from his fear of advocating *a materialistic evolutionary mechanism*. Other evolutionists of Darwin's day spoke of "vital forces," "directed history," "organic striving," and so forth—vague, mystical notions that were easily reconciled with a Christian God who acts through evolution rather than through special creation. But in Darwin's materialistic vision organic design, including the design of the human brain/mind, is the product of random variation and nonrandom replication. The difficulty of reconciling this vision with Christianity and other currents in Western thought (such as the idea that there is a unity and harmony in nature) is probably why Darwin's views did not prevail in biology until the 1940s. The distinguished biologist George C. Williams has argued that "biology would have been able to mature more rapidly in a culture not dominated by Judeo-Christian theology and the Romantic tradition." Outside biology—in psychology, for example—Darwin's view of life has had almost no impact at all. Why? According to evolutionary biologist Michael Ghiselin, "A world populated by organisms striving to no end but rather playing ridiculous sexual games, a world in which the brain is an extension of the gonads . . . simply cannot be reconciled with the old way of thinking."

Gardner's claim that modern Christianity "involves no dogmas that render any aspect of today's science impossible to accept" is tenable only if "dogmas" and "impossible" are defined so restrictively and legalistically as to sap Christianity of its pith, its essence, its very *raison d'être*. Nonfundamentalist Christians are able to accept Darwin evolution so easily because they do not fully understand its implications.

Donald Symons
Department of Anthropology
University of California
Santa Barbara, Calif.

Martin Gardner's "The Relevance of Belief Systems" skirts what seems to me a crucial question for CSICOP: *Is* there any more evidence for specific religious beliefs (i.e., other than a vague feeling of possibility)—life after death, the efficacy of prayer, miracles, salvation, the existence of God, etc.—than for the "claims of the paranormal" that CSICOP examines? I see no logical reason for segregating into two categories such claims and religious beliefs. Some of the latter are manifestly more absurd than others, but "religious views—nowhere in sharp conflict with firmly established science" seems likely to be a class with no members.

I am not of course advocating that CSICOP investigate religious beliefs as claims of the paranormal. Scientific thinking is by no means pervasive enough as yet, and in any case such beliefs are not often definite "claims." Certainly there are psychological and cultural reasons that most people, even including scientists, continue to put religious beliefs and scientific thinking into separate compartments and are not capable of viewing religious beliefs as "extraordinary claims demanding extraordinary evidence."

Isn't it unseemly for an organization like CSICOP to genuflect to certain religions and castigate others (and distasteful to take comfort from what Catholics are *now permitted* to believe)? I find Gardner's position, if I understand it correctly, too close to that of the Irish priest in Honor Tracy's *The Straight and Narrow Path:* "How often must he tell [his parishoners] they were to eschew all superstitions save those approved by Holy Church."

William G. Keehn
Mountain View, Calif.

I replied:

Symons and Keehn have a point, but I suspect neither is aware of the extent to which demythologizing has penetrated liberal Christian, Jewish, Muslim, and Asian religious faiths. Even in the Roman church, the day has long passed when a Catholic biologist like George Mivart could be excommunicated for trying to persuade Rome that evolution must not be condemned. Mivart's battle has been won faster than Galileo's. Evolution in its most "materialistic" form (Darwin, by the way, believed in the inheritance of acquired traits, so for him the variations were not random) is simply taken by liberal theologians around the world as God's method of creation, no more requiring heavenly jabs than the earth requires such jabs to go around the sun.

The rise of the "higher criticism," for which Mivart also fought, has produced millions of Christians today who view the biblical miracles as myths. A top Anglican bishop has recently been in the news for denying the virgin birth and dismissing the bodily resurrection of Jesus as a crude "conjuring trick with bones." Paul Tillich, considered one of the greatest modern Protestant theologians, not only abandoned the miracles but he did not even believe in a personal God or personal immortality. To say that religious views nowhere in conflict with science are held by "a class with no members" is to so narrow the meaning of "religious" that it denies the existence of tens of thousands of the world's best scientists and most eminent thinkers.

Consider such physicists as Protestants Arthur Compton and Stanley Eddington, or David Bohm and his Eastern religious views, or Nobel Prize-winner Abdus Salam, a devout Muslim who sees physics as a form of prayer, and whose deep religious convictions are anathema to Muslim fundamentalists.

Consider such influential Catholic theologians as Hans Küng, Edward Schillebeeckx, or the late Karl Rahner. The present pope is kept from excommunicating them mainly because it would be bad public relations. Consider the Jesuit historian of philosophy F. C. Copleston, whose monumental history is as unbiased as such a history could be. I speak as a Christian outsider, but it seems to me grossly unfair to say that such thinkers either do not comprehend science or should not call themselves Christians. The word *Christian* has become too vague for such a blanket condemnation.

Quite aside from word-quibbling, my basic point is as simple as it is obvious. Black and white are ends of a continuum but that does not make the distinction useless. There is a whopping difference between the research of top "religious" scientists whose metaphysical beliefs play no role in biasing their work and the ignorant babblings of creationists or the crazy claims of scientifically illiterate cults.

9 | Welcome to the Debunking Club

When defenders of a pseudoscience want to put down critics, they like to call them "debunkers." The implication is that debunkers are not open-minded skeptics, eager to learn the truth. The skeptics are accused of relying mainly on ridicule and name-calling instead of rational arguments. Should we skeptics take offense when we are accused of debunking?

The origin of "bunk" is amusing. I happen to live a few miles from Buncombe County, in the mountains of western North Carolina. Back in 1820 the county's representative in the U.S. Congress had a habit of putting colleagues to sleep with long speeches "for Buncombe." Shortened to "bunkum" or "bunk," the word became a synonym for political claptrap. In today's dictionaries *bunk* is defined as nonsense, and *debunking* as the exposing of sham or falsehood. Who could object to that? Nevertheless, it may be that *debunk* is becoming a term of reproach, like the old word *muckraker,* now replaced by the more dignified "investigative reporter."

Stephen Jay Gould is among the many top scientists who do not mind being called debunkers. His splendid book *The Mismeasure of Man*—an attack on historic efforts to link intelligence to race, sex, or the shape of the head—has a section headed "Debunking as a positive science." Gould sees debunking not only as admirable but as essential to the health of science.

Have you noticed that believers in a pseudoscience are all in favor of debunking pseudosciences in which they *don't* believe? Indeed, many times they themselves ridicule believers of other doctrines. Frequently, when they reply to their own detractors, they hurl insults of the very sort they condemn their critics for using.

The thoughts above circulated through my brain while I was reading *Beyond Velikovsky,* by Henry H. Bauer (University of Illinois Press, 1985). A Vienna-born chemist, Bauer is dean of the College of Arts and Sciences at Virginia Polytechnic Institute, in Blacksburg, and the author of several technical books. "Many scientists derisively attacked Velikovsky's theories . . . ," says the book's jacket. "But they seriously undercut their case by resorting to innuendo, ridicule, misrepresentation, *ad hominem* arguments. . . ." In brief, they were debunkers of the worst sort. Because these attackers of V (as I shall henceforth refer to Velikovsky) include such distinguished scientists as Carl Sagan and Gould, science writers like myself, Isaac Asimov, L. Sprague de Camp, and other friends, I opened the book with understandable interest. I expected to find a careful, dispassionate evaluation of everyone involved in the V controversy. To my surprise, I found Bauer writing exactly as he accuses debunkers of doing.

Some samples: V was "an ignoramus masquerading as a sage" (p. 94). He was "quite ignorant of science, and I cheerfully dismiss as nonsense his *explanations* of physical events, where indeed he gives any" (p. 319). V was "unaware of contemporary cosmological views, even to the extent of being unclear about the distinction between the problem of the age and origin of the universe and that of the age and origin of the solar system" (p. 129). "There is warrant to describe him as a pseudo-scientist" and his "ideas about matters of natural science are not worth taking seriously" (p. 133). V is "an arch-dogmatist who regards his own intuition as a more valid guide than all the accumulated body of fact and theory. . . ." (p. 122).

Bauer accuses V of having been a man without humor who saw himself as a heretic and genius in the company of Maxwell and Einstein and who took every opposition to his views as evidence of a vast conspiracy by the establishment. In plain language, V was paranoid. "He misrepresents theories and facts extant at the time he wrote—and not because he had not read about them, for he quotes from authoritative sources: either he did not understand, or he deliberately misrepresented. . . . He uses the jargon of science as though he understands it. His tone is that of one who is discussing subjects with which he is familiar, yet a close look at what he says reveals that he is not competent to carry on such discussions" (p. 121). Bauer is here commenting on V's little-known *Cosmos Without Gravitation,* in which he defends the view that gravity is electromagnetic. On the basis of this book alone, Bauer writes, "I would not hesitate to characterize the author as a crank or a charlatan" (p. 121).

Over and over again Bauer reminds his readers that because V is a crank it doesn't follow that his views are "wrong." What Bauer means is that one can never say with absolute certainty that any theory is right or wrong. Who could disagree? I know of no philosopher who doesn't take this commonplace view for granted. This is not to say that theories can't be evaluated, some with extremely high degrees of probability. Bauer himself often states flatly that V is "downright wrong" and "quite wrong." In this connection it is interesting to note that when Gould debunks V's major geological blunders (in *Ever Since Darwin*) he writes: "Velikovsky is neither crank nor charlatan—although . . . he is at least gloriously wrong."

Naturally I agree with everything Bauer has to say about V in his book and in his excellent review of Alfred de Grazia's *Cosmic Heretics* in the Spring 1985 *Skeptical Inquirer*. But the funny thing is that Bauer is as harsh on V's detractors as he is on V. They are constantly accused of "gross ineptness," yet his own summary of why he decided V was a crank says very little that V's debunkers did not say in more detail and with more cogent arguments. For reasons hard to fathom, Bauer is as eager to bat V's critics on the head as he is to bat V. His technique, borrowed from the Velikovskians, is twofold: (1) say little about the strongest criticism— Gould's essay "Velikovsky in Collision," for instance, is never mentioned, except in the book's excellent bibliography; and (2) nitpick.

A fine specimen of nitpicking is Bauer's attack on Sagan. In his famous lecture on V at a meeting of the American Association for the Advancement of Science, Sagan discusses in detail ten of V's greatest howlers. Bauer ignores all of these criticisms except the one in which Sagan, according to Bauer and others, made a dubious calculation of probability. I come off a trifle better than most debunkers because Bauer credits me with being the first to point out V's enormous debt to Ignatius Donnelly's crank work *Ragnarok,* but other science writers are denigrated in terms as strong as any that Bauer applies to V.

In some cases, Bauer seriously misinterprets. He quotes Asimov: "Velikovsky doesn't accept the laws of motion, the law of conservation of angular momentum, the law of conservation of energy and other such trivialities." Bauer calls this sentence irresponsible, inaccurate, and misleading (p. 141) on the grounds that V did not deny such laws. Now surely it is obvious that Asimov never for a moment thought that V did not accept *some* laws about energy, motion, and momentum. What he clearly meant was that V's wild celestial scenarios violate all classic laws. In other words, V did not accept the laws on which all scientists agree. He accepted only the curious laws he himself invented, laws totally unsupported by evidence, serving no purpose except to bolster V's bizarre interpretations of legends in the Old Testament and elsewhere.

To justify calling V a crank, Bauer acknowledges that he has no objection to anyone calling *him* (Bauer) a crank. Why would anyone do that? Because, he confesses, he firmly believes in the reality of Loch Ness monsters! At first I thought he was joking, but no—he is deadly serious. The book is dedicated to his friend Tim Dinsdale, whose popular books on water monsters Bauer greatly admires. He is convinced that Dinsdale's 1960 film showing a dark spot moving through the loch's waters is an authentic film of the creature's hump. Recalling Bauer's bibliography of references on the Loch Ness monster in *Zetetic Scholar* (no. 7, 1980), I checked it to see what he had to say about this dreary literature. Sure enough, Bauer gives high marks to the two books on sea serpents that Rupert Gould, a British naval officer, wrote in the early 1930s. "Gould's perspicacity is evidenced by his conclusions, borne out by the decades of further investigations." Bauer comments. "Nessie is up to 45 feet long . . . and is a land-locked sea-serpent." Books and articles critical of sea-serpents are either ridiculed or considered unworthy of citing.

Bauer's present opinion is unchanged. On page 139 of his V book he declares: ". . . Just as from personal inquiry I believe Velikovsky to be a pseudo-scientist, so also on the basis of my personal inquiries I believe in the existence of Loch Ness monsters ('Nessies') and of sea serpents. In Loch Ness there is a breeding population of large aquatic animals with powerful flippers, long thin necks, and bulky humped bodies, animals not as yet known to 'science.' I believe that because I myself have examined the evidence of eyewitnesses, of photographs, of sonar observations. So, someone who lumps my Nessies together with the case of Velikovsky loses credibility in my eyes; it indicates to me that he probably takes his opinions at second hand or after only cursory reading."

A footnote on the same page, referring to sonar results and underwater photos, was written before publication in the *Skeptical Inquirer* (Winter 1984-85) of "Sonar and Photographic Searches for the Loch Ness Monster: A Reassessment," by sonar specialists Rikki Razdan and Alan Kielar. In 1983, after finding the evidence for Nessie to be zero, the authors made a careful sonar monitoring of Loch Ness. It lasted seven weeks, searching to a depth of 33 meters in an area where previous contacts had been reported. They found nothing larger than a one-meter fish. It will be interesting to see what Bauer has to say about this in his next book. According to the dust jacket of his book on V, it will be a study of the Loch Ness controversy.

It goes without saying that good debunkers should do their best to understand what they debunk and to avoid as many mistakes as possible. Unfortunately, life is short, scientists are busy, and cranks have a habit of writing lots of books and articles. You can hardly blame scientists for not spending years digging up everything a crank has published, not to mention unprinted manuscripts available only to the master's acolytes.

When V announced that all the craters on the moon were formed a few thousand years ago by the bubbling of its molten surface, can you blame astronomers for not trying to give the public and V's followers a course on ancient lunar impact craters? When V attributed the earth's petroleum to vermin flourishing on Jupiter and being carried to the earth's atmosphere by Venus, can you blame geologists for not regarding this as worthy of a detailed rebuttal? Judging from past history, such attempts to enlighten Velikovskians would have been like trying to write on water. There are times when the claims of a crank are so preposterous, such obvious examples of pure bunk, that ridicule is unavoidable. Welcome, Professor Bauer, to the V debunking club.

Afterword

Professor Bauer's response ran in the *Skeptical Inquirer* (Winter 1985/86):

Readers of Gardner's column will gather that I have displeased him, but it might not be clear how; the answer is probably to be found in pages 141, 143, and 295 of my book *Beyond Velikovsky*. Gardner's column illustrates some of the debunking tactics I criticize, notably misrepresentation by citing out of context, and comments ad hominem; for example, Gardner does not inform your readers that my quoted conclusions about Velikovsky come only after a lengthy setting out of the information and reasoning on which I base those conclusions.

Let me briefly illustrate the differences between Gardner's approach and mine. First, Gardner defends (in his next-to-last paragraph) critics who have not fully done their homework; whereas my book pleads that critics make themselves fully informed, out of plain self-interest if nothing else. Second, Gardner believes (last paragraph) that "there are times when . . . ridicule is unavoidable"; I believe that one always has a choice whether or not to employ ridicule.

Third, the matter of Loch Ness. I chuckled when reading that Gardner at first had thought I was joking in confessing my belief that Nessies are real animals. My purpose in writing that statement had been to produce precisely that sort of response. Immodestly I assume that the statement shocks because hitherto the reader of my book has been led to regard me as rather hard-headed, even intelligent and logical; and one of the major points that I seek to press is that hard-headed, intelligent, and logical people can reach different conclusions and hold different beliefs, quite rationally, on a host of issues for which definite proof and definite disproof are both lacking—for example, concerning the Loch Ness monster.

I value logic and clarity of thought and appreciate them even when they lead others to beliefs different from those I hold. Gardner, on the other hand, appears to be incredulous when others don't admit that his views are correct, and he regards such differences as appropriate occasions for ridicule. In seeking to push the correctness of his own views, Gardner apparently believes that any polemical or rhetorical devices are justified; in other words, regarding what he calls pseudoscience, he seems to believe that the end justifies the means.

Professor Bauer's book on Nessie, *The Enigma of Loch Ness: Making Sense of a Mystery* (University of Illinois Press) was published in 1986. It contains a comprehensive bibliography, lots of photos that resemble UFO pictures in their vagueness, and a list of some 800 sightings. The author is aware that he may be wrong, and he is particularly miffed because Nessie is defended by cranks who believe in such nonsense as astrology, the Bermuda Triangle, UFOs, and other "anomalies" he considers beyond the pale. He has no respect for flaky magazines like *Fate* that regularly defend such things.

This naturally doesn't sit well with Jerome Clark, a *Fate* editor, who reviewed the book unfavorably in *Fate* (February 1987). Clark quotes Bauer: "My own belief in Nessies is grounded on film and photos and the patterns of confirmatory sonar and eyewitness testimony and so forth." Change "sonar" to "radar," writes Clark, and "his sentiments would perfectly express my reasons for 'belief' in UFOs." For more sensible commentary on the book, see Edward Kelly's unfavorable review, "A Too Willing Suspension of Disbelief," in the *Skeptical Inquirer,* Spring 1987; and Owen Gingerich's review "On Trans-Scientific Turf," in *Nature,* April 25, 1985.

How can one explain a scientist's strong disenchantment with Velikovsky followed by an equally strong enchantment with sea monsters? My guess is that Bauer belongs to that small class of scientists and writers who harbor a deep suspicion of establishment science coupled with a passionate desire to latch onto a fringe claim, ridiculed by the mainstream, that will turn out to be right. Of course there is a possibility (in my mind extremely minute) that those of us who scoff at reports of sea serpents could end up red-faced over our failure to take them seriously.

It will be interesting to see whether Bauer's belief in Nessie persists if, for the next decade or two, the situation remains unchanged. Nevertheless, his book, like his blast at Velikovsky, is a valuable history of a fringe controversy kept alive by the media. Perhaps the Blacksburg chemist will soon give us a Bauer book on Bigfoot.

What about the future of Velikovskyism? Since V's death in 1979 and Bauer's 1985 blast, defenders of the faith have been slowly abandoning their sinking scow. In December 1986 C. Leroy Ellenberger, a senior editor and former executive secretary of the pro-V journal *Kronos,* resigned from the magazine. He had finally faced up, as he put it, to the "cruel truth" that his former hero was a pathological crank. (See his "A Lesson From Velikovsky," in the *Skeptical Inquirer,* Summer, 1986, pp. 380-381). That *Kronos* continues to be published is a striking tribute to the persistence of irrational beliefs on the part of humorless acolytes—the outstanding example is Lynn Rose, professor of (of all things) philosophy at the State University of New York at Buffalo—whose minds are set in concrete. A journal devoted to defending Percival Lowell's Martian canals would be just as useful to science; certainly more fun to edit and read.

For an informative exchange of letters between Ellenberger and Rose, see *Nature,* August 1, 1985; October 10, 1985; and November 21, 1985. The letters were prompted by Gingerich's review, cited above, of Bauer's book. Gingerich's response is in *Nature,* January 9, 1985. See also Henrietta W. Lo's excellent article on "Velikovsky's Interpretation of the Evidence Offered by China in his *Worlds in Collision,*" in the *Skeptical Inquirer,* Spring 1987. Ms. Lo finds V's book so riddled with errors of fact and logic that historians were fully justified in refusing to take seriously V's clumsy efforts to reconstruct world history.

10 | The Great Stone Face

Clouds often take the shapes of animals and human faces. The same is true of rock formations, such as the Great Stone Face in the White Mountains of New Hampshire, made famous by Hawthorne's tale. Draw a wiggly vertical line. It's easy to find spots where you can add a few more lines to make the profile of a face. On the left and right sides of the maple leaf on the Canadian flag you'll see the faces of two men (liberal and conservative?) arguing with each other. A few decades ago the Canadian dollar bill had to be re-engraved because the face of a demon accidentally turned up in the Queen's hair just behind her left ear.

This tendency of chaotic shapes to form patterns vaguely resembling familiar things is responsible for one of the most absurd books ever written about advertising: *Subliminal Seduction,* by journalist Wilson Bryan Key (Prentice-Hall, 1973). The Signet paperback had on its cover a photograph of an ice-filled cocktail with the caption "Are you sexually aroused by this picture?" It was the author's contention that hundreds of advertising photographs are carefully retouched to "embed" concealed pictures designed to shock your unconscious and thereby help you remember the product. The hidden pictures include words ranging from *sex* to the most taboo of four-letter words, but there are also phallic symbols and all sorts of other eroticisms. In the ice-cube in an ad for Sprite, the author professed to see a nude woman cohabiting with a shaggy dog. It's hard to imagine anyone taking this nonsense seriously, especially since the author's many references to "recent studies" never disclosed where they took place or who the experimenters were. More amazing still, the Canadian Catholic philosopher Marshall McLuhan wrote the book's laudatory introduction. Key has gone on to write two even more bizarre books about the sneaky ways modern advertising is subliminally seducing us.

More recently, UFO enthusiasts have been playing the hidden-picture game with the moon and Mars. They pore over thousands of photographs of cratered surfaces until—aha!—they find something suggesting the presence of alien creatures. An early anticipation of this pastime occurred in 1953,

Do you see the demon in the Queen's hair? Some did, and the Canadian dollar bill had to be re-engraved as a result.

when H. Percy Wilkins, a retired British moon-mapper, discovered what looked like a man-made bridge on the moon. Frank Edwards wrote about it in *Stranger Than Science* (1959), and UFO cranks lost no time seizing on this as evidence of lunar life. Donald Keyhoe, in *The Flying Saucer Conspiracy* (1955), reported that spectroscopic analysis had identified the bridge's metal! When astronomer Donald Menzel said he couldn't see the bridge, Keyhoe called him an "army stooge" collaborating on a vast government conspiracy to conceal the truth about UFOs. (See James Oberg's article, "Myths and Mysteries of the Moon," in *Fate,* September 1980.)

As late as 1976, UFO buff George H. Leonard was claiming that bridges on the moon are among the "least controversial things about the moon." Alas, all bridges vanished when the Apollo photographs were obtained. The "bridges" were nothing more than illusions created by lights and shadows, yet the myth of moon bridges still persists in UFO fringe literature.

The same thing happened to mysterious spires on the moon. Photos in 1966 of the moon's surface showed objects casting such long shadows that UFOlogists decided they had to be rocket ships or radio beacons— at least *something* built by aliens. A Russian periodical called *Technology and Youth* featured a wild article about the spires in its May 1968 issue. The spires turned out to be ordinary boulders, their long shadows caused by the sunlight hitting them at extremely low angles.

George Leonard, in *Somebody Else Is on the Moon* (David McKay, 1976), carried this kind of speculation to such extremes that he managed to write one of the funniest books ever written by a UFO buff. Leonard is an amateur astronomer and retired public-health official in Rockville, Maryland. Photos of the moon's surface, he insists, show rims of craters sliced away by giant machines, jets of soil spraying out (caused by mining operations), and tracks of huge vehicles. "No, I do *not* know who they are," Leonard told the tabloid *Midnight* (February 8, 1977), "where they come from or precisely what their purpose is. But I do know the government is suppressing the discovery from the American people."

Leonard quotes an unnamed NASA scientist: "A lot of people at the

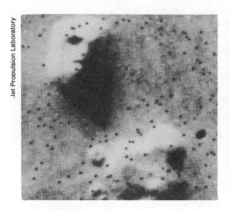

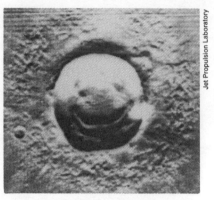

The Great Stone "Face" photographed by the Viking 1 orbiter. The feature is one mile across. Shadows in the rock formation give the illusion of a nose and mouth and bit errors, caused by problems in transmission, create the abundant speckles on the photo. Planetary geologists at the Jet Propulsion Laboratory attribute the formation to purely natural processes.

"Happy Face." This otherwise typical Martian impact crater seems to show a smiling mouth and eyes. They're both formed by fractures caused by the original meteor impact. JPL jokingly refers to the 5-mile-wide crater as the largest known Happy Face in the solar system.

top are scared." He thinks the aliens live underground and that seismic quakes on the moon are caused by their undersurface activities. "NASA is simply lying to the American people about UFOs," he told *Midnight*. He suspects the aliens are waiting patiently to take over the earth after we blow ourselves up.

Seeing familiar anomalies on Mars has been common ever since the invention of the telescope. Percival Lowell found the red planet's surface so honeycombed with canals that he wrote three books about how the Martians, desperately in need of water, built the canals to bring water from polar regions. Now, of course, we know the canals were only figments in Lowell's mind, distinguished astronomer though he was. Unfortunately, this has not deterred seemingly intelligent people from similar self-deception.

Here and there on Mars are formations with gridlike structures. "Did NASA Photograph Ruins of an Ancient City on Mars?" is the headline of a *National Enquirer* article (October 25, 1977). A photo of a region near Mars's south pole shows a series of squarelike formations called "Inca City" because they somewhat resemble a decayed Indian village.

In 1977, electrical engineer Vincent DiPietro came across a 1976 photograph taken by the Viking spacecraft that orbited Mars. At first he thought it was a hoax. The photograph showed a remarkably human-looking stone face about a mile wide. NASA had released the photo shortly after it was taken in 1976, and planetary scientists emphasized that it was a natural

formation. DiPietro thinks it isn't. Computer scientist Gregory Molenaar used image-enhancement to explore details of the face, and in 1982 DiPietro and Molenaar published a 77-page book, *Unusual Martian Surface Features,* about their results. ("Face in Space," *Omni,* April 1982, was an excerpt from this book.) The authors concede that the face may have been produced by erosion but they suspect otherwise. They claim that computer enhancement shows an eyeball in the face's right eye cavity, with a pupil near the center, and what looks like a teardrop below the eye. "If this object was a natural formation," they write, "the amount of detail makes Nature herself a very intelligent being."

West of the big stone face, in the shadow of a pyramidlike formation, is a gridlike pattern suggesting a lost city with an avenue leading toward the face. (See "Metropolis on Mars," an unsigned article in *Omni,* March 1985). Skeptics have pointed out that the so-called pyramid is much cruder than scores of pyramids found as natural rock formations in Arizona.

Top drumbeater for the view that the stone face proves that an alien race once flourished on Mars is writer Richard Hoagland. He is completing a book about it that could make him lots of money, especially if he can tie the face into UFOs and get a chapter published in *Omni.* Fred Golden, writing the "Skeptical Eye" page in *Discover* (April 1985), ridiculed Hoagland's claims and ran a photo of another spot on Mars, where the topography resembles Kermit the Frog.

Let us not underestimate the public's scientific illiteracy. Dr. Emil Gaverluk, of East Flat Rock, N.C., is now lecturing around the country about the Martian face. A story in the Hendersonville, N.C., newspaper of February 16, 1985, reported that Dr. Gaverluk was speaking at the First Baptist Church on "the meaning of the gigantic face and pyramids and the laser of tremendous power that have been discovered on Mars." Why are these things on Mars? It's all explained in the Bible, Dr. Gaverluk told the newspaper columnist who wrote about him.

Dr. Gaverluk was identified as an expert on communications science

and the holder of a doctorate in edu-
cational technology, whatever that is.
His lectures on science and faith are
sponsored by the School Assembly
Service, of Chicago. Dr. Gaverluk il-
lustrates his talks with chalk draw-
ings. He is a member of the American
Association for the Advancement of
Science and the Creation Research
Society.

The great stone face can teach
a serious lesson. If you search any
kind of chaotic data, it is easy to
find combinations that seem remarkable. Every page of a book of random

Kermit the Frog's there too! This Martian feature
was formed by flowing lava. A small impact
crater in the flow resembles an eye.

numbers contains patterns with enormous odds against them if you were
to specify the pattern before generating the random numbers. Every bridge
hand you are dealt would be a stupendous miracle if you had written down
its exact pattern before the deck was shuffled.

Let someone close his eyes and talk for 15 minutes about a scene
he imagines. You'll have no trouble finding amazing correlations between
his description and any randomly selected scenic spot. Let a psychic crime-
solver rattle on for an hour about clues to a missing corpse. It's inevitable
she'll have made some lucky hits if and when the body is found. If you
don't have a tape of everything she told the police, how can you evaluate
her accuracy? Jeane Dixon's few good hits seem impressive until you see
a list of her thousands of whopping misses.

If hundreds of ESP tests are performed around the world during any
given week, and only a few successful ones are published, the normal operations of chance are effectively concealed. J. B. Rhine was notorious in
his belief that unsuccessful tests in his laboratory were not worth reporting;
and equally notorious during his youth in finding patterns in data to support
correlations that the experiment had not been designed to find. Today's
better parapsychologists are aware of such statistical pitfalls, but a failure
to understand them casts a deceptively strong glow of success over the
results trumpeted in the early naive years of modern parapsychology.

Let's take a closer look at that great stone face on Mars. Rotate the
picture 90 degrees clockwise and what do you see? On the left is the nude
torso of a woman, complete with dark pubic hair, small breasts, and an
enlarged belly button slightly off center. I'm surprised Ken Frazier would
allow such a picture in his family magazine.

Afterword

An interesting letter from British reader Christopher Allan informed me that the first discovery of the moon bridge was by the American science writer John J. O'Neill. Wilkins merely confirmed the observation and lectured about it. H. P. Wilkins, he adds, should not be confused with the UFO writer Harold T. Wilkins. Surprisingly, the two men not only lived in the same town, but both died in 1960. Willy Ley, Allan says, debunked the bridge as early as 1962 in his book *Satellites, Rockets, and Outer Space.*

In September 1986, Dr. Gaverluk lectured for four days at Hendersonville's Wesleyan Church. His last lecture was titled "What Are the Astonishing Mile-Wide Human Face, the Mile-High Pyramids, and the 40-Mile-High Laser Beam Doing on Mars?" The local paper quotes him as saying: "The discoveries on Mars could mean a quantum jump into the Milky Way Galaxy. It relates significantly to the Second Coming of Jesus Christ."

Where did Gaverluk get the notion of a laser on Mars? It is from the opening sentence of Allen Soraiko's article "Lasers" in *National Geographic* (March 1984): "Each morning, in the soft coral flush of daybreak, a laser dawns on Mars." Reading further, one discovers what the author means. Carbon dioxide in Mars's atmosphere acts like a laser by absorbing infrared sunlight and radiating energy over the planet's surface.

There Are No Alien Bases on the Moon, by selenologist Francis Graham, was published by William L. Moore (Burbank, Calif.) in 1984. This 32-page work contains a trenchant critique of Leonard's absurd claims, as well as of other crank books like Fred Stockling's *We Discovered Alien Bases on the Moon,* Don Wilson's *Our Mysterious Spaceship Moon,* and William Brian's *Moongate.* The latter argues that the Apollo landing on the moon was a government hoax.

In spite of Graham's book and an admirable debunking by Carl Sagan in *Parade* (June 2, 1985), reputable newspapers continued to play up the Face. The *San Francisco Chronicle,* for example, in its "This World" section (July 14, 1985) devoted four outrageous pages to the Face without consulting a single scientist or even its own science editor, David Perlman.

In 1986, North Atlantic Books (Berkeley, Calif.) issued *Planetary Mysteries,* a paperback anthology edited by Richard Grossinger. It features a long interview with Hoagland. Later that same year, in its November issue, *Analog Science Fiction* published Hoagland's adolescent gee-whiz article "The Curious Case of the Humanoid Face on Mars."

Why do Carl Sagan and other scientists ridicule Hoagland's claims? Because, Hoagland writes, the existence of the Face "is almost a literal insult to an entire generation of evolutionary biologists steeped in the work of George Gaylord Simpson. . . ." Hoagland recommends a book edited by medical anthropologist Rafael Pozos, *The Face on Mars: Evidence for a Lost Civilization?* (Chicago Review Press, 1986), and his own *The Monuments of Mars: A City on the Edge of Forever* (North Atlantic Books, 1987).

Pozo's book is an edited version of the proceedings of a teleconference on the Face, so absurd that one could almost believe it to be a parody on scientific reasoning. As Jon Muller said in his review (*Skeptical Inquirer,* Spring 1987), many of the participants were directly or indirectly associated with SRI International, that prestigious think tank that authenticated the psi powers of Uri Geller. It is useful, writes Muller, to recall a comment in Carl Sagan's *Cosmos* about the Martian canals that were the basis of books by Percival Lowell: "Lowell always said the regularity of the canals was an unmistakable sign that they were of intelligent origin. This is certainly true. The only unresolved question was which side of the telescope the intelligence was on."

That *Analog* would publish lunar hogwash is bad enough; but to make things worse, the magazine's editor, Stanley Schmidt, wrote an editorial headed "Cold Feet" lambasting skeptics for not taking the Face seriously. How did establishment scientists respond to the Face and to the Martian city? They got cold feet. Confronted with "something concrete," something that could be the first evidence of ETI (extraterrestrial intelligence), what did they do? They "shrugged it off with reactions ranging from indifference to dismissal of the evidence as meaningless. At least one such dismissal that I saw [in my column?] seemed to me little more than handwaving, relying on vague analogies with things like rock 'profiles.'"

Why does someone like Sagan behave this way? "Could it be," Schmidt asks, "fear of being upstaged . . . of having the first confirmation of ETI come from somebody else's data rather than his own, or having a Mars expedition mounted for reasons other than his?"

Well, pseudoscience is on a sliding scale; but when it becomes as ridiculous as a stone face and a city on Mars, scientists have more important things to do than treat such claims soberly. "If you want to talk about the Face," Sagan told a Face enthusiast who tried to interview him, "I can give you less than five minutes."

Now that I think about it, what a waste of time to be typing such a lengthy afterword!

11 | From Phillips to Morris

In 1985 the McDonnell Foundation, which funded the McDonnell Laboratory for Psychical Research at Washington University, St. Louis, announced it had withdrawn funding. A wise decision. The lab had become an albatross around the university's neck after Randi's notorious Alpha experiment (see Chapter 1) made clear that Peter Phillips, the lab's director, though a competent physicist, had no comprehension of how to test supposed psychics.

When psychics start bending metal, rotating motors, moving objects, and performing other feats that imitate conjuring, there are only two sensible ways to conduct an investigation. Either have a knowledgeable magician present during the testing, or take a few years off to learn the art of close-up magic.

One of the dreariest aspects of psi history is the failure of otherwise intelligent researchers to understand this simple fact. Everyone now knows that Uri Geller is a con artist, except for a few diehards who still think he doesn't cheat *all* the time; but consider the damage Uri has already done to the psi community. Over and over again researchers and writers, ignorant of conjuring, have made fools of themselves by declaring their belief in metal-bending. Professor John Taylor, a British mathematical physicist, was duped into writing a preposterous book about the "Geller effect" before he discovered he had been hoodwinked. Physicist John Hasted produced an even funnier book about the wonders of metal-bending. Neither Taylor nor Hasted deemed it worthwhile to seek the help of conjurors before starting their amateur investigations. To Taylor's credit, he later rejected metal-bending, but to this day he has been too embarrassed to admit how gullible he was.

In the United States the damage done to psi research by Uri has been equally great. Both Helmut Schmidt and E. H. Walker, the two leading proponents of the quantum-mechanical explanation of psi, were taken in by Geller. As far as I know they may still be on the fence with respect to Geller's "sometime" powers. Science writer Charles Panati was so overwhelmed by Uri's simple tricks that he edited *The Geller Papers,* a

Daniel Douglas Home

book so worthless that it will be years before the damage Uri inflicted on Panati's career can be repaired.

I could go on and on with other recent cases of parapsychologists who never grasped the fact that magicians are the only experts on close-up deception. Jule Eisenbud, as far as I know, still believes Ted Serios could project his thoughts onto Polaroid film, although magicians have explained how Ted could have faked it with a palmed optical device. I suspect that every leading parapsychologist in the country now realizes that Eisenbud was deceived, but are too timid to say so. It never occurred to Charles Honorton to ask magicians how his friend Felicia Parise moved a pill bottle across her kitchen counter before he wrote a paper about this great event. Does Honorton still think Felicia did not use an invisible nylon thread? Apparently he does.

What makes this so hilarious is that it has all happened before, in the days of the great mediums. Did Conan Doyle or William Crookes or Oliver Lodge ever take a disguised magician to a séance? If so, I never heard of it. Among British journalists, the most tireless drumbeater for spiritualism was W. T. Stead, who died in the sinking of the *Titanic*. It would be hard to decide who was the biggest mark, Stead or Doyle. Stead thought it terrible that the Society for Psychical Research would try to apply scientific methods to mediums. In 1909, he attacked the Society by picturing himself as shipwrecked and drowning. (Believers in precognition have seized on this speech as evidence for psi premonition!) Suppose, said Stead, that instead of throwing him a rope someone shouts: "Who are you? What's your name?"

"I am Stead!" he imagined himself shouting back. "I am drowning here in the sea. Throw me a rope." His rescuers continue: "How do we know you are Stead? Where were you born? Tell us the name of your grandmother."

"What are known as psychical research methods were abhorrent to him," wrote spiritualist Edith Harper in her book *Stead the Man* (1914).

An artist's conception of Home levitating.

"He held them truly unscientific. . . . He said he would rather die in the workhouse than believe that anyone would tell him a deliberate falsehood for the mere purpose of deceiving him." I once had lunch with an occult journalist who made an almost identical remark about his inability to believe that a charming fellow like Geller would ever try to flimflam anybody.

Recently I obtained a copy of one of the strangest books on spiritualism ever written, or rather ghostwritten. It is *Lights and Shadows* by that magnificent charlatan D. D. Home. Doyle was furious with Home because in this book the Scottish medium exposed the methods of rivals who produced phenomena unlike his own—slate-writing, for instance. Of course Home carefully avoided any mention of his own methods. Even when he heard it from the medium he most admired, poor gullible Doyle couldn't believe that other mediums cheated as much as Home said they did.

Over and over again Home chastises his rivals for conducting séances in darkness, always adding that his own were in the light. Is it true that Home's séances were in the light? It is not. Home always *began* his sittings in the light. There would be table vibrations, raps, singing, talking, and praying; then the gaslights would be dimmed or extinguished. The room was seldom totally dark because it was necessary to see such things as fluttering white hands.

Pause to meditate on the absurdity of such darkness. Why would friendly spirits, anxious to contact loved ones, refuse to manifest themselves in significant ways except in the dark? If Home could flit about a room near the ceiling, as he often did, why did he always do this in rooms so black that the only proof he was up there was his own voice describing these Peter Pan flights? An article by Robert Bell in the *Cornhill Magazine* (August 1860) contains a dramatic account of Home floating around in "pitch darkness." How did the sitters know Home was really up there? As he had done hundreds of times, Home left a mark on the ceiling!

It is often said that Home was never caught cheating. Well, it all depends on what you mean by "caught." In the same *Cornhill* article, Bell tells how he broke one of Home's cardinal rules by taking his hands off the table and clutching a spirit hand. "It was palpable as any soft substance, velvet or pulp, but pressure reduced it to air." White rubber gloves that glow in the dark were the stock-in-trade of nineteenth-century mediums. There are other records that strongly suggest ways in which Home cheated. In France, Baron Morio de l'Isle looked under the table and saw an empty shoe. After a woman said a spirit had touched her, Morio saw Home's foot slip back into his shoe. It is said that this ill-fated séance was one reason for Home's abrupt departure from France.

Such incidents are rare in Home's career, as they are in Uri's, and for a simple reason. Like Geller, Home would not perform in the presence of magicians or even skeptics unless he sized up the skeptic as simple-minded. If a sitter in one of Home's séances so much as hinted doubts, the spirits would ask the skeptic to leave. Would not such negative thoughts dampen the spirits' spirits? We hear the same rationalizations today from psi investigators who want to exclude magicians and skeptics as observers.

The result of course is that dramatic PK phenomena—metal-bending, translocations, levitations, poltergeist activity—always occur when nobody capable of detecting fraud is watching. I write at the time of Edinburgh University's announcement that Robert Morris, of Syracuse University, has been appointed to Edinburgh's new Chair of Parapsychology, endowed by half a million pounds from the late Arthur Koestler's estate. Will Morris do a better job in Scotland than Phillips did in Missouri? Or will he too find excuses for excluding magicians when he starts testing extraordinary powers?

Morris is a firm believer in the paranormal, though more cautious than most of his colleagues. He has what he once called "a high tolerance for ambiguity." As a younger man he was not always so cautious. While getting a doctorate in psychology at Duke University—his thesis was on the mating habits of ring-necked doves—he also worked at the nearby Psychical Research Foundation. This had been set up in 1960 to investigate evidence for survival after death, with William Roll, the well-known authenticator of poltergeists, as director. Morris was Roll's research assistant.

The best known of Morris's many experiments were his investigations of the powers of Blue Harary, a "psychic" who recently teamed up with Russell Targ to form a new psi-research organization and to coauthor their book *Mind Race* (see Chapter 8). Morris's tests strongly confirmed Harary's ability to go "out of body" to a nearby lab where his spirit influenced the spirit of Spirit, Blue's pet kitten.

Another notable experiment was designed to test precognition in rats. The clever scheme was this: Monitor the behavior of a group of rats, select a few animals randomly, kill them, then see if anything in their previous behavior suggested foreknowledge of their doom. According to D. Scott Rogo, who describes these experiments in his *Parapsychology: A Century of Inquiry,* the rat test was "inconclusive." Morris tried again with goldfish. This time the fish were not killed, but simply held out of water long enough to cause "stress." Success! "Those goldfish that had been removed from the tank," Rogo writes, "were the ones who had been more active in the base-line period." This, Rogo informs us, could have been due to "an ability of the animals to show anxiety because of an awareness of what would be happening to them."

Morris, then at the Psychical Research Foundation, in early experiments with animal psi.

As these experiments indicate, Morris has been intensely interested in "animal psi." His paper "The Psychobiology of Psi," in Edgar Mitchell's *Psychic Explorations* (1974), is a readily accessible introduction to his views. Unfortunately, this survey of outstanding results on animal psi included Walter Levy's research at Dr. Rhine's laboratory on the PK power of live chicken eggs, having been written before Levy was caught cheating.

"Evidence for psi seems obtainable from a wide range of species and central nervous system complexity levels . . . ," Morris concludes. "In many ways, animals appear to respond to psi tasks in the same way that humans do—psi missing under negative conditions, habituation, response bias effects, and so on." He adds the warning that a major difficulty in such tests is that an experimenter's PK may bias results. He cites "evidence" that researchers can influence the movements of paramecia and wood lice, and Schmidt's famous tests with cockroaches, in which the results suggest it was Schmidt who influenced the randomizer because he hates cockroaches.

In recent years Morris has moved away from animal psi to other areas. In May 1984 *Omni* reported an experiment to test the abilities of humans to influence computers. Out of 33 subjects, the computer crashed with 13. Morris reported that these 13 were significantly more skeptical of PK than the others. The crashing may not have been the result of PK, Morris admitted—his high tolerance for ambiguity coming to the fore—but he added: "Why then did it occur so consistently in relation to the attitude of the people involved?"

In brief, Morris is a believer, but more hesitant than most parapsychologists in making extraordinary claims without extraordinary evidence. It will be interesting to see what results emerge from the Edinburgh laboratory. Let us hope that the lesson taught by the St. Louis fiasco will not be forgotten and that before Morris tests a psychic who performs what looks exactly like mediocre magic he will have the foresight and the courage to have someone on the scene capable of detecting fraud.

Afterword

John Beloff, a parapsychologist at the University of Edinburgh who played an important role in his university's appointment of Robert Morris, did not like my account of Home's self-levitations. The following letter from him was published in the *Skeptical Inquirer* (Summer 1986):

> Martin Gardner gives such a distorted account of D. D. Home's self-levitations that, with your permission, I would like for the sake of your readers to set the record straight.
>
> It is true that, in contrast with his table-levitations, which took place in good light, and for which no credible normal explanation has ever been proposed, his self-levitations, for whatever reason, took place in semi-darkness and so are inevitably more controversial. On the other hand, they did not occur in total darkness, as Gardner would have us believe, so that the only evidence for Home having risen would be his voice or the cross he marked on the ceiling. If that had been the case we could indeed dismiss such claims as a bad joke.
>
> Gardner cites the authority of Robert Bell, a contemporary writer and editor whose account of a sitting with Home appeared in the *Cornhill Magazine* for August 1859. It was then edited by the well-known English novelist, William Thackeray, a close friend of Robert Bell. The relevant passage in Bell's account is as follows:
>
>> I was sitting nearly opposite to Mr. Home, and saw his hands disappear from the table, and his head vanish into the deep shadow beyond. In a moment or two more he spoke again. This time his voice was in the air above our heads. He had risen from his chair to a height of four or five feet from the ground. As he ascended higher he described his position, which at first was perpendicular, and afterwards became horizontal. He said he felt as if he had been turned in the gentlest manner, as a child is turned in the arms of a nurse. In a moment or two more, he told us that he was going to pass across the window, against the grey silvery light of which he would be visible. We watched in profound stillness, and saw his figure

pass from one side of the window to the other, feet foremost lying horizontally in the air. He spoke to us and told us that he would turn the reverse way, and recross the window; which he did. His own tranquil confidence in the safety of what seemed from below a situation of the most novel peril gave confidence to everybody else; but, with the strongest nerves, it was impossible not to be conscious of a certain sensation of fear or awe.

Nor was Bell the only witness whose testimony we have. The physician Dr. James Gully (well known in his day as the pioneer of hydrotherapy and suchlike nature cures) wrote to the *Morning Star* newspaper to confirm Bell's account. There he writes: "Even when the room was comparatively darkened light streamed through the window from a distant gas-lamp outside, between which gas-lamp and our eyes Mr. Home's form passed, so that we distinctly perceived its trunk and limbs; and most assuredly there was no balloon near him, nor any machinery attached to him."

Thus we see that it is only Martin Gardner who speaks of "pitch darkness" as prevailing during the levitations. I would suggest that the reason for the mark on the ceiling was not because the sitters could not see him during the ascent but to convince themselves afterwards that they had not been hallucinating, which even then was a favorite counterexplanation.

It is interesting to note that the readers of the *Cornhill Magazine* must have been rather like readers of the *Skeptical Inquirer*. They were furious with Thackeray for publishing such rubbish, and a group of scientists that included the physicist John Tyndall descended on him to remonstrate. Thackeray is reported to have told them that it was all very well for them to protest because they had never seen any spiritualist manifestations whereas he, Thackeray, had been present with Home when a heavy dining-room table covered with decanters, glasses, and dishes had risen in the air.

Finally, we would be foolish to ignore the testimony of William Crookes. He writes (*Quarterly Journal of Science,* January 1874): "The most striking cases of levitations which I have witnessed have been with Mr. Home. On three separate occasions have I seen him raised completely from the floor of the room. Once sitting in an easy chair, once kneeling on his chair, and once standing up. On each occasion I had full opportunity of watching the occurrence as it was taking place."

I have no quarrel with Martin Gardner for expressing doubts concerning the authenticity of Daniel Home, but he can no more *know* that Home was a charlatan than I can *know* that he was not. Home no longer exists and there is no one at the present time who is remotely like him, so we can but wonder. Meanwhile, let us at least be careful to allow the evidence to speak for itself.

My reply appeared in the same issue:

What a strange response! Professor Beloff totally ignores my statement that during Home's séances "the room was seldom totally dark because it was necessary to see such things as fluttering white hands."

Let me quote more fully from Robert Bell's article "Stranger than Fiction," which ran in the *Cornhill Magazine* in August 1860—not 1859, as Beloff has it.

The guests sat around a table near a window. Home's spirits had asked that the gaslights be extinguished, and the only light came from a dying fire and from the window. "We could see but scarcely distinguish our hands upon the table," Bell writes. After the usual minor miracles, a spirit hand pulled down the blind, "and the room was thrown into deeper darkness than before." The major miracles now began. Some sitters thought they saw Home's accordion move. "I could not," writes Bell. "It was as black as pitch to me." Later he thought he saw it move.

The grand climax was Home's flotation. All Bell could see of *this* miracle was a vague shape crossing the grey light of the window.* He points out that the only way sitters could judge Home's location in the air was from his voice growing fainter when he moved farther away. Bell felt a foot touch his shoulder. At least he assumed it was a foot. But when Bell placed his hand on it, Home uttered a cry of pain and the "foot" quickly withdrew. What a disaster if Bell had tried to explore the ankle or leg!

While Home was floating here and there, "the accordion, which we supposed to be on the ground under the window"—"supposed," because it was too dark to see it—"played a strain of pathos in the air." I dislike giving away magic secrets, but Home's accordion music was almost certainly produced by a tiny harmonica, easily concealed in the mouth and played without hands. The country singer June Carter is among many entertainers today who do this expertly. It is amusing to learn that the favorite airs the spirits played on Home's accordion were simple tunes like "Home Sweet Home" that do not require sharps and flats, only the single octave these little mouth organs have.

Just two theories can explain why the great physical mediums of the past century (where are such giants today?) performed their wonders in almost total darkness. (Absolute darkness, by the way, is not only useless for such séances but impossible to obtain except in windowless rooms.) The theories are:

A. Something in the nature of light has a negative effect on whatever psi force lifts the medium. What would have happened if some awful skeptic, who had managed to get past Home's careful screenings of guests, had suddenly turned on the gaslight while Home said he was making his usual mark on the ceiling? Does Beloff think Home would have dropped to the floor? Otherwise, why not levitate in the light so there would be no question about it? It would be interesting to know Beloff's answer.

B. It is a thousand times easier for a fake medium to cheat when lights are off than when they are on. Indeed, it is like shooting fish in a barrel. Here is how *Punch* (August 18, 1860) reacted to the *Cornhill* article:

---

*There are several ways Home could have made the shape resemble a man on his back. The simplest would be to put his boots on his hands, stretch his arms out horizontally, throw back his head, and walk slowly in front of the window, pausing a moment in mid-passage to suggest a longer distance between feet and head. Shoes on the ends of two sticks would make the illusion perfect.

HOME GREAT HOME!

(Respectfully dedicated to all Admirers of that mighty Medium)

Through humbugs and fallacies though we may roam,
　　Be they never so artful, there's no case like HOME.
With a lift from the spirits he'll rise in the air,
　　(Though, as lights are put out, we can't see him there).

Spring-blinds will fly up or run down at his word
　　(If a wire has been previously fixed to the cord).
He can make tables dance, and bid chairs stand on end
　　(But, of course, it must be in the house of a friend).

Robert Bell was a journalist, a spiritualist, and a friend of Home. That a parapsychologist of Beloff's reputation can still take seriously eyewitness accounts of Home's levitations, by true believers sitting in almost total darkness, in equally total ignorance of methods used by the great charlatans of the time, is almost beyond belief. I suppose it is some sign of progress that modern psychics perform their tricks in daylight.

As for Dr. Gully, "A gull indeed!" was Robert Browning's comment. (It took only one séance for Browning to spot Home as a fraud—a "dungball" he once called him.) William Crookes is a long story. I content myself with saying there is ample evidence he was as gullible as Conan Doyle and totally unreliable in reporting what he saw in near darkness. It is astonishing how often spiritualists, describing what they "saw" in a séance, neglect to add that the room was almost pitch black.

Concerning Beloff's incredible response, I couldn't have asked for a more dramatic confirmation of my column's central theme.

My response produced a second letter from Professor Beloff. It ran in the *Skeptical Inquirer's* Winter 1986-87 issue:

Martin Gardner expresses astonishment that I should challenge his interpretation of Home's self-levitations. Why else, he asks, should a medium choose to perform in darkness except that it makes it so much easier to cheat? If you will bear with me once more I would like to respond.

I have no doubt that, in the overwhelming majority of cases, Gardner's commonsense explanation is the correct one. There are, however, good reasons for doubting whether this was so in the case of Home. We must remember that Home produced some of his most powerful and impressive phenomena, e.g., his table levitations, in full illumination. There are a great many circumstantial accounts of these from a variety of witnesses, and the fact is that no one, to this day, has ever offered a plausible natural explanation for them. Given the size of the tables, the heights to which they were elevated, and the conditions obtaining, the idea that Home might have been using some sort of concealed machinery is so ludicrous as not to be worth discussing. Yet the only alternative, as far as I can see, is to suppose that the tables never left the ground but that all the sitters when in the presence of Home dutifully hallucinated their rising. But this would be to ascribe to Home a power that was hardly less miraculous than the one in question and even more exceptional. Of course it could be that, having given a display of genuine table-levitation, Home turned down the lights and proceeded to give a display of fraudulent self-levitations, but I cannot imagine that Martin Gardner would find this plausible. It seems to me more likely, therefore, that the self-levitations, although performed in semi-darkness, were also genuine.

I agree that, if Home possessed genuine paranormal powers, it is curious that he should have resorted to the cloak of darkness. In fact, somewhat belatedly, he himself realized that he had made a tactical error. In his book *Lights and Shadows of Spiritualism* (1877), written toward the end of his life, he expresses regret that he had ever given séances in anything less than full light. "Light," he insisted, "is the single test necessary and it is a test which can and must be given." At the same time he pointed out that "every form of phenomena ever occurring through me at the few dark séances has been repeated over and over again in the light." Nor was this an empty boast. William Crookes, speaking at the Society for Psychical Research, some ten years after Home's death, had the following to say:

> Home always refused to sit in the dark. He said that with firmness and perseverance the phenomena could be got just as well in the light and, even if some of the things were not so strong, the evidence of one's eyesight was worth making some sacrifice for. In almost all the séances I had with Home there was plenty of light to see all that occurred and not only to enable me to write down notes but to read my notes without difficulty.[1]

So much for Gardner's insinuation that Crookes was really just fooling around in the dark. Crookes also remarks on this occasion:

> During the whole of my knowledge of D. D. Home, extending over several years, I never once saw the slightest occurrence that would make me suspicious that he was trying to play tricks. He was scrupulously sensitive on this point and never felt hurt at anyone taking precautions against deception.

Evidently Martin Gardner is unimpressed by Crookes, whom he calls "gullible" and "unreliable." Indeed, he seems to prefer the opinion of the lampoonist from *Punch* who, we may be sure, never attended a sitting with Home, or even that of Robert Browning (who found no fault with his sitting at the time but later developed a pathological hatred toward Home), to that of Crookes, who had had numerous sittings with Home. I do not grudge Gardner his prerogative in seeking to discredit a witness whose testimony conflicts so sharply with his own suppositions; but, when that witness happens to be someone who, in due course, attained, successively, a knighthood, an

Order of Merit, and the presidency of the Royal Society, Gardner must not be surprised if he is suspected of special pleading.

Be that as it may, it was certainly not Crookes's fault that his fellow scientists could not be persuaded to pay attention to Home's phenomena. To quote once more from Crookes's reminiscences:

> I think it is a cruel thing that a man like D. D. Home, gifted with such extraordinary powers, and always willing, nay anxious to place himself at the disposal of men of science for investigation, should have lived so many years in London, and with one or two exceptions no one in the scientific world should have thought it worth while to look into the truth or falsity of things which were being talked about in society on all sides.

One of these few honorable exceptions among his contemporaries was Francis Galton. Galton took no special interest in psychical research, but he was conscientious enough to attend a sitting with Home at which Crookes was officiating. It is clear, from a letter he wrote afterward to his cousin Charles Darwin, that he did not share Gardner's low opinion of Crookes. "Crookes, I am sure, so far as it is just for me to give an opinion, is thoroughly scientific in his procedure. I am convinced the affair is no matter of vulgar legerdemain. . . ."[2] Galton, indeed, reserved his criticism for his fellow skeptical scientists: "I really believe the truth of what they [the mediums] allege, that people who come as men of science are usually so disagreeable, opinionated and obstructive and have so little patience that the séances rarely succeed with them."[3]

So much then for Home. But Martin Gardner raises the more general question, of interest in its own right, of why for so long it was thought necessary to resort to darkness or dim illumination when investigating psychical mediumship, especially if materializations were involved. Broadly speaking there were two basic hypotheses, which we might call the physical and the psychological. According to the physical hypothesis the action of light was antagonistic to the phenomena. Crookes himself seems to have accepted this view, almost universal at the time among both spiritualists and their investigators. Although, as we have seen, he did not consider darkness essential, he accepted "as a well ascertained fact that, when the force is weak, a bright light exerts an interfering action on some of the phenomena."[4] Home, it was thought, could afford to operate in the light only because he was so much more powerful than other mediums. However, in answer to Gardner's query about what would have happened if someone had turned up the gaslight while Home was aloft, the effect, I presume, on this hypothesis, is that he would have come crashing down—like Icarus!

The more modern view would be to adopt a psychological hypothesis, and this could take various forms. For example, most people, as we know, find it easier to fall asleep and stay asleep in a darkened room, although it is quite possible to sleep in daylight. If entering a deep trance was necessary for most mediums before producing physical phenomena, then it is understandable why darkness was at a premium. Modern parapsychologists stress the importance of a psi-conducive atmosphere in experiments, and here again darkness might be a positive psychological factor. According to Batcheldor, some degree of ambiguity in the situation is essential if we are to avoid inhibiting the phenomena; in other words, it helps if we can reassure ourselves that the phenomena might not be paranormal after all.

But these are all speculations that I put forward with due diffidence only because Gardner challenged me to lay my cards on the table. I can, unfortunately, see no prospect at present of deciding between these rival hypotheses. The trouble is that physical mediums (or, at any rate, ones who are amenable to testing) are an extinct species. All I can say to Martin Gardner, with any degree of assurance, is that the enigma of Daniel Home remains unsolved.

Notes

1. *Journal of the SPR,* 6 (1893–94): 341-345; reprinted in R. G. Medhurst, ed., *Crookes and the Spirit World,* Souvenir Press, London 1972.

2. The letter is dated 19 April 1872 and has been published in Karl Pearson, *Life, Letters and Labours of Francis Galton,* 3 vols., Cambridge University Press, 1914-1930; also in R. G. Medhurst and K. M. Goldney, "William Crookes and the Physical Phenomena of Mediumship," *Proceedings of the SPR,* 54 (1964): 42.

3. See Note 2.

4. See Note 1.

I did not reply to Beloff's even more astonishing second letter because I did not want to prolong our debate in the *Skeptical Inquirer.* Here I will make a few brief comments.

Randi's Alpha Project has taught Beloff nothing. Note that to support his beliefs about Home he quotes only from scientists whose knowledge of magic was zero. He seems to think that because Crookes was knighted, and honored in other ways, it made him capable of detecting fraud! Sir Arthur Conan Doyle was also knighted and honored. Not only was he incapable of recognizing crude fairy photographs as faked, he actually believed Houdini was a powerful medium because he, Doyle, couldn't figure out how Houdini did his escapes!

Beloff's assertion that no one has offered any plausible explanation of how Home could have levitated heavy tables in the light confirms once again my belief that most psi researchers have no inclination to learn anything about modern magic. There are dozens of ways to levitate tables in the light, none using "concealed machinery"; but to learn about them Beloff would have to ask someone like Randi or to consult the magic literature.

On one count Beloff is absolutely correct. Physical mediums "amenable to testing" have indeed become an extinct species. It would be good to know why Beloff thinks this has happened. My own guess is simple. In gaslight days it was difficult for skeptics at a dark séance to get up, cross the room, and light the gas without giving a medium time to prepare for the illumination. Today, if a glowing trumpet is floating around, or white hands are touching sitters, or the medium is pretending to be up near the ceiling, all a skeptic has to do is turn on a flashlight. Physical mediums are now so easy to trap, is it any wonder they resist testing? But who can trap a channel medium who does nothing more than take a few deep breaths, go into a trance, allow a discarnate entity to take over his or her vocal cords, then chatter boringly about a sitter's previous incarnations on this planet or how beautiful things are on the astral plane.

The following letter from the British philosopher Antony Flew appeared in the Fall 1987 *Skeptical Inquirer:*

My friend John Beloff is impressed by the testimony of William Crookes, "who, in due course, attained, successively, a knighthood, an Order of Merit, and the Presidency of the Royal Society." So was I until I became a student of the works of Trevor Hall, which curiously neither Beloff nor Gardner appear to have noticed.

The first findings of Hall's researches into "The Story of Florence Cook and William Crookes" were published in Hall's *The Spiritualists* (London: Duckworth, 1962), published by Prometheus Books as *The Medium and the Scientist* in 1984; and these were later supplemented by the chapter "Florence Cook and William Crookes" in Hall's *New Light on Old Ghosts* (Duckworth, 1965). To my mind these works demonstrate decisively that, at least in spiritualist matters, the testimony of Crookes was worthless: that, in a word, Crookes was a crook and the medium was his mistress.

This does not of course prove that Crookes was equally unreliable in his tributes to Home, with whom he was—presumably—not sexually involved. But Hall has also contributed to resolving *The Enigma of Daniel Home* (Buffalo, N.Y.: Prometheus, 1984). And Beloff should surely give more weight to his own observation that "physical mediums . . . are an extinct species," and to the suggestion of others that this extinction was consequent upon the development of infrared photography.

12 | George McCready Price

Andrew White's monumental *History of the Warfare of Science with Theology in Christendom* was published in 1896. By "theology," White meant the doctrines of Christian conservatives who believe the Bible to be literally true in its history, and therefore an infallible guide on all questions where science and the Scriptures come in conflict.

A few decades later, the battle for a broader interpretation of the Bible —one that would allow the ancient writers to be wrong on scientific topics— seemed to have been won. At least it seemed won in mainstream churches. Fundamentalism became a minority viewpoint, confined largely to southern churches whose members and clergy were poorly educated, to Pentecostal denominations, and to such fundamentalist sects as Jehovah's Witnesses and Seventh-Day Adventism.

Then, a few decades later, an amazing thing happened. The liberal churches began to decline in attendance, while the fundamentalist churches began to grow. Even students in secular colleges were caught up in the trend. As we all know, the great fundamentalist-evangelical resurgence (the two groups are hard to distinguish) is still on the upswing and rapidly gaining political clout. Fundamentalist pressures on politicians in several states have led to bitter court battles over the teaching of evolution in schools and colleges. Major publishers of science textbooks, motivated by nothing higher than making money, found it necessary to water down references to evolution as a "fact" and to present it, if at all, as unconfirmed theory. Even President Reagan went on record as favoring the teaching of creationism in public schools. If any sociologist predicted this revival of fundamentalist theology in America, I am not aware of it. Indeed, predictions were just the reverse—that fundamentalism was dying.

Lessons learned from the famous "monkey trial" in Dayton, where William Jennings Bryan came off as a seedy ignoramus in his clashes with Clarence Darrow, have vanished in the wind so far as fundamentalist leaders are concerned. During the trial Bryan relied heavily on the work of America's top creationist of the day, George McCready Price (1870-1963). There were,

Clark's book about his one-time friend and teacher.

of course, a few other fundamentalists who were writing books and pamphlets attacking evolution, but these without exception were on a scholarly level far below Price. Price wrote clear, persuasive prose and seemed extremely well informed in all areas of science, especially geology. His *New Geology* (1923), a college textbook of 726 pages, is in my opinion one of the great classics of modern bogus science. As crazy as its theories are, about the origin of the earth and its fossils, I rate it as cuts above the fantasies of Velikovsky. (Velikovsky, by the way, has many favorable references to Price in *Earth in Upheaval.*) One needs to know only a little astronomy and physics to see that Velikovsky's cosmology is hogwash; one has to know a lot about geology to penetrate Price's ingenious arguments.

Although Price is a name unfamiliar now to the general public, it is his work that underpins the writings of the country's top creationist, Henry M. Morris. Trained as a hydraulics engineer, Morris is founder and president of the Institute for Creation Research, the most influential of several institutions that pretend to be doing serious empirical studies that discredit evolution and support a creationist model. Morris is the author of numerous books, articles, and pamphlets and a tireless crusader for the creationist cause. *The Genesis Flood* (1961), which he coauthored with John Whitcomb, Jr., is by all odds the most significant attack on evolution to have been published since the Scopes trial of 1925.

You will have to search hard through this 518-page tome to find a Priceless idea. The arguments are all from Price, even some of the book's pictures, yet Price is scarcely mentioned except in passing. Why? The reason is easy to understand. Price was a devout Seventh-Day Adventist. Morris is a Southern Baptist. Today's fundamentalist leaders, including such famous preachers as Billy Graham, Jerry Falwell, Jimmy Swaggart, Oral Roberts, Pat Robertson, and others, do not like to give credit for their arguments against evolution to a member of a sect that teaches doctrines they consider false.

In light of this reluctance, I was pleased to see that Morris, in his recent *History of Modern Creationism* (1984), speaks highly of Price, and of the enormous influence Price's writings had on him:

Although I never met George McCready Price, his tremendous breadth of knowledge in science and Scripture, his careful logic, and his beautiful writing style made a profound impression on me when I first began studying these great themes, back in the early 1940s.

I first encountered his name in one of Harry Rimmer's books . . . and thereupon looked up his book *The New Geology* in the library at Rice Institute, where I was teaching at the time. This was in early 1943, and it was a life-changing experience for me. I eventually acquired and read most of his other books as well.

Price's knowledge of geology was entirely self-taught. After carefully studying the writings of his church's inspired prophetess, Ellen Gould White, and all the geological literature he could get his hands on, Price concluded that the most basic of all arguments for evolution rested on circular reasoning. Evolutionists tell us that fossils show a steady progression from simple life forms in the oldest sedimentary rocks to more complex forms in beds of a later date. And how do geologists know the ages of the strata? Why, said Price, they date the beds by the kinds of fossils they contain!

In Price's theory, based on Mrs. White, who in turn based her creationism on earlier theories, all fossil-bearing strata are of the same age. The fossils are records of life that perished during Noah's flood. The earth, according to Price, was created in six solar days, just as Genesis reveals. A few thousand years later the great flood destroyed all living things except those preserved in Noah's Ark. Ocean life would tend to be captured by the first beds of sediment laid down by the flood. Mammals would be in higher strata; and birds (who kept flapping about), in still higher layers. In general, however, one would expect to see a mixture of all types of fossils in the same beds. If that is the case, there should be outcrops of rock here and there with fossils in an upside-down order with respect to evolutionary theory. This, Price maintained, is exactly what we *do* find.

Price formulated what he called the "great law of conformable stratigraphic sequences. . . . Any kind of fossiliferous beds whatever, 'young' or 'old,' may be found occurring conformably on any other fossiliferous beds, 'older' or 'younger.' " Early in his career Price offered a thousand dollars "to anyone who will . . . show me how to prove that one kind of fossil is older than another."

The New Geology contains many photographs of upside-down outcrops. Geologists try to get around these anomalies, Price argued, by inventing totally imaginary faults and folds in the strata to explain how the fossils got into the wrong order. It is here that Price discloses his vast ignorance, but how is a reader to know without some background in paleontology?

Geologists have all sorts of ways to determine when faulting and folding have occurred. Thrust faults display the planes along which strata slid. If you find fossil trilobites on their backs, you know a fold has turned over the bed. All of Price's (and Morris's) cherished instances of wrong-order fossils are easily explained by historical events that can be identified by a variety of techniques—not to mention modern methods, getting more accurate every year, for dating the ages of rocks in ways that have nothing to do with faulting or folding or evolutionary theory. If you are interested, you can learn more about Price and his simple-minded views in my *Fads and Fallacies in the Name of Science,* and in the only biography of Price, *Crusader for Creation* (1966), by his one-time friend and student Harold W. Clark. Another excellent reference on Price, as well as on Morris and other modern creationists, is "Creationism in 20th-Century America," by Ronald L. Numbers, in *Science* (vol. 218, November 5, 1982, pp. 538-544).

In the forties a violent quarrel erupted between Price and Clark, then teaching biology at a small Adventist college in California. As Numbers tells it, Clark became convinced that Price's *New Geology* was out of date and inadequate as a college text, although Clark still believed in a six-day creation and a universal flood. Price accused Clark of suffering from "the modern mental disease of universityitis" and of seeking the favor of "tobacco-smoking, Sabbath-breaking, God-defying" evolutionists. "Price kept up his attack for the better part of a decade," Numbers tells us, "at one point addressing a vitriolic pamphlet, *Theories of Satanic Origin,* to his erstwhile friend and fellow creationist."

Price had occasional lapses into modesty, but there are no such lapses in the writings of Morris. Like all fundamentalists, he believes that Jesus is about to return to earth, but before he does it will become clear to everyone that evolution is a false doctrine coming straight from the Devil. Nothing can shake Morris's conviction that the entire universe was created about 10,000 years ago, in seven literal days. He knows this not just because the Bible reveals it, and God cannot lie, but also because, he is firmly persuaded, there is now *more* scientific evidence to support such a model than evidence to support an evolutionary model! Any scientist or religious leader who thinks otherwise, in Morris's primitive theology, is doing the work of Satan. Here is a sample of Morris's rhetoric:

> Creation is not merely a religious doctrine of only peripheral importance, as many people (even many evangelical Christians) seem to assume. Rather, it is the basis of all true science, of true Americanism, and of true Christianity. Evolutionism, on the other hand, is actually a pseudoscience masquerading as a science. As such, it has been acclaimed as the "scientific" foundation

of atheism, humanism, communism, fascism, imperialism, racism, laissez-faire capitalism, and a variety of cultic, ethnic, and so-called liberal religions, by the respective founders and advocates of these systems. The creation/evolution issue is, in a very real sense, the most fundamental issue of all.

I find it a bit frightening that a British edition of *The Genesis Flood* was published in 1969 and that (as Numbers reveals) by 1980 Morris's books had been translated into Chinese, Czech, Dutch, French, German, Japanese, Korean, Portuguese, Russian, and Spanish. "Creationism," Numbers concludes his paper, "had become an international phenomenon."

If you would like to know the best arguments available today for creationism, my advice is to skip the derivative scribblings of Morris and his friends. Go directly to the source. Try to locate a copy of Price's long-out-of-print masterpiece. I wish some publisher would reprint it, with an introduction and annotations by a paleontologist of the stature of Stephen Jay Gould. I have a feeling, though, that Gould would consider this more a waste of time than I did the writing of this column.

Afterword

An amazing thing happened in 1986. The creationists actually abandoned one of their favorite arguments.

For some 40 years creationists have made a big thing about a riverbed in Glen Rose, Texas, where dinosaur tracks appear alongside what seem to be human footprints. You'll find a photograph of the bed on page 167 of *The Genesis Flood.* In 1980 Henry Morris's son John wrote an entire book about it: *Tracking Those Incredible Dinosaurs and the People Who Knew Them.* Of course if dinosaurs and humans lived at the same time, the entire fossil record, as evidence for evolution, becomes suspect.

In 1986 Glen Kuban, a biology student who is also a creationist, began to have doubts about the human prints. After a careful investigation, he found strong evidence that they were made by a bipedal dinosaur that walked on its heel and sole, leaving toeless prints that resembled human footprints. Faint impressions of the toes could have later filled with mud or some other material, or maybe erosion eliminated them. (See *Time,* June 30, 1986, and *Discover,* August 1986.)

"Everyone knows that they are dinosaur tracks," commented paleontologist Stephen Jay Gould. "It's been a non-issue for a long time." The big surprise was that John Morris capitulated. He agreed that the creationist interpretation of the prints had become too shaky to defend. The Institute

Mourning Dove, a painting by the Texas brothers Scott and Stuart Gentling. The bird is standing by a giant footprint of one of its dinosaur ancestors, in a river bed in Glen Rose, Texas.

for Creation Research, where John is a professor of geology, withdrew his book from circulation, and also its movie on the topic.

13 | Wonders of Science

> A man is a small thing, and the night is very large and full of wonders.
>
> Lord Dunsany, *The Laughter of the Gods*

Parapsychologists and psi journalists are fond of an argument that goes like this: Orthodox science is making such colossal strides, putting forth such bizarre theories, that no one should hesitate to accept the reality of psi. It is a theme that pervades Arthur Koestler's influential *Roots of Coincidence*. As parapsychology becomes "more rigorous, more statistical," Koestler writes on the very first page, theoretical physics becomes

> more and more "occult," cheerfully breaking practically every previously sacrosanct "law of nature." Thus to some extent the accusation could even be reversed: parapsychology has laid itself open to the charge of scientific pedantry, quantum physics to the charge of leaning towards such "supernatural" concepts as negative mass and time flowing backwards.
>
> One might call this a negative sort of rapprochement—negative in the sense that the unthinkable phenomena of ESP appear somewhat less preposterous in the light of the unthinkable propositions of physics.

It is true that modern science is making discoveries and formulating theories that contradict experience and boggle the mind, but this has always been the case. I suspect that most people are less boggled today by the wonders of science than they were boggled in the past by the notion that the earth rotates and goes around the sun. Indeed, all the evidence of the senses suggests that the earth is immovable and the heavens rotate. The centuries that elapsed before the Copernican theory became entrenched in the common beliefs of the civilized world—including the beliefs of Catholics and Protestants, who fought the theory as long as they could—testify to the cultural shock of such a monumental paradigm shift, to use Thomas Kuhn's fashionable phrase.

Today the public is much less bewildered by the paradoxes of relativity and QM (quantum mechanics), not just because it has grown accustomed to the surprises of science but because the paradoxes are too technical to understand. If a twin takes a long space trip at fast speeds and returns to earth, he will be younger than his stay-at-home twin. If he goes far enough and fast enough, he could return to find that centuries on earth had gone by. Most nonphysicists, unless they read science fiction, have never heard of the paradox.

The same can be said of recent confirmations of the notorious EPR paradox that Einstein and two friends (E, P, and R are the initials of the three last names) devised to show that QM is incomplete. Two particles, separated by vast distances, can under certain circumstances remain "correlated" in the sense that, if one particle is measured for a property, the other is altered even though there is no known causal connection between the pair. Who is troubled by what Einstein called the "telepathy" of his paradox except physicists and philosophers of science?

The Big Bang, black holes, pulsars, and other awesome aspects of modern cosmology have been dramatic enough to reach the general public, but I see no evidence that the public is disturbed. If *Time* reports that some physicists now think all particles are made of inconceivably tiny "superstrings," vibrating in spaces of ten dimensions, it is not likely to be a topic of cocktail-party chatter except in science circles. The only establishment claim now arousing strong public emotion is evolution, and that is because of the astonishing revival of Protestant fundamentalism.

From the beginning, science has been upsetting and drastically modifying history. It does not, however (as Koestler writes), progress by breaking sacrosanct laws. No laws of science are sacrosanct, and "breaking" is a poor word for the meandering process by which laws are refined. Great paradigm-shifts build on what went before. Ancient astronomers were good at predicting the motions of planets long before astronomy accepted a central sun. Let $1/c$, where c is the speed of light, reduce to 0 in the formulas of relativity, and you have Newton's formulas. Let Planck's constant equal 0, and QM becomes classical mechanics. The great revolutions of science are better described as benign evolutions. They refine what was known before by placing that knowledge within new theoretical frames that have superior power to explain and predict.

There are other reasons that the progress of science is cumulative and increasingly rapid. Every decade the number of working scientists increases. In Galileo's day you could count the number of physicists on your fingers. Today tens of thousands of journals report the latest scientific discoveries and conjectures, many of the conjectures (as Koestler rightly perceived) more outlandish than the claims of parapsychology. Instruments of observation get better and better. Galileo's telescope was a child's toy. Microscopes using particles other than photons have greatly increased the range of observation of the small. Giant particle accelerators provide empirical underpinnings for strange new theories of matter that could not possibly have been devised even in Einstein's day. Space probes have disclosed more facts about the planets in the past 20 years than in the previous 200.

Koestler is right in one sense. The results of science should instill in all of us a strong awareness of how mysterious and complex nature is. In the words of J. B. S. Haldane, which occult journalists love to quote, the universe is queerer than we can suppose. Every scientist and every layperson should be open to any scientific claim no matter how preposterous it may seem. If it turns out that the human mind can view a remote scene by clairvoyance, or influence a falling die or a random-number generator, this surely would be no more surprising than thousands of well-confirmed natural phenomena.

Does it follow from such admirable open-mindedness, from what the American philosopher Charles Peirce called the "fallibilism of science," that we should all accept the ability of psychics to bend paperclips with their psi powers? It no more follows than it follows from modern cosmology that (as Velikovsky maintained) the moon's craters are only a few thousand years old, or (as Jerry Falwell firmly believes) that the earth was created in six literal days and dinosaurs were beasts that perished in Noah's flood.

We can now say what is wrong with Koestler's rhetoric. The extraordinary claims of modern science rest on extraordinary evidence. No physicist today would be bothered in the least by the seemingly paranormal aspect of the EPR paradox if it did not follow inescapably from firmly established laws of QM, and from carefully controlled laboratory tests. But the extraordinary claims of parapsychology are *not* backed by extraordinary evidence.

For reasons that spiritualists have never been able to explain, the great mediums of the nineteenth century could perform their greatest miracles only in darkness. The equivalent of that darkness today is the darkness of statistics, and why psi phenomena flourish best in such darkness is equally hard to comprehend. If a mind can alter the statistical outcome of many tosses of heavy dice, why is it powerless to rotate a tiny arrow, magnetically suspended in a vacuum to eliminate friction? (J. B. Rhine's laboratory, by the way, made many unsuccessful experiments of just this sort, but they were never reported.) The failure of such direct, unequivocal tests is in my opinion one of the great scandals of parapsychology.

Why is it that the most respectable evidence today for PK, the work of Helmut Schmidt and Robert Jahn, involves sophisticated statistical analyses of thousands of repeated events? The skeptic's answer is that, when a supposed PK effect is so weak that it can be detected only by statistics, many familiar sources of bias creep into the laboratory. In the case of S. G. Soal, once hailed as England's top parapsychologist, we now know that the bias was outright fraud. Even when researchers are totally honest, it is as difficult to control the effect of passionate desires on methods of getting and analyzing data as it is to keep sealed flasks free of bacterial contamination.

No skeptic known to me rules psi forces outside the bounds of the possible. They are merely waiting for evidence strong enough to justify such extraordinary claims. Their skepticism is not mollified when they find the raw data of sensational experiments sealed off from inspection by outsiders or when failures of replication by unbelievers are blamed on unconscious negative vibes.

I am convinced that today's skeptics would have not the slightest difficulty —I certainly would not—accepting ESP and PK the instant evidence accumulates that can be reliably replicated. Unfortunately, for 50 years parapsychology has rolled along the same murky road of statistical tests that can be repeated with positive results only by true believers. Psi forces have a curious habit of fading away when controls are tightened or when the experimenter is a skeptic—sometimes even when a skeptic is just there to observe.

Surely every parapsychologist worthy of respect now knows (even though he won't say so) that psychics are unable to bend spoons, move compass arrows, or produce thought photographs if a magician is watching. As for the more responsible and more modest claims that rest on statistics, they are too often obtained solo or by a small band of researchers who will not let an outsider monitor what is going on. Raw data is often kept, as is most of it at SRI International, permanently under wraps.

Parapsychologists are forever accusing establishment psychologists of wearing blindfolds that make it impossible for them to see the results of the new Copernican Revolution. If the results are as claimed, it is indeed a paradigm shift more sensational than most of the great shifts of the past, and Rhine deserves to rank with Copernicus, Newton, Einstein, and Bohr. Alas, the claims remain as poorly verified as nineteenth-century claims that character traits correlate with bumps on the head.

It would be good for every parapsychologist to study the history of phrenology. The number of scholarly journals devoted to this "science" once far exceeded the number of journals that are today devoted to parapsychology; and, at one time, the number of distinguished scientists who believed that phrenology had been strongly confirmed far exceeded the number of distinguished psychologists today who believe that parapsychology has established the reality of the phenomena it studies.

14 | Tommy Gold

No clear line separates good science from bad; or, to put it more technically, no solution is known for what philosophers of science call the "demarcation problem" of finding sharp criteria for the ways good science should operate. This is hardly surprising, because all values have fuzzy boundaries. Who knows how to be sure when a novel is good or bad, or a painting, or a person, except at the extremities of spectrums? On the other hand, we couldn't talk at all if we didn't constantly make useful distinctions like day and night, even though twilight is ambiguous.

Sociologists who love to browbeat the scientific establishment for its rigid orthodoxy are seldom concerned with the speculations of those genuinely creative scientists who are often called "mavericks" because they delight in needling their peers with wild theories. Such a maverick is Thomas, or "Tommy," as he is known, Gold. His career is a thousand times more interesting and more significant than that of an irrelevant crank like Velikovsky. He is a distinguished scientist who may be—I stress the word *may*—on the threshold of triggering an authentic "paradigm shift" in geology.

Born in Vienna in 1920 and educated in England, Gold began his career as an engineer, designing radar equipment for England's Royal Navy during World War II. In 1959 he became chairman of the Astronomy Department at Cornell University, where he is now a professor, and where he founded and for 20 years directed the Center for Radiophysics and Space Research.

No top scientist of recent decades has been less timid than Gold in publishing brilliant but highly unorthodox theories that range over many sciences. Unlike the dogmas of crackpots, Gold's conjectures are almost always based on hard data and a thorough knowledge of the relevant science. His theories are carefully reasoned, usually testable, published in orthodox journals, and strongly debated by other experts. Babe Ruth was famous for his home runs, but he also had unusually high numbers of strikeouts. Gold's record is similar. The price a maverick scientist pays for constantly tossing out bold theories is that most of them turn out to be wrong. But the hits can be spectacular.

It would take a book by someone better informed than I am about Gold's career to cover all of his speculations, so I must be content with sketching a few highlights. His biggest miss was the famous steady-state theory of the universe, developed in 1948 with Hermann Bondi and Fred Hoyle. In this theory, the universe did not have a Big Bang origin. It has always been and always will be like it is now, expanding, with new matter forever being created in space to replace the matter that constantly flees outward. The theory collapsed with the discovery of background radiation from the primeval fireball, although, like Hoyle, Gold still thinks it may be revived someday in a more complex form.

Gold's biggest hit was his explanation of pulsars. When these strange stars, with their regular pulses of radio waves, were first discovered, Gold published in *Nature* his conjecture that they are extremely dense, fast-spinning neutron stars. Hardly anyone took this seriously. When the first conference on pulsars was held in 1968, Gold was refused platform time and had to air his views from the floor. Many scientists then found, and still find, his tone abrasive. Some still refuse to share a platform with him. Nevertheless, a few months after the conference Gold's predictions (that faster pulsars would be found and that their pulse rate would be slowing) were confirmed. Today, the standard explanation of pulsars is that they are rotating neutron stars.

Many of Gold's guesses have been half-right. A typical example was his much-publicized warning before the first moon-landing that the spacecraft might be swallowed by a thick layer of dust—"Gold dust," it was called. This didn't happen, but neither were astronomers right who expected the moon's crust to be solid rock. It is more like sand on a beach. The dust is there, just not nearly as deep or as powdery as Gold feared.

Almost every new satellite photograph of a planet or a moon starts Gold's mind buzzing with bizarre ideas. Most astronomers think the huge plumes erupting on Io, one of Jupiter's four giant moons, are active volcanoes. Not so, says Gold. Io's spinning in the mother planet's strong magnetic field generates enormous electric currents on Io's surface. They heat up spots that explode. This is probably another miss, but nobody really knows.

The most controversial, perhaps the most important, theory in Gold's career—it produced the cover article by David Osborne in the February 1986 *Atlantic*—is his theory that petroleum has a nonorganic form. This is an old theory, and one still held by some Soviet geologists, but in recent years Gold has revived and defended it with enormous energy.

Conventional geological wisdom says that almost all the earth's oil and natural gas is organic—"fossil fuels," they are called. Gold grants that *some* oil and gas is organic, but most of it, he is persuaded, comes from methane that formed when the earth was young and still slumbers deep beneath our planet's granite mantle. From these vast reservoirs it slowly seeps upward into sedimentary, fossil-bearing strata, where it gets trapped under the nonporous limestone domes into which oil and gas wells penetrate.

In Gold's opinion, earthquakes are partially caused by the pressure of this methane. It cracks the strata above, perhaps lubricating the faults. Escaping methane often catches fire and produces the lights in the sky so often reported during major quakes. Although methane is odorless to us, perhaps animals can smell it. If so, it could explain the widely reported strange behavior of animals preceding big quakes. It might also explain the booming sounds, the bubbling of gas in the ocean, and the deaths of fish. Gold first published his theory of the nonorganic origin of gas and oil in the February 1979 issue of the *Journal of Petroleum Geology*. *Scientific American* (June 1980) gave a more popular account of the theory, written by Gold and Steven Soter, who is also at Cornell.

In the years since, there have been mild confirmations of Gold's theory from the Soviet Union, where a deep hole was drilled into granite in the Kola peninsula, but the major test has just got underway in Sweden. About 360 million years ago, a huge meteorite crashed in central Sweden to form a crater that became Lake Siljan. The Swedish government intends to drill more than 15,000 feet into this crater's bedrock, using a rig about 20 stories high. The cost is an estimated $20 million, and it may take several years to reach the required depth. The project is partly funded by the Gas Research Institute, a United States firm whose president, Henry Linden, is a strong believer in Gold's theory. Indeed, he considers Gold a modern Copernicus.

Most geologists around the world think the theory is utter nonsense. One has likened it to the view that sugar-plum fairies cure cancer. "I am confident I'll be proved right," Gold said in an interview featured in *Omni* (December 1980).

My own guess is that the Swedish well will be dry, but that doesn't mean that scientists like Gold are not valuable to have around. In spite of his obvious pleasure in ridiculing peers, he is always (unlike cranks) open to changing his views when evidence turns against them. If the Swedes do strike black gold or methane in the crater's granite, it could alter history. Oil and gas will suddenly cease to be fossil fuels that are rapidly running out. Enormous reservoirs of oil and gas may be there deep below us, all over the earth, to supply cheap energy and cleaner air. In a few years we may know if Tommy Gold has struck out again or whether he has hit the longest home-run yet in his colorful career.

Afterword

The following two letters appeared in the *Skeptical Inquirer* (Spring 1987):

> I enjoy the *Skeptical Inquirer,* particularly the columns by Martin Gardner. However, in his Fall 1986 column, "The Unorthodox Conjectures of Tommy Gold," there are some statements regarding Gold's lunar work that I feel are misleading to the lay reader.
>
> Mr. Gardner refers to Gold's lunar guesses as "half-right," whereas I believe that the phrase "almost totally wrong" is more appropriate. Gold predicted in the pre-Apollo era that the lunar maria (dark areas) were large "dust bowls," i.e., that these large depressions served to accumulate fine powder, levitated by electrostatic force and transported by gravity from the highlands into topographic lows. He further asserted that the moon was a body shaped totally by cold accretion and that large-scale melting and chemical differentiation never occurred (a perfectly respectable position in those days, shared by Harold Urey, among others).
>
> Gardner then says that Gold's prediction about the sinking of spacecraft in thick layers of dust didn't occur, but "neither were astronomers right who expected the moon's crust to be solid rock." The differences between *crust* and *surface* are confused here. To my knowledge, no one predicted in the pre-Apollo era that the *surface* of the Moon would be solid rock; this was well known before any lunar missions from the properties of light reflected from the moon, which indicate a ground-up, powdery surface layer. The impact bombardment of the moon over geologic time has completely pulverized the surface rocks into a chaotic mass of material called the "regolith." The production of the regolith was well understood before Apollo 11, based on analysis of images returned by the unmanned precursor missions (mostly Surveyor). The *crust* proper, which comprises roughly the outer 70 kilometers of the moon, *is* in fact rock, albeit fractured and broken by impacts. Some of these impacts formed craters more than 1,000 km in diameter. The evidence from lunar sample analysis and remote-sensing strongly indicates that the early moon underwent intensive melting (possibly on a global scale) to form the crust and partial melting episodes continued to produce volcanic eruptions for at least 1.5 billion years after the moon formed.
>
> It is no crime in science to be wrong, if you are willing to revise your ideas when the data so direct. The statement that I find most offensive in Mr. Gardner's article is that "[Gold] is always (unlike cranks) open to changing his views when evidence turns against them." To my knowledge, Gold has not done this regarding the moon. In what I believe to be his last published paper on the moon (*Proc. Royal Society London,* A285, 1977), Gold essentially rehashes all of his (pre-Apollo) views on lunar evolution and totally ignores the overwhelming evidence accrued during post-Apollo analysis for early lunar differentiation (melting) and subsequent volcanism. In contrast, and to his credit, Harold Urey, a staunch advocate of a cold, primordial moon, publicly

proclaimed that his pre-Apollo ideas about the moon were wrong. I have little doubt that, no matter what is found in the Swedish drill-hole, Gold will see the results as confirmation of his ideas.

Paul D. Spudis
Flagstaff, Ariz.

I have long thought that Professor Thomas Gold's pronouncements form an excellent example of the lack of clear boundary between science and nonscience; I therefore was amused to see Martin Gardner's column on Dr. Gold's speculations. Unfortunately, however, I think that Mr. Gardner attaches more weight to Dr. Gold's speculations than the record warrants, and indeed there seem to be some points in Dr. Gold's career for the skeptical community to ponder.

It *is* good to know that Dr. Gold has occasionally connected with his speculations; I was unaware, for example, that the current conventional wisdom on pulsars is due to him. On the other hand, the phenomenon of "shotgun prediction" is well known, as documented so well in *SI* itself, and one might expect a prediction to connect once in a while on that basis alone.

The part of Dr. Gold's record of which I'm aware is much worse. His "deep lunar dust" hypothesis was not nearly so soundly based as Gardner implies, and I moreover am one of those geologists who feel that his abiogenic oil theory is probably "utter nonsense." . . . It seems even less soundly based than his lunar dust speculations. Quite apart from the vast literature based on empirical data, on the occurrence of oil, which Dr. Gold ignores completely, there are also geochemical constraints on oil formation. . . . Quite apart from the evidence Gold has had to ignore to advance his theory, he has not put money where his mouth is. If he is correct, his idea would literally be worth billions. But it is very easy to make media-worthy pronouncements from the security of a tenured faculty position; much more difficult to actually take the risk of acting on them. It would be easier to take his idea a bit more seriously if it seemed he did too. As it is, it merely seems a device to get featured prominently in the forums far removed from the professional scientific literature, such as the *Atlantic*. (As pointed out repeatedly by *SI*, moreover, it is typical of fringe science that it is presented in the popular press rather than in refereed journals.) . . .

Now for some philosophy. I suppose I am particularly unimpressed with Gold's presentations because I have been involved in the rocky and thankless task of actually taking an academic technique and making it into an oil-industry tool. But this leads to my last point: economic applications of science as a tool of skepticism. Applications give great urgency to the question "Does it *work?*" Experiments can often be argued around or interpreted in various ways. It is much more difficult to do so when a stark economic objective is present. . . . The large economic outlay that can hinge on the correctness of one's interpretations furnishes special motivation to ensure the interpretation is correct. If you're going to spend several million dollars drilling a well you want it to be in the right place. The economic application forces a "real-world" evaluation of *what* the discrepancy represents. It is impossible to take refuge in might-be's and go running back to the National Science Foundation for more funding. . . .

Does it *work?* That should be a primary question of skeptics. The jury is still out on Dr. Gold's abiogenic oil idea, but certainly his track record— and his method of presentation—are not such as to inspire confidence in his theory. In any event, the economic significance of his idea is such that it is not likely to remain an academic dispute much longer.

Stephen L. Gillett
Consulting Geologist
Pasco, Wash.

My reply to the above letters:

On all counts I yield to Paul Spudis and Stephen Gillett, who obviously know far more than I about the moon's geology and the origin of oil. I tried to lean over backward to give Thomas Gold the benefit of the doubt, basing my remarks about his moon dust prediction on the account given by David Osborne in his cover story on Gold in the *Atlantic* (February 1986). I am now convinced that I should have distrusted Osborne and given more space to Gold's critics, who surely outnumbered his defenders by an enormously wide margin.

Highlights in Science (Pergamon, 1987), edited by Australian physicist H. Messel, contains four lectures by Gold. One of them, titled "Moon," defends his view that the moon's surface consists of compacted powder that may go to a depth of several kilometers. "I believe," Gold concludes, "that the whole story of the evolution of the Moon will be completely rewritten one day when one has recognized the surface transportation processes of the powder . . . and when less haste and a freer attitude, together with a more diversified set of opinions, can be brought to bear on this programme."

In another paper, "The Origin of Natural Gas and Petroleum," Gold predicts that drilling in the Siljan crater will uncover "hundreds of times more [oil and gas] than was estimated on the basis of the biological origin theories." There will be no need for nations to "fight over the regions that supply fuels; it will be much easier to find one's own." Gold is currently writing a popular book about his petroleum theory.

15 | Rupert Sheldrake

I have an impression that most parapsychologists around the world—I don't know about those in the Soviet Union—have given up the notion that psi phenomena can be explained by any known force of nature. At any rate, the fashionable trend in the United States and England is to conjecture that somehow the phenomena can be identified with a yet-to-be-discovered force-field that would also account for those paradoxes of QM in which information seems to be transmitted either instantly or at a speed faster than light.

Many paradoxes in QM appear to require such a field, but none is more debated at the moment than the notorious EPR paradox. The letters refer to Einstein and two young colleagues, Boris Podolsky and Nathan Rosen. In 1935 the three published a paper in which they argued that QM was incomplete because it does not explain how two particles can remain "correlated" over vast distances without being causally connected.

The EPR paradox has numerous forms, but the easiest to explain is a version first proposed by physicist David Bohm. It involves a property of particles called "spin" because in some ways it resembles ordinary spin. Like a top, a particle can spin in either of two directions, usually called plus and minus, or up and down. Certain interactions produce a pair of particles that speed off in opposite directions. Regardless of how far apart they get, they remain correlated in the following way: If you measure one for spin, the other particle must have opposite spin.

At first thought you might suppose there is nothing more mysterious about this than tossing two frisbies in opposite directions and giving them opposite spins. But in QM a particle does not *have* a spin until it is measured. At the moment of measurement its wave function is said to "collapse" and nature decides by chance whether to give the particle a plus or a minus spin. If the other particle is, say, light-years away, the same wave-function collapse will give it an opposite spin. Put another way, the two particles remain a *single* quantum system with a single wave-function.

The question Einstein asked was this: How does the other particle "know"

Sheldrake, maven of M-fields.

what spin to acquire unless the two particles are in some manner causally connected? Einstein was a realist who took for granted that the universe has a mathematical structure independent of observing minds and that instant or faster-than-light "action at a distance" is ruled out by relativity theory. The correlation of the two particles, he argued, proves that QM is not the final word. A "little voice" inside him, he liked to say, told him that someday new parameters would be discovered that would explain the correlations without having to invoke what he derisively called "telepathy."

Physicists by and large were not troubled much about the paradox. It was no more than a curious "thought experiment" that could not at the time be verified. Then in 1964 physicist John S. Bell discovered what is called "Bell's theorem." The theorem provided for the first time a way of testing the EPR paradox in a laboratory. Many such tests have since been made, with even better ones now under way. The EPR paradox has been strongly confirmed, at least for short distances. It is possible that the two particles will lose their correlation at longer distances; but, if QM is correct, the correlation will never be lost as long as the particles continue to travel through space.

Working physicists today may still shrug and say: "So what? We knew it all along. That's just the way QM works." But the troubling question won't go away. What connects the particles? Bohm has always maintained, with Einstein, that QM is incomplete—that some type of field, on a level not yet explored, provides the "connectedness" that keeps the two particles in a single quantum system.

It is easy to see why so many paraphysicists have turned to QM for an explanation of ESP and psychokinesis (PK). (The leading theoretician of this approach is E. H. Walker, and the most productive experimenter is Helmut Schmidt.) Other fringe scientists are similarly turning to QM for support of unusual conjectures. A notable recent example is the British plant physiologist Rupert Sheldrake. In his book *A New Science of Life* (1981) Sheldrake defends the notion that there are "morphogenetic fields" (M-fields), not yet detected. They link every pattern in the universe, from particles to galaxies to human minds, with all other patterns of a similar type. These M-fields operate instantaneously—no energy is transmitted— on a sub-quantum level outside space and time. They give the universe the "wholeness" stressed by Bohm, by Eastern religions, and by such philosophers as Alfred North Whitehead.

You must not think of Sheldrake's M-fields as fixed laws. They are created whenever a new pattern emerges in our evolving universe, and they change as the patterns change. For example, Sheldrake maintains that the first time a particular crystal is formed it can grow in different ways, but that once it forms, it creates an M-field that makes it easier for other crystals to grow the same way. All snowflakes are now hexagonal because countless snowflakes in the past have imposed that pattern strongly on their M-field. The first time an organic compound is synthesized, its M-field makes it easier for other scientists to synthesize it.

How does an egg "know" how to become a chicken? It is following the pattern of its M-field. Behavior of animals, including humans, also creates and modifies M-fields. If you teach mice in Moscow how to run a maze, the M-field for that species makes it easier to teach mice in Paris how to run the same maze. The more often a poem is memorized, the easier it is for others to memorize it. "Within the present century," Sheldrake writes (p. 196), "it should have become progressively easier to learn to ride a bicycle, drive a car, play the piano, or use a typewriter, owing to the cumulative morphic resonance from the large number of people who have already acquired these skills." M-fields not only explain how quantum information gets around so fast, they also underlie such alleged phenomena as ESP, PK, and the Law of Karma. "Morphic resonance" also guides the evolution of life in ways that Sheldrake thinks Darwinian theory cannot explain.

Almost all scientists who have looked into Sheldrake's theory consider it balderdash. When his book was first published in England, an editorial in *Nature* called it "the best candidate for burning there has been for many years" and said it would be a waste of time and money to test its conjectures. On the other hand, some believers in psi have heralded Sheldrake's theory as a great leap forward.

Newsweek (July 7, 1986) reported on three winners of a contest sponsored by the Tarrytown Executive Conference Center, Tarrytown, New York, for tests of Sheldrake's theory. The $10,000 first prize was split between Gary Schwartz, a Yale psychologist, and Alan Pickering, of Hatfield Polytechnic, Hatfield, England. Schwartz showed three-letter Hebrew words, half of them real and half of them nonsense, to Yale students who knew no Hebrew. He claims that students did better than chance in recognizing the true words, presumably guided by the M-fields of all those today and in the past who have read Hebrew. Pickering did a similar test using real and nonsense words in Persian. The third winner, Arden Mahlberg, a clinical psychologist in Madison, Wisconsin, used true and nonsense words in Morse code. Sheldrake is quoted as saying he is delighted and encouraged by these results, but finds all of them "inconclusive." As he sensibly added: "With such a radical hypothesis, a larger weight of evidence is needed."

According to Michael Kernan, in his report on the Tarrytown awards ("Can We Learn from Learning of the Past?" *Washington Post,* July 11, 1986), Sheldrake "hopes to monitor the marketing of a new puzzle in England and to study how fast people learn to solve it." Kernan recalls the enormous popularity a few years ago of Rubik's Cube: "At first it was so hard to solve that people actually published books on the subject, but soon it became relatively easy to solve, and faded from sight." Did it occur to Kernan that it became easy to solve because so many books explained how to solve it?

In 1987 Random House is expected to publish Sheldrake's second book, *The Presence of the Past.* Kernan quotes Sheldrake's explanation of how a lost fingernail knows how to grow back to its original form: "Plato held that somewhere there was an eternal, archetypal fingernail. I say that the field is caused by actual fingernails of the past, a kind of pooled memory."

Back to EPR. No one has yet found a way that the spin correlation, or any other kind of correlation of two particles, can be used to send a message. If relativity is correct, no signal can be sent faster than light. When you measure the spin of a particle, nature makes it plus or minus with equal probability. No "hidden variables" dictate these choices. They are pure chance events. If you measure a stream of particles, their spins are like random sequences of heads and tails.

Imagine a coin correlated in some mysterious way with another coin thousands of miles distant. At both locations the coins are flipped simultaneously. Each time this is repeated they fall with opposite sides up! It is not a bad model of the EPR paradox. Can such a strange correlation be used to send a message faster than light? The answer is obvious: not unless you can influence one coin to fall heads or tails at will. Unfortunately, there is no known way to give a particle a desired spin when it is measured; and, if you could, the correlation with the other particle would contradict relativity theory.

So where do matters stand? It certainly can't be ruled out that a subquantum field, yet undiscovered, provides the connectedness that Bohm invokes to explain the EPR and other QM paradoxes. If such a field is ever found, it will turn out that Einstein was right after all in his famous clashes with Niels Bohr. QM *is* incomplete. It may be embedded in a deeper theory, similar to the way Newtonian physics is embedded in relativity theory.

David Mermin, a physicist at Cornell University, recently divided physicists into three classes with respect to their attitude toward the EPR:

1. Those who are troubled by it.

2. Those who are not troubled, but invent explanations that either are wrong or miss the point by doing no more than restate the formalism of QM.

3. Those who are not troubled, but refuse to say why.

The last position, Mermin added, "is unassailable."

Afterword

When this chapter ran as a column, I made an unforgivable blunder. I said that if one of two correlated particles is measured a second time for spin, it again acquires plus or minus spin with equal probability, and the other particle goes at once into the opposite state.

I should have known better. "Quantum mechanics may seem spooky," said physicist John McGervey in one of many letters I received about the error, "but it is not *that* spooky." (Professor McGervey's letter was published in the *Skeptical Inquirer,* Summer 1987, with my red-faced reply.)

Were the situation as I described, it would be possible in theory to violate relativity by sending a binary-coded message at a speed faster than light. If a particle had the wrong spin for a given bit of information, one could (in principle) simply keep measuring it until it shifted to the right spin. The fact is that the spin of a particle does not alter if a prompt second measurement is made. For a good nontechnical explanation of the EPR paradox, and its recent verifications, I recommended David Mermin's article "Is the Moon There When Nobody Looks? Reality and the Quantum Theory," in *Physics Today,* April 1985.

Physicist Jon J. Thaler consoled me by saying in his letter: "A couple of years ago I had a student (physics major) who was interested in studying the possible connection between QM and ESP phenomena, particularly clairvoyance, telepathy, and remote sensing. It took nearly an entire semester (it was an independent-study project) for him to understand the problem of measurement in quantum mechanics well enough to analyze the situation properly. Measurement in quantum mechanics is a difficult subject and is the least satisfactory aspect of the theory."

16 | The Anomalies of Chip Arp

> We have watched the farther galaxies fleeing
> away from us, wild herds of panic horses—
> or a trick of distance deceived the prism. . . .
> Robinson Jeffers

In his splendid book *The Drama of the Universe* (1978) the late astronomer George Abell speculates on what generates the enormous energies emitted by quasars (quasi-stellar sources). Quasars are almost surely the most distant known objects in the universe. Their gigantic redshifts indicate that some are moving outward at velocities close to 90 percent of the speed of light. They occupy positions believed to be very near the "edge" of the light barrier, a boundary beyond which nothing could ever be observed from our galaxy.

"All these ideas," writes Abell, referring to alternative theories about the nature of quasars, "and many more (except, probably, the right one), have been suggested. . . . But I must say, the situation isn't helped any by certain catalogs of crazy-looking objects. One nasty person who has given us such a catalog, and who keeps adding to it, is Halton C. Arp. I don't know what the 'C' stands for, but all his friends call him 'Chip.' He's in danger of losing all those friends, if he keeps up what he's doing now!

"Now mind you, I am kidding, because I am very fond of Chip Arp. In fact, we were graduate students at Caltech together. But in those years he was nice."

An astronomer at Hale Observatories, in California, Chip Arp is still adding to his collection of crazy objects, and still making sharp rapier jabs at his more orthodox colleagues. (Actual sword fencing, by the way, is one of his major hobbies.) Like Thomas Gold, the subject of Chapter 15, Arp is a competent, well-informed scientist who delights in the role of gadfly. His peculiar anomalies are quasars that seem to be connected by bridges of luminous gas, but which have markedly different redshifts, or high-redshift quasars that appear joined to low-redshift galaxies. "Arpian objects" they are sometimes called. If such objects really are connected, they cast grave doubts on the establishment view that a redshift is an accurate indicator of a quasar's distance and receding speed.

Of course no one can be absolutely sure the orthodox view is correct—in science you can't be certain of anything—but powerful arguments support it. The redshift is a "Doppler" effect similar to changes in the pitch of sound from objects moving rapidly toward or away from you. Light from objects moving away has its wavelength shifted to the red side of the spectrum; light going in the opposite direction is blueshifted. The effect is strongly confirmed by the motions of nearby stars and galaxies for which there are other ways to estimate distances and velocities, but for quasars the redshift is the only way to gauge distances and speeds. Could the shift have causes other than outward motion?

One theory, for which there is not a shred of evidence, is the old "tired light" hypothesis of Fritz Zwicky. This proposes that, when light travels long distances through space, something not yet understood makes it shift toward the red. Very few astronomers support this conjecture, although it is periodically revived with new and exotic explanations of what causes the light to alter.

Another strongly discredited theory is that the quasars are indeed moving rapidly away from us but are objects ejected violently from our galaxy. This could give them huge redshifts, but allow them to be nearby rather than extremely far away. Such a "local theory" of quasars is held by a minority of astrophysicists who simply can't believe that quasars near the rim of the universe could generate enough energy to be as bright as they are.

If quasars are ejected from our galaxy, one would expect similar stellar objects to be blown out from other galaxies, and those moving toward us would be blueshifted. No blueshifted quasar has yet been seen. Proponents of the local theory argue that blueshifts move the spectrum into the ultraviolet, where it is harder to detect than shifts into the infrared. Maybe blueshifted quasars *are* out there. We just haven't found them.

A third conjecture, allowing quasars to be nearby, is that most of their redshifting is caused not by receding velocity but by what is called the "gravitational redshift" of relativity theory. Strong gravity fields jog light toward the red. Judging by closer stellar objects, gravitational redshifts are too weak to account for quasar redshifting even if there are massive black holes at their centers, as many cosmologists suspect. Arp's view is that nobody knows what quasars are or what causes their redshifts. He believes the quasars are nearby and that his anomalies prove that their redshifts are not proportional to their distances or velocities.

Arp's opponents, the majority of astrophysicists, think his peculiar objects with their "discordant redshifts" are nothing more than optical illusions. If you look long and hard enough at the heavens, they say, you can expect to find many spots where one quasar seems linked to another, or to a galaxy, when actually one object is millions of light-years in front of or behind the other. The situation is like searching for peculiar patterns in a table of random numbers. You are sure to find unusual patterns that, after you apply *a posteriori* statistics, seem highly unlikely. Arp and his supporters claim he has found more anomalies than chance can explain. Opponents insist that his statistics are faulty. If he is right, cosmology will be in a shambles.

As a science writer with only a dim grasp of astrophysics, I would bet against high odds that Arp is wrong. "The people who were antagonistic toward Arp in the past," said astronomer Wallace Sargent, "have been afraid that he might be right. They're not, for the most part, afraid anymore. He's like a pebble in your shoe. After a while you don't notice the irritation anymore."*

On the other hand, it has always been hazardous to be certain about cosmological theories, and today may be no exception. If, for example, it is discovered that photons (carriers of light) have a slight rest mass, quasar redshifting could indicate high temperatures rather than high velocities. In addition, collisions of such photons with the blackbody radiation that permeates the universe (a remnant of the primeval explosion) might also shift quasar light toward the red. In 1986, Emil Wolf, at the University of Rochester, reported evidence supporting his theory that certain kinds of coherent light, possibly coming from quasars, can shift toward the red in going long distances.

It has been said that cosmologists, more than most scientists, incline toward dogmatic rhetoric. Here, for instance, is Fred Hoyle defending his once-popular steady-state theory in the 1960 revision of *The Nature of the Universe:* "Is it likely that any astonishing developments are lying in wait for us? Is it possible that cosmology of 500 years hence will extend as far beyond our present beliefs as our cosmology goes beyond that of Newton? It may surprise you to hear that I doubt whether this will be so."

Five years later, it was Hoyle who was surprised. That was when two teams of New Jersey scientists, working independently, found the microwave radiation that can be plausibly explained only as a residue of the ancient fireball. It was Hoyle, incidentally, in the first edition of the same book,

---

*As quoted in "The Most Feared Astronomer on Earth: Halton C. Arp," by William Kaufmann III, *Science Digest,* July 1981.

who invented the term *Big Bang*. He intended it as a phrase of derision. "When we look at our own galaxy," he wrote, "there is not the smallest sign that such an explosion occurred."

Other famous cosmologists have been just as dogmatic as Hoyle— and just as mistaken—about their theories of the origin of the universe or the origin of our solar system. However, from my novice's seat, it now looks as if Big Bang theory will last 500 years and that Arp's anomalies will prove to be just what his opponents say they are—perspective illusions. "Call halton eatwords," wrote James Joyce in *Finnegans Wake*. Let Abell have the final comment:

> It is always the *un*explained phenomena and the observations we *do not* understand that lead us to new insights about the nature of the physical world. Most of us strongly expect that when we know enough, we shall be able to understand quasars and other peculiar galaxies in terms of known laws of physics. But consider the delight of the scientist when he finds something really new, and you will realize why many of us, deep inside, hope *not*.

17 | Thoughts on Superstrings

Goaded by the realization that science is fallible and by the efforts of pragmatists to eliminate "truth" from the vocabularies of science and philosophy, a line of study emerged early this century called the "sociology of knowledge." Its practitioners fall on a rough spectrum. At one end are the sociologists and historians who recognize that science makes steady progress toward understanding how nature works, but who like to stress how that progress is shaped by social influences. At the other extreme are those so smitten by the uncertainty of science that they are almost incapable of making value judgments about the relative merits of competing theories.

Voices from the latter group are perpetually raised about the baleful influence of the "establishment," the keepers of scientific orthodoxy, in opposing offbeat theories that challenge prevailing opinions. It is this group that keeps reminding us, over and over again, about how Aristotelian astronomers fought Galileo's cosmology, how orthodox doctors scorned the germ theory of Ignaz Semmelweis, how conservative geologists ridiculed continental drift, and how stubborn astronomers refused to believe stones could fall from the sky.

One important aspect of the history of science that these extreme sociologists of knowledge tend to overlook is the accelerating speed with which the scientific enterprise is growing and improving its methods and investigative tools. In Galileo's day the number of experiments taking place around the world was minuscule, and the telescope was literally a child's toy. At the time of Semmelweis, medicine was at a stage comparable to astrological astronomy. When Alfred Wegener argued for continental drift, his theory had almost no supporting evidence. Astronomers who did not believe in meteorites knew little about the solar system.

This century's increase in scientific knowledge and techniques has been staggering. Tens of thousands of researchers around the world now make tens of thousands of observations and experiments every year, and report them in hundreds of periodicals. Communication of significant new discoveries is rapid. There are two recent examples: the discovery of the nearest supernova in 383 years, and the creation of materials that superconduct electricity at much higher temperatures than hitherto thought possible. Reports of these dramatic events spread by telephone to laboratories around the world even before they made headlines. Astronomers immediately began observations of the supernova. Physicists instantly began making and testing the new superconducting compounds.

This is not to say that "paradigm shifts" no longer occur, but when they start to occur they are seldom dismissed today by a hostile establishment. The shifts are increasingly welcome, increasingly rapid, and usually fast roads to fame for the shifters. Moreover, scientific revolutions never totally overturn past dogmas. Relativity and quantum mechanics did not overthrow classical physics; they refined classical physics. The DNA revolution did not overthrow traditional genetics; it advanced traditional genetics. Modern evolutionary theory is not discarding Darwin; it is correcting and improving Darwin's work on the basis of knowledge Darwin could not have had.

At the moment, the world of physics is in enormous ferment over a bizarre new conjecture called "superstring theory." Whether it will turn out to be fruitful or just a passing fad may soon be clear, or it may not be clear for decades. In any case, it is a superb instance of how quickly a wild theory, with no empirical support, can capture the enthusiasm of many of the world's most conservative theoretical physicists.

On the last page of my *Ambidextrous Universe* I quoted a famous remark by Niels Bohr. When physicist Wolfgang Pauli had finished lecturing in 1958 on a new conjecture about particles, Bohr arose and said: "We are all agreed your theory is crazy. The question which divides us is whether it is crazy enough to have a chance of being correct. My own feeling is that it is not crazy enough."

Well, the crazy theory is here, and I suspect that if Bohr were around he would be entranced. Edward Witten, a noted Princeton physicist, has described superstring theory as "beautiful, wonderful, majestic—and strange." He thinks the next 50 years will be devoted to work on the theory's implications and possible testing. On the other hand, Sheldon Glashow, who shared a Nobel prize with Steven Weinberg and Abdus Salam for unifying the weak and electromagnetic forces, has jingled:

> Please heed our advice
> > That you too are not smitten.
> The book is not finished,
> > The last word is not Witten.

Glashow thinks superstring theory has only sociological interest, not for the way some physicists are opposing it, but for how eagerly other physicists are leaping on the bandwagon. Is he right? That's not the point. The point is that within the short span of two years a novel theory has so impressed top particle physicists that dozens of papers about it are appearing every month, not to mention popular articles like Gary Taubes's cover story, "Everything's Now Tied to Strings," in (November 1986) *Discover*.

To suggest how crazy superstring theory is, let me give a hopelessly inadequate precis of its major ideas. All matter is believed to be made of pointlike particles that belong to two classes: the quarks (of which there are six varieties not counting their antiparticles) and the leptons (also six varieties not counting antiparticles). The most important lepton is the electron. Until now it has been regarded as a geometrical point with no known spatial structure—only quantum properties.

In superstring theory, basic particles are modeled not as points but as inconceivably tiny one-dimensional strings. In the most promising superstring theory, they are closed, like rubber bands. These loops should not be thought of as made of smaller entities, the way elastic bands are made of molecules. They are the quantized aspects of string fields. The infinitesimal loops move, rotate, and vibrate in a space of ten dimensions: one of time, three that are the familiar dimensions of our experience, and six that are "compacted" in the sense that they are curled into invisible hyperspheres at every point in 3-space. When the loops move they follow geodesics that trace minimal surface areas on what is called a "world sheet."

Superstring theory is the latest dramatic instance of how mathematicians construct theorems and formal systems of no known utility that suddenly turn out to have practical applications. Notable past examples include the Greek conic-section curves; Riemann's work on non-Euclidian spaces that became so essential in relativity theory; work on matrices, group theory, and statistics that became part of quantum mechanics; and Boolean algebra that underpins the designing of computer circuitry. In superstring theory it is the work of topologists on two-dimensional surfaces embedded in higher-dimensional spaces. To their vast surprise, topologists now find themselves frantically teaching topology to particle physicists while simultaneously struggling to master quantum mechanics. Weinberg recently speculated that some mathematicians sell their souls to Satan in exchange for information on what new areas of pure mathematics will have profound applications in science!

Are the higher dimensions of superstring theory "real" or are they artificial constructs like the infinitely dimensional Hilbert spaces of quantum mechanics? Physicists are dividing over this question. Some see the compacted dimensions as no more than useful artifacts. Others see them as no less real than 3-space.

A similar debate concerns the reality of superstrings. At this moment, any prediction about the outcome would be foolhardy. Ernst Mach, the Austrian physicist who so strongly influenced Einstein, could not believe that atoms and molecules were anything but mathematical abstractions; useful, yes, but no more "out there" than the curves that represent a functional relationship between two variables are out there. Atoms now have passed from theoretical entities to "observables" that can be seen in microscopes. Superstrings obviously are not like ordinary strings or elastic bands; nevertheless they could model structures as much "out there" as molecules, trees, and stars.

String theory goes back to the late 1960s, when no one took it seriously. It was not until about 1980 that John Schwarz of Caltech and Michael Green of London's Queen Mary College transformed strings into superstrings by combining them with grand unified theories (GUTs) based on the supersymmetry of force-fields immediately after the Big Bang and the symmetry breaking that occurred as the superhot universe expanded and cooled. A few years later Green and Schwarz succeeded in purging superstring theory of the numerous inconsistencies that had plagued it. It was this purging that ignited the current big bang of interest in superstrings.

For the first time, apparently, there is now a plausible, elegant way to account for all the forces of nature as well as for the properties of all the particles, especially the yet-undetected graviton. The graviton belongs to a family of bosons, the so-called virtual particles that are the carriers of forces. Other GUTs incorporate gravity, but superstring theory is the first to require gravity as an essential part of the theory. The graviton is the simplest mode of vibration the little loops can have. Without gravity, the strings fall to the ground.

Superstring theory is what some physicists like to call a "TOE," an acronym for "Theory of Everything." Of course it doesn't really explain everything. For one thing it hasn't explained (yet) why the universe, after the primeval fireball, curled up six space dimensions into tight little hyperspheres while the other three, along with time, expanded. And of course it doesn't explain why nature selected equations that describe the behavior of shimmering strings to build a universe, including you and me. Why is there something rather than nothing? And why is that something mathematically structured the way it is? These are metaphysical questions that clearly, at least to me, are in principle beyond the reach of both science and philosophy.

My own opinion is that the Big Bang was a laboratory experiment; that TOE refers to the big toe of a hyperphysicist who used her toe to press the button.

18 | The Third Eye

Since 1950, almost every top publishing house in the United States has been issuing books that its editors know to be occult garbage. Why? The answer is obvious. Like worthless diet books, they make lots of money. I am sure I speak for everyone in CSICOP when I say we are all firmly opposed to government, at any level, telling publishers what they can't print. There are, however, moral issues involved. Just as publishers have the democratic freedom to print books that mislead and do harm,· so we citizens have the freedom to express ethical outrage.

Hundreds of shabby books could be cited as examples, but I'll confine this chapter to just one, because it has an amusing history and because it ties in with one of the craziest of New Age fads—using acupuncture to arouse memories of previous lives. In Shirley MacLaine's latest autobiography, *Dancing in the Light,* she tells about her treatment in a village near Santa Fe by Chris Griscom, a trance medium who also practices acupuncture. (This is not the book I will be attacking; Shirley's four autobiographies have redeeming merit as works of fiction.) Shirley writes:

> The yoga tantra tradition maintained that there was unlimited energy locked in the central nervous system located along the spinal column. . . . If it is released, it flows up and down the spine. Along the way it passes through the seven centers of energy (chakkras) that govern various functions of the body. The chakkras, they say, are the knots of centered energy by which the soul is connected to the body.
>
> With yoga and proper meditational techniques, the energy at the base of the spine (*kundalini* energy) can be aroused until it moves up through each chakkra dissolving the knots binding the soul until it reaches the brain and a feeling of the liberation of the soul is achieved.

In most people, Shirley continues, the seven chakras (I adopt the conventional spelling with one *k*) are "closed," permitting "only the barest amount of vibrational current necessary for functioning. The person is walled into himself and sees the world from a closed and limited perspective. When the chakkra centers are opened, he sees with a more unlimited vision."

To open Shirley's chakras, Chris followed the instructions of her spirit guides, the principal one being an ancient Chinese acupuncturist. He was, Shirley assures us, "always present when she [Chris] worked." After Chris went into her meditation, and her guides took over, Shirley felt frigid air blow over her body. This, she says, "always accompanies the presence of a spiritual guide in the room."

Chris began her treatment by inserting three thin gold needles into Shirley's *ajna chakra*—more popularly known as the Third Eye—and then twirling them gently. "You have scar tissue in here," said Chris. "Your Third Eye is holding some traumatic pain."

Shirley recalls that when she visited an Inca museum in Lima, Peru, she walked by a glass case containing several skulls. Each skull had a hole in the center of its forehead.

> The museum keeper had not even needed to tell me that the Inca high priests had chiseled holes in the center of the forehead to open up the psychic energy of the Third Eye. The Third Eye is an especially sensitized area for spiritual awareness. Clairvoyant capacity, perceptive levels of discernment, the eye of God are supposed to center in the Third Eye. It is the eye that "sees" beyond the earth-plane dimension.

Soon Chris was pushing needles into Shirley's other chakras—at her shoulders, ears, chest, under her chin, and below her navel. Shirley doesn't say whether Chris poked a needle into her *muladhara chakra,* located between the anus and the genitals. In Eastern religions and theosophical traditions, psychic energy is often pictured as a serpent coiled asleep at the base of the spine in the *muladhara chakra.* Charles W. Leadbeater, a famous British theosophist, wrote an entire book about the chakras in 1921. You can learn still more about them in the recent popular books on kundalini by Gopi Krishna.

In Eastern occult traditions, the Third Eye is usually associated with the pineal gland, a small gland about the size of a pea that lies behind the forehead. (Sometimes the Third Eye is also related to the nearby pituitary gland.) The philosopher René Descartes, following an ancient belief, thought that the pineal gland was the seat of the soul. In certain reptiles, fish, and amphibians, the gland is light-sensitive and probably was an actual eye in some prehistoric reptiles. In humans it is a vestigial organ, like the appendix, of no known use. It is often conjectured that psi powers originate in the Third Eye. In recent years, vague efforts have been made to tie it somehow into the holographic theory of the brain.

When Shirley's Third Eye was "opened" by needles, she began to have colorful visions of her previous lives. This notion that spiritual awareness can be heightened by probing the Third Eye is looked down upon by almost all leading gurus of Eastern religions, as well as by theosophists, but in 1956 the notion got a tremendous boost from one of the most sensational best-sellers of this century's occult mania. I refer to *The Third Eye,* by T. (for Tuesday) Lobsang Rampa—not to be confused with Ramtha, one of Shirley's spirit guides.

Rampa claimed to be a Tibetan monk. On his eighth birthday, his superiors opened his Third Eye. The curious instrument they used was made of steel, resembling a bradawl, except it was U-shaped, with little teeth around the U's edge. After sterilizing it in a flame, Rampa wrote, one of the lamas "pressed the instrument to the center of my forehead and rotated the handle. . . . There was a little jolt as the end hit the bone. He applied more pressure. . . . There was a little 'scrunch' and the instrument penetrated the bone. . . . Suddenly there was a blinding flash. . . ."

"You are now one of us, Lobsang," the lama said. "For the rest of your life you will see people as they are and not as they pretend to be."

"It was a very strange experience," Lobsang rambles on, "to see these men apparently enveloped in a golden flame. Not until later did I realize that their auras were golden because of the pure life they led. . . ."

The operation gave Rampa enormous psi powers. He was able to diagnose diseases from the shapes and colors of human auras. His book swarms with such wonders as levitation, Abominable Snowmen, and a visit to see the mummy of one of his previous incarnations. Astral (out-of-body) traveling is something anyone can easily learn, he wrote, but levitation takes lots of practice. He claimed to have been an advisor to the Dali Lama, a medical officer in China, and a prisoner in Russian and Japanese concentration camps.

A long list of Lobsang's blunders about life in Tibet aroused the suspicion of a group of British skeptics. After some fancy detective work they discovered that Tuesday Lobsang was one Cyril Henry Hoskin, the son of a Devon plumber. While a clerk in London, Hoskin had shaved his head, grown a beard, donned Chinese robes, changed his name to Kuan Suo, and had begun hack-writing for magazines. In 1956, a literary agent persuaded him that his manuscript on the history of women's corsets wouldn't sell, but that his Third Eye fantasy would. Hoskin had never been near Tibet, though later he claimed that, when an accident injured his head, his body was taken over by the spirit of a Tibetan lama. *Time* magazine exposed all this in an article titled "Private v. Third Eye" (February 17, 1958). It printed a photograph of Hoskin, taken when he was ailing in a house near Dublin. His totally bald head showed no sign of a scar.

Ballantine's sixteenth printing of Rampa's hoax book still gives no hint that it was exposed as a fraud 30 years ago.

Time, February 17, 1958

Private v. Third Eye

"He pressed the instrument to the center of my forehead and rotated the handle . . . There was no particular pain as it penetrated the skin and flesh, but there was a little jolt as the end hit the bone . . . Suddenly there was a little 'scrunch' and the instrument penetrated the bone . . . there was a blinding flash . . . The Lama Mingyar Dondup turned to me and said: 'You are now one of us, Lobsang. For the rest of your life you will see people as they are and not as they pretend to be. It was a very strange experience . . ."

Thus a mysterious Tibetan calling himself T. (for Tuesday) Lobsang Rampa described the operation that at the age of eight opened his "third eye," giving him, in addition to clairvoyant and telepathic powers, the ability to diagnose a person's state of health and humor from his "aura." (a cleaning man with a temper looked like "a figure smothered in blue smoke, shot through with flecks of angry red"). This was a mere overture to a long vaudeville show of astonishment presented in Rampa's account of his Tibetan life, *The Third Eye* (Doubleday; $3.50). Other attractions included levitation, riding in kites ("horrible swayings and bobbings did unpleasant things to my stomach"), man-mauling Siamese cats, Abominable Snowmen, and a visit to the mummified remains of one of his own previous incarnations.

Rampa claimed to have been a confidant and adviser to the Dalai Lama, to have served as a medical officer in the Chinese army during World War II. I have done time in Japanese and Russian concentration camps and to have visited the U.S. "We Tibetans," wrote Rampa, "believe that everyone before the Fall of Man had the ability to travel in the astral,

TIME, FEBRUARY 17, 1958

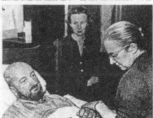

CYRIL HENRI HOSKIN WITH WIFE (RIGHT) & DISCIPLE
But where is the hole in his forehead?

ing quietly with his English wife outside Dublin. One of these insiders, pretty Mrs. John Rouse, wife of a London businessman, lives with the Kuans, serves as Dr. Kuan's secretary.

Not all *Third Eye* readers were fans. Among the doubters were British barber Marca Pallis, whose *Peaks and Lamas* was a bestselling account of his Tibetan mountain climbing in the 1930s; and Diplomat Hugh Richardson, who had served at chief of the British mission in Lhasa for eight years before and after World War II. They compiled lists of Rampa inaccuracies, *e.g.*, mention of gold candlesticks unknown in Tibet; description of Rampa's mother wearing a single earring, a privilege restricted to male officials, a certain rank. Joining forces with Austrian Author Heinrich Harrer (*Seven Years in Tibet*), Pallis and Richardson decided to go to work on three-eyed Rampa with a private eye of their own.

In four weeks and 3,000 miles of traveling, Detective Clifford Burgess and his agents and assistant turned up enough to make Tuesday Lobsang long for a sanctuary. For, announced Burgess, his name

Brooks suggested he forget corsets and set to work on *The Third Eye* instead.

As a result, Hoskin, 47, was nearly $50,000 richer last week as he lay ill in his Irish cottage. Outside, flocks of tourists, startled by front-page treatment of the exposé in the British press, trampled the lawn. The embarrassed publishing firm of Secker & Warburg suspended plans for publication of Hoskin's next book, *Medical Lama*, and a U.S. spokesman for Doubleday. "We expected that people would think it was good reading, but not necessarily true. "I am surprised," said Agent Brooks, "he possesses extraordinary powers of telepathy." Aiding Hoaxer Hoskin the says he has both Scott divorce and consort, insisted in a tape recording made for a British commercial TV program, that his book was all true—he had merely allotted it for a ghost.

"Some time ago," he said, "I had the strangest premonition, the strangest urge, and even against my will I was compelled to change my name . . . I feel a slight accident, I had concussion. And my body was actually taken over by the spirit of an Easterner.

Time magazine's article on the hoax.

After learning of the hoax, Hoskin's British publisher at once canceled plans for Hoskin's next book. A spokesman for Doubleday, his U.S. publisher, was less forthcoming: "We expected that people would think it good reading, but not necessarily true." This is a frequent rationalization by publishers of occult trash.

T. Lobsang Rampa, age 70, shuffled off to his next incarnation in 1981, when he died at a hospital in Calgary, Canada. He and his wife had become Canadian citizens to escape high British taxes on his royalties. The 1956 hoax had no discernible effect on the sales of some 18 subsequent whoppers. Most of them are still in print in the United States, including such inspiring works as *My Visit to Venus* and *You Forever.* I don't know whether you can still buy Rampa's Meditation Kit. It contained such useful things as a Tibetan robe, incense and burner, and an LP record of Tibetan chants.

Now comes the main point of this chapter. In 1964 Ballantine Books (a subsidiary of Random House) reissued *The Third Eye,* and they have kept it in print ever since. A copy I bought a few months ago is identified as the sixteenth (May 1986) printing. In his 1964 foreword Rampa dismisses all the charges against him as the product of "vicious hatred" by enemies. "Let me again state that everything I have written in my books is true. All my claims are true."

There is not a line, on the cover or inside of the Ballantine paperback, to let poor, gullible, hole-in-the-head readers know that the book is a fraud from beginning to end. Ballantine has, of course, broken no laws. Dare we hope, however, that its editors and blurb writers feel at least a few twinges of conscience over letting sheer greed override all sense of honesty and fairness?

Afterword

Dr. Larry R. Squire was among several readers who supplied information about recent research on the human pineal gland. Like the pineal gland of certain vertebrates, it is known to produce the hormone melatonin, but whether this plays a role in the health of humans is controversial. The secretion of melatonin is low during the day, higher at night, but beyond that not much is known. Some psychiatrists have conjectured that the melatonin functions as an antidepressant, explaining why depression for some persons seems to be seasonal—higher in the long-night months of winter, lower in the spring—but evidence for this is shaky. It has also been conjectured, though far from established, that the secretion plays a role in the onset of puberty.

In 1988 the *Skeptical Inquirer* received a request from Paul Carden, director of the Instituto Cristão de Pesquisas, in São Paulo, Brazil, to translate and distribute my article. "Brazil greatly needs this kind of information," he wrote, "because Rampa's entire collection of books sells terrifically well here, year after year. Who among his readers would dream that the man was exposed thirty years ago?"

19 | Irving Kristol and the Facts of Life

Fundamentalists all consider Genesis an accurate account of how God created the universe in six days, a process that culminated in forming Adam out of the dust, then fashioning Eve from one of Adam's ribs. (Can you think of a myth more insulting to women than one explaining how Eve was created as a "helpmeet" by putting Adam to sleep and then fabricating her from one of her husband's minor bones?) Fundamentalists differ, however, over many details of the Genesis account, especially over whether its "days" were 24 hours or whether they were long patches of time.

The "young earthers" argue that the entire universe was created in six literal days about ten thousand years ago and that fossils are records of life destroyed by the great Deluge. Because light is coming to us from stars that are millions of light-years away, young-earthers must assume that God created light waves "on the way" from stars and galaxies that did not exist when the light was created.

It is amusing to note that this difficulty about light is similar to difficulties about traces of the past histories of plants and animals. Did Adam and Eve have belly buttons? For centuries there were furious debates among Bible scholars over this weighty question, as well as over hundreds of other features of living things that imply a nonexistent past: rings of trees, chambers of the nautilus, laminae on a turtle's carapace, tusks of elephants, human hair, teeth, fingernails, and so on. It was evident that, if God created the universe in six literal days, he had to create plants and animals "on the way" from a past they never had.

British zoologist Philip Gosse, father of the writer Edmund Gosse, had a bizarre inspiration. Why not extend this "on the way" notion to the fossil record? Just as God created light on the way from nonexistent stars, so he created an ongoing universe with records of prehistoric life that never existed. Gosse wrote a marvelous book about this called *Omphalos*, the Greek word for navel. "It may be objected," he argued, "that to assume the world to have been created with fossil skeletons in its crust—skeletons of animals that never really existed—is to charge the Creator with forming

Did Adam and Eve have navels? A celebrated 1504 copper engraving by Albrecht Dürer.

objects whose sole purpose was to deceive us. The reply is obvious. Were the concentric timber-rings of a created tree formed merely to deceive? Was the navel of the created man intended to deceive him into the persuasion that he had a parent?"

As I pointed out in my *Fads and Fallacies* (Dover, 1952), Gosse even considered coprolite, or fossilized excrement. Does not dinosaur coprolite prove that dinosaurs once roamed the earth? No more, Gosse countered, than the existence of waste matter in the intestines of Adam and Eve, and the chyle and chyme that result from food intakes and which are essential components of blood. I find Gosse's reasoning so flawless that I often wonder why modern creationists refuse to embrace it. Incidentally, a few of today's physicists, smitten by the subjective aspects of quantum mechanics, come dangerously close to Gosse's vision by denying that the universe was "real" before minds had evolved to observe it.

Another ingenious way to harmonize science and Genesis is the so-called gap theory. According to Ronald Numbers, in his spendid history, *Creation by Natural Law* (University of Washington Press, 1977), the gap conjecture was first advanced in 1814 by the Scottish "old earth" theologian Thomas Chalmers. In England it was promoted by Oxford geologist William Buckland, and in the United States by Edward Hitchcock, a Congregationalist minister and president of Amherst College (see his 1840 textbook *Elementary Geology*). During the pre-Darwinian period of the 1830s and 1840s, Numbers tells us, the gap theory was the most widely held way of squaring Genesis with the fossil record. It got a tremendous boost in 1909 when another Congregationalist minister, the American fundamentalist Cyrus Ingerson Scofield, defended gapism in his note on Genesis 1:1 in the enormously influential *Scofield Reference Bible*. This is an annotated Bible still greatly admired by fundamentalists.

According to the gap theory, a vast stretch of time elapsed between the first and second verses of Genesis. "In the beginning God created the heaven and the earth." This included at least one creation, perhaps more, of plant and animal life on earth. God destroyed the pre-Adamic creation, leading to the second verse: "And the earth was without form and void. . . ." Then about 10,000 years ago he started over again, replenishing the earth in the manner described in Genesis. You don't have to be puzzled over why Noah didn't take two dinosaurs of each species on his Ark. It wasn't because they were too big, but because they no longer existed.

Among today's self-declared Bible experts, the Pentecostal televangelist Jimmy Swaggart is the loudest drum-beater for the gap theory. If you write to Jimmy Swaggart Ministries, Baton Route, LA 70821, you can buy his booklet *The Pre-Adamic Creation and Evolution* (1986) or his cassette tapes with the same title. According to Swaggart, scientists are right in their estimates of the advanced age of the earth. Before the creation described in Genesis, our planet was the domain of Satan and the angels. When the devil fell, dragging one-third of the angelic hosts with him (how did Jimmy arrive at *that* fraction?), God utterly destroyed this creation. Fossils are not records of life buried by the Flood, as young-earthers maintain. They are records of pre-Adamic life.

Like other old-earth gapists, Swaggart believes that the Adamic creation took place in six 24-hour days. "Evolution," he proclaims in his booklet, "is a bankrupt speculative philosophy, not a scientific fact. Only a spiritually bankrupt society could ever believe it." Only atheists, he goes on to say, could accept this satanic theory.

Like his brother fundamentalists, Swaggart here reveals an ignorance so total that it could only spring from a monstrous ego, a sin of pride that renders him incapable of learning even the most elementary facts of biology and geology. Evolution is as much a fact as the earth turning on its axis and going around the sun. At one time this was called the Copernican theory; but, when evidence for a theory becomes so overwhelming that no informed person can doubt it, it is customary for scientists to call it a fact. That all present life descended from earlier forms, over vast stretches of geologic time, is as firmly established as Copernican cosmology. Biologists differ only with respect to theories about how the process operates.

Swaggart is also dead wrong in supposing that evolution implies atheism. Hundreds of the most distinguished modern Christian thinkers, both Catholic and Protestant, have accepted evolution, but Swaggart is too busy preaching, rereading the Bible, and studying books by other Pentecostals to be aware of them. Millions of evangelicals who share Jimmy's born-again faith long ago decided to interpret the days of Genesis as long periods of time. Non-Christian theists—Thomas Jefferson and most of the other Founding Fathers, for instance—have had no difficulty seeing evolution as God's method of creating. I know of no contemporary Protestant or Catholic theologians outside fundamentalist circles who have not accepted the fact of evolution, though they may insist on God's directing the process and infusing souls into the first humans.

In view of the sharp distinction between the fact of evolution and theories about how it operates, it is distressing to find some distinguished political conservatives giving aid and comfort to fundamentalists by adopting their blurring of this distinction. A recent horrendous example was "Room for Darwin and the Bible," a mini-essay by neoconservative Irving Kristol on the Op Ed page of the *New York Times* (September 30, 1986). After stressing divisions among scientists over the precise mechanisms of evolution,

Kristol informs us that a "significant minority" of top scientists doubt that evolution occurred at all! "The current teaching of evolution in our public schools does indeed have an ideological bias against religious belief," Kristol writes, "teaching as 'fact' what is only hypothesis."

Kristol's source for this remark, which repeats a favorite tactic of know-nothing fundamentalists, is probably Tom Bethell's careless, misleading article "Agnostic Evolutionists," in *Harper's* (February 1985). Bethell discusses the views of a small noisy group of iconoclasts known as "transformed cladists." As Kristol puts it: "Many younger biologists (the so-called cladists) are persuaded that the differences among species . . . are such as to make the very concept of evolution questionable." Kristol neglected to do his homework. The cladists have never denied the fact of evolution. They merely classify life forms by methods that in their opinion cast doubts only on prevailing beliefs about ancestral linkages.

Why a respected writer who harbors no conservative religious opinions—if Kristol is even a philosophical theist, he has kept it carefully concealed—should go out of his way to write a piece that could have come straight from Jerry Falwell, beats me. It is sad to find him belaboring the science community for its united opposition to ignorant creationists who want teachers and textbooks to give equal time to crank arguments that have advanced not a step beyond the flyblown rhetoric of Bishop Wilberforce and William Jennings Bryan. Could his motive be to shore up Ronald Reagan's friendship with Falwell, and the president's support for teaching creationism in public schools? I will say no more because Stephen Jay Gould, with his usual clarity and elegance, has explained the facts of life to Kristol in "Darwinism Defined: The Difference Between Fact and Theory" (*Discover,* January 1987). It is an essay I commend to all my readers.

Afterword

Since writing this I have discovered where Brother Swaggart got his one-third figure. It is from Revelation 12:3-4: "And there appeared another wonder in heaven, and behold, a great red dragon, having seven heads and ten horns, and seven crowns upon his heads.

"And his tail drew the third part of the stars of heaven, and did cast them to the earth. . . ."

THE NEW AGE

PART 2

20 | The Great SRI Die Mystery

Writing in *Nature* (vol. 251, October 18, 1974) on their 1972-73 experiments with Uri Geller at the Stanford Research Institute, Harold Puthoff and Russell Targ described one sensational experiment as follows:

> A double-blind experiment was performed in which a single 3/4-inch die was placed in a 3″ × 4″ × 5″ steel box. The box was then vigorously shaken by one of the experimenters and placed on the table, a technique found in control runs to produce a distribution of die faces differing nonsignificantly from chance. The orientation of the die within the box was unknown to the experimenters at that time. Geller would then write down which face was uppermost. The target pool was known, but the targets were individually prepared in a manner blind to all persons involved in the experiment. This experiment was performed ten times, with Geller passing twice and giving a response eight times. In the eight times in which he gave a response, he was correct each time. The distribution of reponses consisted of three 2s, one 4, two 5s, and two 6s. The probability of this occurring by chance is approximately one in 10^6.

Surely this experiment deserves to rank with the famous test in which Hubert Pearce, a student at Duke University, correctly called 25 ESP cards in a row as J. B. Rhine repeatedly cut a deck and held up a card. In one respect, the die test with Geller is more significant because it rules out telepathy. Of course it does not rule out the possibility that Geller used precognition or that he decided on a number while the box was being shaken and then used PK to joggle the die to that number. In any case, the experiment seems to be a simple, foolproof, monumental violation of chance.

On the other hand, as in the case of Rhine's informal account of Pearce's equally miraculous run of 25 card-hits, P and T describe the die test with a brevity that seems inappropriate for so extraordinary a claim. We are not told who shook the box, where or when the test was made, who observed the trials, how long Geller took to make each guess, whether he was allowed to touch the box, whether there were earlier or later die-box tests with Uri, or whether the experiment was visually recorded.

This article originally appeared in the *Skeptical Inquirer,* Winter 1982-83, and is reprinted with permission.

Uri Geller and Russell Targ during die box experiments in 1973.

When P and T released their official SRI film about their five-week testing of Geller, one of the die-box trials appeared on the film. It was accompanied by the following voice-over:

> Here is another double blind experiment in which a die is placed in a metal file box (both box and die being provided by SRI). The box is shaken up with neither the experimenter nor Geller knowing where the die is or which face is up. This is a live experiment that you see—in this case, Geller guessed that a four was showing but first he passed because he was not confident. You will note he was correct and he was quite pleased to have guessed correctly, but this particular test does not enter into our statistics.

The box is seen to be a metal one of the sort used for 3-by-5 file cards. The same box appears in two photographs that accompany an article on Geller in the July 1973 issue of *Psychic* magazine (now called *New Realities*). One picture shows Geller recording his guess, the closed box near his hand. The other shows Geller opening the box to check his guess.

John Wilhelm, in *The Search for Superman* (Pocket Books, 1976) reports that he was told by P and T of many other tests they made of Geller with a die in a box. Some of them took place in Geller's motel room, with Uri doing the shaking. "He's like a kid in that he had something that made a lot of noise and he just shook it," Targ told Wilhelm. Targ also said that during the experiment reported in *Nature* Geller was allowed to place his hands on the box in "dowsing fashion."

Targ also informed Wilhelm that they had a "good-quality videotape" of another die test in which Geller, five times in succession, correctly wrote down the die's number *before* the box was shaken. "We think it's precognition," said Targ. "We think maybe even on his original experiment it wasn't that he knew what was facing up, but that he had precognition as to what he would see when he opened the box."[1]

Wilhelm gives other details about the original test. Puthoff was the experimenter who usually shook the box. Many different dice were used, each etched with a serial number to guard against switching. To avoid ambiguity in guessing, Geller was asked to draw a picture of the spots rather than write a digit. "The experimenters also insist that a magician who examined the videotape of these performances found 'no way' in which Geller could have cheated."

Note that Wilhelm was told the experiment had been videotaped. In 1976, in a letter published in the *New York Review of Books* (reprinted on page 108 of my *Science: Good, Bad and Bogus*), I wondered if the test shown on the SRI film was part of the original test or a later one. If part of the actual test, I urged P and T to allow magicians to see the film of the entire experiment. James Randi, in *The Magic of Uri Geller* (the revised edition, *The Truth About Uri Geller,* was published by Prometheus Books in 1982), suggested a method by which Geller could have secretly obtained peeks into the box. Seeing the film of all ten trials (not just a trial on which he passed; obviously if Uri had a way of cheating he would pass whenever circumstances made it impossible to make the needed "move") would provide valuable information concerning Randi's hypothesis. "Come, gentlemen," I concluded my letter, "let us see the entire tape! If we are wrong, we will humbly apologize."

After Randi's book appeared, P and T issued an eight-page "Fact Sheet" intended to correct what they considered serious errors in the book. They mention Randi's "elaborate hypothesis" about the die test and reply as follows: "Fact: Film and videotape show otherwise, and magicians examining this material have failed to detect a conjuring trick."

Now this statement clearly implies that the experiment had been videotaped or filmed in its entirety. Who were the magicians who examined the film? They could not have included Milbourne Christopher, a professional who visited SRI, because he told me he saw no film of the die test. There are only two possibilities. One is Targ himself, who had a boyhood interest in magic. The other is Arthur Hastings, a close associate of P and T and a strong supporter of their work. P and T used him frequently as a judge in their remote-viewing experiments. Hastings claims some knowledge of conjuring techniques, but in my opinion his knowledge is extremely limited.

In the fall of 1981, almost ten years after the die test, Puthoff finally revealed an astonishing fact. No film or videotape was ever made of Uri's eight successful guesses!

This revelation came about only because Randi, in his latest book, *Film-Flam!,* concluded on the basis of privately obtained information, that the episode on the SRI film, showing Uri passing, was a reenactment of the experiment. Both Puthoff and Zev Pressman, the research engineer who made the film, have since vigorously denied that it was a reenactment. In reply to an inquiry, Puthoff unequivocally told me in a letter (September 10, 1981): "Only one trial was filmed, and that is the one that appears on the film . . . the entire series of trials was *not* filmed."

Why? Because, Puthoff explained, Pressman's filming was done primarily to record PK efforts. As the Christmas holidays of 1972 approached, Puthoff said, they decided to "slip" in some die-box trials, "without making a big deal of it," to see if Geller could succeed in a pure clairvoyance test. These trials, Puthoff added, were "spaced-out over a few-day period" just before Geller left. When Puthoff saw they were getting hits, he decided that a film record of their protocols would be useful. Puthoff asked Pressman to make the record and he came over to do it. "We broke up for the holidays," Puthoff continued, "assuming that eventually we would get more trials on film, but we never came back to it, going on to other things. . . . I hope this clears it up for you."

Well, not quite. It seems passing strange that in a test of this importance P and T would see fit to film only the single trial on which Uri passed. Moreover, I was puzzled by the vagueness of the statement that the test had been spaced out over a "few-day period." I wrote again on September 14 to ask Puthoff if he could recall the exact number of days. Puthoff replied (October 5) that the experiment was spread over a "two or three day period, a few trials per day, sandwiched in among other experiments, until a total of ten trials were collected." He added that the length of time per trial, "from when I began the shake to when I opened the box, was relatively short—30, 40, 50 seconds. The one you see on the film is quite typical, and it is well under a minute."

I had asked for the "exact number" of days, but Puthoff's answer of "two or three days" was almost as vague as his "few-day period." D. Scott Rogo, writing about the die experiment in *Fate* (November 1981) said that P and T told him that Uri had found the die test difficult. It is hard to imagine that Uri would have considered the test difficult when he obtained eight hits in a row in trials that lasted less than a minute

Psychic magazine

Geller opening die box during 1973 experiments.

each. Nevertheless, Rogo continues, "he did only one or two trials a day over a period of a week. . . . He made a total of ten trials. . . . Only *one* of these trials was ever filmed. . . . This is the only SRI film ever made of any die-throwing tests."

Now there is a big difference between two or three days and a week. I was further mystified because Puthoff had also told Randi personally, at a parapsychology conclave in Toronto in 1981, that the die test had taken a week. Was it a week, or two or three days?

An incredible thought struck me. Could it be possible that P and T had not considered it worthwhile to keep a written record of the trials giving all the details about when and where each trial was made and who was present on each occasion? I sent Puthoff the following letter:

Dear Hal: 8 Oct 81

Your reply of 5 Oct was much appreciated. I did not even know, until I got your letter, that you were the experimenter in these tests.

May I assume from your statement of "two or three days" that the trials were not recorded and dated when they took place? It is the only way I can explain the ambiguity. (Rogo, by the way, in the latest issue of *Fate,* reports that he was told the trials took place during a period of a week, which only adds to the confusion.)

Perhaps I have regarded the test as more significant than it was considered at the time—especially since it ruled out the possiblility of telepathy. If the die test was considered not important, and made more or less at random, with no keeping of records, then I can understand the confusion over the number of days. . . .

My assumption, Puthoff replied, was dead wrong. "Careful records were kept." He said he had now checked those records and determined that "the trials were carried out over a three-day period." Wilhelm, he added, confused two separate die tests. One was the test reported in *Nature,* of which only the passed trial was filmed. It used a red transparent die. Later a series of similar tests were carried out in a motel room in San Francisco when they were there for the *Psychic* article. These were videotaped. Puthoff closed by saying that he continues "to entertain Randi's hypothesis" but considers it ruled out by the SRI film. "Go back and view the film— that's what we have to deal with."

I found it curious that Puthoff would place any value on the filmed trial because, assuming Geller used a peek move for his hits, he obviously would not use it when being filmed. I wrote to Puthoff again (October 18) asking him if I could pay for the cost of having the original records photocopied. This is how I justified my request:

In the interest of seeking the truth about this historic test (in which the results were so unambiguous and so overwhelmingly against chance), it would be enormously helpful to see these records. I want to be completely open. I know a great deal about dice-cheating techniques, and it is my belief that Geller did indeed peek by a method similar to the one Randi conjectured. The written records may cast no light on the matter, but at least they could be of help in pinning down the exact protocols.

The letter was never answered.

What conclusions can we reach from all this? The most important is surely that what seemed to any reader of *Nature* to be a carefully controlled die test has now become little more than a collection of anecdotes. At the very least P and T should make a full disclosure of all the details of the test, including photocopies of whatever records were made at the time. We also should be told the results of the videotaped tests made in San Francisco, and whether Wilhelm was accurate in reporting that a videotape was made of a successful precognition test with a die and box.

As it stands, the ten-trial test at SRI should not be called an experiment. There were too many ways Uri could have cheated (the peek move is only one)—ways that could be ruled out only if a knowledgeable magician had been present as an observer, or if a videotape had been made of all ten trials from start to finish, with no time breaks. In the absence of such controls for guarding against deception by a known charlatan, the die test was far too casual and slipshod to deserve being included in a technical paper for a journal as reputable as *Nature*. It belonged more properly in a popular article for *Fate*.

Notes

1. Both P and T are strong believers in precognition. Indeed, this was the topic of Targ's paper, "Precognition and Time's Arrow," delivered at the 24th annual meeting of the Parapsychological Association, at Syracuse University, August 1981. Targ gave his reasons for thinking that precognition does not violate quantum mechanics and that it could be explained only by assuming time-reversed causality. He defended Helmut Schmidt's experiments that supposedly confirm backward causality, and cited William E. Cox's paper on precognition in the *Journal of the American Society for Psychical Research* (vol. 50, 1956, pp. 99–100), reporting a study of 28 train wrecks that occurred between 1950 and 1955. Cox concluded that (in Targ's words) "significantly fewer people chose to ride trains on days when they were going to crash, than rode them on previous corresponding days of the week in earlier weeks or months."

2. Here is how Wilhelm reported what P and T told him about this die test *(The Search for Superman,* p. 95):

> "We only talk about the more conservative miracles," muses Targ. "We have another tape of Geller that's not reported because it's more outlandish. We have a very good-quality videotape in which Geller, on another visit, said, 'I don't want to repeat that, I have a new way of doing that dice experiment.' The new way is to write down on a piece of paper a number on the table. Then I [Targ] take the box and shake it vigorously. Then he takes my shaken box and he shakes it vigorously, dumps the dice out on the table, and it comes up the number he wrote down. We did that five times in a row."
>
> According to Puthoff, the dice was thrown "way up in the air, landing on the table, bouncing all over, and then coming up the [guessed number]." The die belonged to SRI.

In view of the fact that this entire test was videotaped, in contrast to the original test, which was not, it was a much better controlled test than the one reported in *Nature*. Does a tape of this test exist? If so, why has it not been made available to psi researchers?

Afterword

It has been 15 years since P and T made their notorious die tests with Uri Geller, and no outsider has yet seen any records or videotapes of any of those tests. The sole exception continues to be the film of one shake, totally worthless as evidence because it was a test on which Uri "passed." Had he been cheating on unfilmed tests, obviously he wouldn't cheat on the only test filmed.

In my column I mentioned that using the "peek" method was only one way Uri could have cheated. Although I am reluctant to mention other ways because they give away professional magic secrets, I shall allude here to one possible method. Let's assume that on some of the tests Uri made his prediction on a card or tablet that was turned face down until the die box was opened. After the lid was raised, Uri then turned over the card or pad to reveal that his prediction was accurate. There is nothing in the report by P and T to rule this out. It is true that a photograph in *Psychic* shows Uri writing down his prediction while Targ observes what he is writing, but this could have been a picture specially posed for the magazine.

If Uri's prediction was not disclosed until *after* the box was opened, the simplest way he could have cheated would have been to use a device that magicians call a "nail writer." This also would have been the easiest way to cheat on the five tests in which Geller wrote down the number before the box was shaken. This test, we are told, actually was videotaped.

I favor the peek explanation over the nail writer because I cannot imagine that, even in 1983, P and T would have been unfamiliar with nail writers and would not have taken all precautions to rule them out. But who knows? It is such possibilities that make it so necessary to make time-unbroken videotapes and to keep thorough records of every detail when a miracle is performed by a known magician who pretends to be a psychic. Perhaps the videotape of the five precognition tests would rule out the use of a nail writer. If so, it would be a service to science if SRI would allow those tapes to be seen.

P and T are no longer at SRI International. Does SRI still have the videotapes under lock and key, or did P or T take them when they left? I have not been able to learn the answer to this question.

21 | Perpetual Motion

A perpetual-motion machine is often defined as one that never stops running, but a better definition is a machine that puts out more energy than it takes in. It is not hard to build devices that, aside from the inevitable wearing out of parts, will run virtually forever. Perpetual clocks, for instance, which go back to the eighteenth century, are perpetually rewound by changes in air pressure or temperature, but of course they are no more perpetual-motion devices than a watch that is rewound by the motions of the person who carries it.

Windmills, water wheels, and machines that run on tidal or solar energy are other examples of pseudo-perpetual motion because they require outside energy. The earth's rotation and revolution, the Brownian movements of particles in liquid suspension, the motions of molecules in a gas, of electrons in an atom, of electrical currents in supercooled substances—all such motions are of no help in making a device that will produce more energy than it extracts from its source.

Another way to define a perpetual-motion machine is to call it a device that violates the first law of thermodynamics. This is the law stating that energy (in relativity theory one must speak of mass-energy) is always conserved. It may alter in form, but the total energy output of a machine can never exceed its total input. Because of unavoidable heat loss from friction, air resistance, electrical resistance, and other retarding forces, all machines with no outside power source will eventually stop for the same reason that a spinning top soon falls over. Although the conservation of energy law is empirical, it is so firmly entrenched in modern physics that searching for a counterexample is as foolish as trying to lift yourself by your own bootstraps.

It is important to remember, however, that before the conservation of energy was well understood, the search for perpetual motion was thorough-

This originally appeared in *Foote Prints* (the house organ of Foote Mineral Company), vol. 47, no. 2 (1984), and is reprinted with permission.

ly reasonable. There was nothing irrational about attempts by early mathematicians to square the circle or to prove Euclid's parallel axiom before proofs of impossibility were found. Even less irrational was the tendency of seventeenth-century scientists like Robert Fludd and Robert Boyle to take perpetual motion seriously. Newton and Leibniz assumed intuitively that such machines were impossible, but by the end of the nineteenth century grounds for believing them impossible became so overwhelming that all knowledgeable physicists abandoned the search.

No one knows who designed the first perpetual-motion machine. It was probably either a wheel intended to turn endlessly by the force of gravity, or a water wheel that operated a mechanism for carrying water

FIGURE 1. A gravity wheel used for advertising a cafeteria in Los Angeles (reproduced from *The Strand,* 43 [1912] p. 598). If the device had produced perpetual motion, the proprietor of McKee's Cafe could have retired, having grown rich beyond the dreams of avarice.

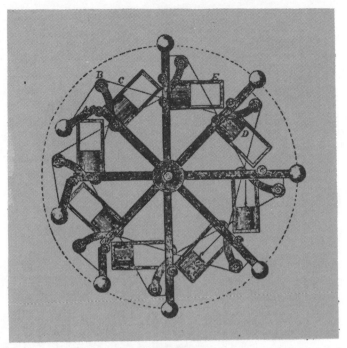

FIGURE 2. This gravity wheel was designed by James Ferguson, an 18th-century Scottish astronomer and Fellow of the Royal Society. As the weights fall inside the cylinders, they operate pulleys that draw outward the weights at the ends of the hinged rods.

back to its source. Until recent decades, most machines purporting to produce perpetual motion were of the gravity-wheel type.

The extremely simple gravity wheel (see Figure 1) reproduced from a 1912 issue of *The Strand* is based on a centuries-old idea. It shows a rotating wheel (probably secretly powered by electricity) that served as a large advertising sign for a cafeteria in Los Angeles. On one side of the wheel, the steel balls roll outward from the center, and on the other side, inward toward the center. Consequently, the wheel seems permanently overbalanced, like an imaginary polyhedron that is unstable on all faces. Because it is always the same side of the wheel that seemingly outweighs the other, will not the wheel perpetually rotate?

A slight elaboration of the same scheme used levers with elbow joints instead of weights. Thousands of more complicated wheels, some using mercury and other liquids for weights, were designed in the eighteenth and nineteenth centuries. Figures 2 and 3 show typical models.

Occasionally, an optimistic inventor would add a brake to his wheel to keep it from spinning too fast! Obviously, none of these devices will

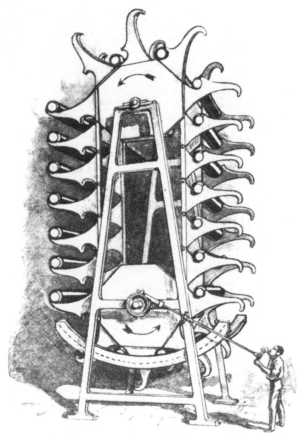

FIGURE 3. Two versions of overbalanced rotary devices, depicted in the March 1925 issue of *Science and Invention.* The man on the right is operating a brake that the optimistic inventor added to prevent his machine from going too fast. Making provision for braking a perpetual motion machine must surely count as one of the great acts of faith in the history of mankind.

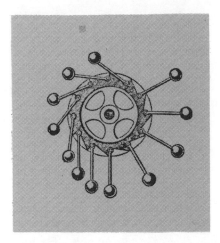

FIGURE 5. George Lipton, a British inventor, designed this self-turning wheel in the mid-nineteenth century. A steel ball rolls down the incline from *D* to *C*, where it is caught in a cup at the end of a flexible, jointed arm. The arm carries the ball back to *D*, where it is deposited back on the incline. The seven balls are supposed to keep the wheel perpetually overbalanced. Like all the other inventors of perpetual motion devices, Lipton demonstrated the human weakness for self-deception in the perpetual triumph of hope over experience.

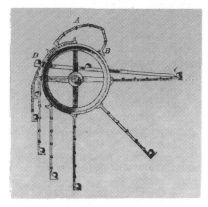

keep on turning longer than an ordinary wheel suspended vertically by its horizontal axle; some will not turn nearly so well. The modified wheels may be temporarily overbalanced, but they quickly reach equilibrium because there is no way to design them so that the sum of the moments (products of each weight and its distance from the axle) on one side is always greater than the sum on the other side.

One of the earliest and most famous of overbalanced wheels was built during the seventeenth century in England by Edward Somerset, Sixth Earl and Second Marquis of Worcester, "for exhibiting self-motive power." While no picture of the device survives, it was said to be 14 feet in diameter. It carried 40 weights of 50 pounds each, and rotated on an axle supported by two upright shafts.

Jean Ernest Elie-Bessler, an eccentric German engineer designated on a portrait as "The High Hessian Councillor of Commerce, Professor of Mathematics, and Inventor of Perpetual Motion," who added the outlandish name of Orffyreus (Was this perhaps an allusion to Orpheus, the legendary Thracian poet-musician?) to his given name, created quite a stir in the early eighteenth century with his persistent claims for a gravity wheel. He apparently destroyed it in a fit of anger over the skeptical rebuff of scientists and never dabbled in perpetual motion thereafter.

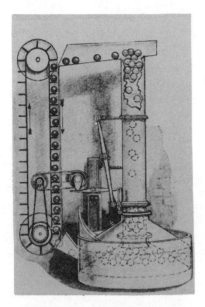

FIGURE 6. Spherical floats rise inside this machine's tank of water, then roll out of a valve to drop into compartments on the endless belt. Their weight in open air carries them down to be fed back through another valve into the tank. (From *Science and Invention*, March 1925.)

You can find the most detailed history of such mechanisms, as well as other kinds of perpetual-motion machines, in Henry Dircks's comprehensive two-volume *Perpetuum Mobile* ("History of the Search for Self-Motive Power from the 13th to the 19th Century"), published in London in two volumes: 1861 and 1870.[1]

On April Fool's Day in 1978, science writer Robert Schadewald disclosed his tongue-in-cheek Gravity Engine.[2] The joke was based on a conjecture by renowned English physicist Paul Dirac and other physicists that gravity may be slowly decreasing as the universe expands. Schadewald's simple machine is nothing more than a large vertical wheel with a heavy weight on the rim. Gravity pulls the weight down on one side. By the time it rises on the other side, the weight has slightly decreased, thereby allowing its inertia to carry it back to the top with momentum to spare. Since the weight will always be a trifle heavier going down than it was going up, the wheel should continually gain in speed.

Unfortunately, this scheme contains a built-in pitfall. Even if the decline in gravity were large and rapid enough to make a difference, relativity theory would prevent the device from working. In Einstein's theory, gravity and inertia are two names for the same force. This means that the wheel's momentum would also steadily decline, allowing friction to take its usual toll.

There used to be much speculation about the possibility of making a shield through which gravity could not penetrate. This is now ruled out by relativity theory, in which gravity is not a conventional force but a distortion of spacetime. Early science-fiction writers often made use of gravity shields, notably H. G. Wells in *The First Men in the Moon*. He describes a gravity-screening substance called Cavorite; its use effectively lofts a spaceship to the moon. In more recent science fiction, James Blish has solved the problem of transportation in outer space with an antigravity

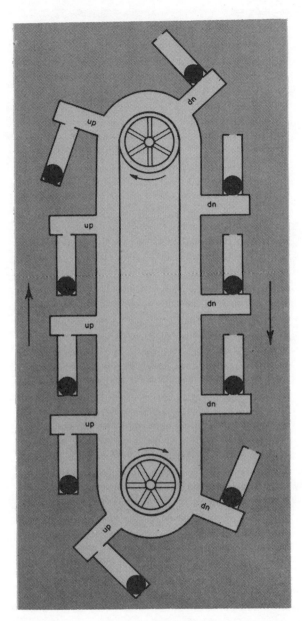

FIGURE 7. Would you invest in a company that announced its intention to build this "foolproof" perpetual motion device? On the left, the falling rubber balls draw air into cylinders, making them buoyant. When they drop on the right, they allow water to enter the cylinders, at the same time compressing the air and forcing it into the cylinders on the left. The amount of air inside the device remains constant. In my *Scientific American* column on Mathematical Games (February 1972), I called this a "dynamaforce generator," attributing its invention to the savvy numerologist Dr. Irving Joshua Matrix.

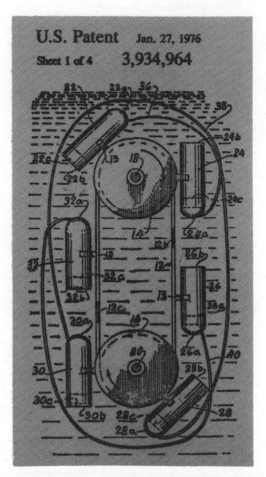

FIGURE 8. The U.S. Patent Office granted this patent in 1976, apparently unaware that the "Gravity-Actuated Fluid Displacement Power Generator" was a perpetual motion machine of a type that had been popular, if not functional, in the 19th century. An appropriate date of issuance would have been April 1, but probably neither the Patent Office nor the inventor would have found any humor in the situation.

device called a "spindizzy." If such a screen could be made, perpetual motion would at once become feasible. Simply put the screen under one side of a vertical wheel! The operator of such a machine might even need a brake.

The buoyancy of water is of course the effect of gravity. It is not surprising that hundreds of ingenious gravity wheels would be designed to rotate underwater by the liquid's upward force. One absurd plan specified that floats on one side of the wheel would rise, then enter a tube of air on the other side where their weight would pull that side of the wheel

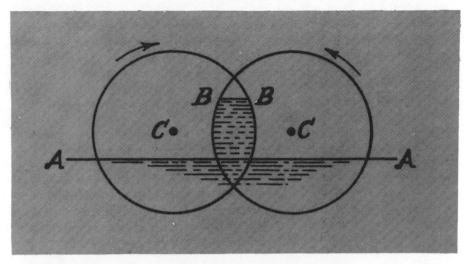

FIGURE 9. The April 22, 1911, issue of *Scientific American* presented in its correspondence columns an ingenious variation on run-of-the-mill perpetual motion machines. Two disks, arranged to rotate readily on their axes, are placed in some suitable container with the water level indicated by the line AA. A thin space between the two disks allows water to rise between them at the overlap area by capillary action. The weight of this lifted water is supposed to turn the wheels in the direction shown by the arrows and thus "furnish a continuous and perpetual supply of power." The editor commented: "Our readers may find it interesting to search out the fallacy of this ingenious device."

down. One of the many variations is shown in Figure 6. Here unattached spheres float up through a tank of water, then emerge through a valve to fall into compartments on an endless belt that carries them back to the tank's bottom. One catch: no designer of this kind of contrivance ever solved the problem of getting the floats through two watertight valves.

A better scheme is an underwater machine I once described in *Scientific American*.[3] As you can see in Figure 7, rubber balls on the right drop down inside the cylinders, pushing air into the cylinders on the left where the falling balls create suction. Scores of machines of this type were proposed in the nineteenth century. To make the cylinders airtight, each weight was often attached to the center of an elastic membrane that covered the opening. This allowed the balls to descend into the cylinders on one side and hang out of them on the other. Note the *up* and *dn* words I added to the device. They are my improvements over earlier joke wheels with 6s or IXs on one side that become weightier 9s or XIs when inverted on the opposite side.

Why it won't work—and it won't—is harder to explain for this model than for any of the other gravity-powered models. Perhaps that is why, incredible as it seems, two years after I wrote about this machine, a patent for it (see Figure 8) was filed (August 15, 1974) by David Diamond, of

Brooklyn. In a lapse into carelessness, the Patent Office actually granted the patent! It is Number 3,934,964, and can be obtained from the Patent Office for a dollar. Diamond called his machine a "gravity-actuated fluid displacement power generator." I was peeved to learn that my machine's finest features, *dn* and *up,* were omitted from the patent.

Water has been used in many other ways to propel perpetual-motion mechanisms. Some early machines had siphons designed to carry water back up to the top to be used over again to turn a wheel. Nor did inventors overlook capillary action. The specifications for one such whimsical device were published in *Scientific American,* April 22, 1911. (See Figure 9.) The two disks are partially submerged. Capillary action causes the water to rise in a thin space between the disks, and the weight of this water is supposed to turn the wheels in opposite directions.

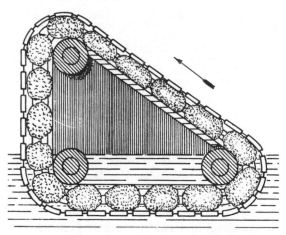

FIGURE 10. Sir William Congreve, politican and inventor of the Congreve rocket used by the British navy in the War of 1812, also dabbled in perpetual motion and invented a 16 spongepower machine, or "spongewheel." The operation of this device is simplicity itself. The joined sponges absorb water on the left, move in a counterclockwise direction, and as they go up the incline the attached weights squeeze the water out. The watersoaked sponges on the left or vertical side are heavier than those coming up the incline and naturally pull the latter up. For obvious reasons, this alternative source of power never threatened the coal industry.

Another capillary-action machine (see Figure 10) was proposed about 1827 by the British inventor and politician Sir William Congreve, whose improved rockets pummeled American ships and forts in the War of 1812 severely enough to be noted by Francis Scott Key in his phrase, "the rockets' red glare." The connected sponges on the left draw water upward by capillary action and become heavy. On the triangle's sloping side, the weights compress the sponges to which they are attached, making them lighter. Congreve's was another splendid idea, the only defect of which was that it did not work.

Can a water wheel somehow pump water back up to its source? This question must have been asked by the ancients, but not until the seventeenth century are such devices on record. One of them was proposed by the British physician and Rosicrucian, Robert Fludd. (See Figure 11.) The cylinder, with its helical pipe, is an invention attributed to Archimedes. It will indeed lift water to a higher level and until recent times was actually used for this purpose around the world. Additional power, usually horsepower, is needed to turn the cylinder.

FIGURE 11. The English mystic philosopher, Rosicrucian, and physician, Robert Fludd, designed this grinding machine in 1618. The water that operates the wheel is carried back to the top by the helical tube around the cylinder that is rotated by the wheel that is rotated by the water that is carried back to the top by the helical tube around . . . etc., etc., etc.

Numerous perpetual-motion machines based on Archimedes' screw, as it was called, were proposed in the seventeenth century. Sometimes the water was replaced by hundreds of little balls. They turned the wheel that operated the cylinder that presumably would carry the balls back to the top to be used over and over again.

In the same century, Bishop John Wilkins, the English mathematician, suggested using a loadstone (a kind of magnet). As suggested in Figure 12, the magnet is supposed to pull the ball to the top of the incline, where it falls through a hole and rolls back to its starting place.

Unfortunately, if the loadstone is strong enough to draw the ball up, it is then too strong to let it go. How about substituting an electromagnet for the loadstone? The ball could then trip a switch at the top of the slope; this would turn off the current and let the ball drop. The modified device would work, but it would no more be a perpetual-motion machine than an electric doorbell.

Since the discovery of electricity, thousands of perpetual-motionists have sought ways to use electrical energy, frequently combining it with gravity wheels and other devices. All such schemes are doomed by the laws of thermodynamics. But, because the idea of free energy is always newsworthy, even today an inventor of a totally useless device can sometimes snag fantastic amounts of newspaper and even television coverage.

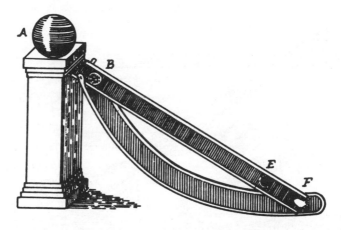

FIGURE 12. Bishop John Wilkins, whose intellectual interests combined theology and mathematics, argued, contrary to Copernicus, that the earth was not a planet, and believed that the moon was inhabited. Not surprisingly, he also joined the perpetual motion cavalcade. He thought that a loadstone (A) could pull a steel ball (E) up the incline. At the top the ball would drop through a hole at (B), then roll down a curved track to (F) from whence it would be pulled up to the top again. What spoiled the classic simplicity of this scheme was the fact that any magnet strong enough to pull the steel ball to the top of the incline would not easily let go of it.

In 1981, for example, NBC News gave extensive publicity to William Lucas, of Big Sandy, Texas, who claimed to have a machine that generated more electrical power than it needed to start it and keep it going. Lucas's contraption consists of an overbalanced wheel aided by electricity and compressed air. "They laughed at Fulton and Edison," said the gullible NBC reporter, "but they're not laughing at Bill Lucas." If NBC News had bothered to ask a physicist for advice, it would have quickly discovered someone who laughed. Lucas is still trying hard to get his machine patented.[4]

Early in 1984, a CBS station trumpeted a perpetual-motion machine invented by Joseph Wesley Newman, of Lucedale, Mississippi. Newman's

Rube Goldberg mechanism is based on electromagnetic particles unknown to physicists. They are said to spin like gyroscopes. The machine supposedly takes energy from these particles to run a motor; then the energy is fed back to the source. This marvelous device has the endorsement of a solid-state physicist who works for a major corporation and who should know better. Newman is convinced that his particle theory explains sunspots, tornadoes, dowsing, gravity, and ESP. He recently sued the Patent Office for rejecting his application.[5]

Because any attempt to build a perpetual-motion machine has to be an exercise in sheer folly, we must ask what sort of person becomes so obsessed by such a task that he can squander a lifetime on it. There are three main character types:

1. The honest but ignorant inventor who does not know enough physics to realize the hopelessness of his efforts.

2. The charlatan who knows his contrivance won't work, but who is out to fleece as many suckers as possible out of as much money as possible.

3. The pious fraud, who combines sincerity of motive with artful opportunism.

Sincere belief mixed with crafty deception is conspicuous by its prevalence in the history of bogus science. Among the great spiritualist mediums of the past, for instance, many believed they could really communicate with the dead. They also discovered they could greatly boost their income and reputation by secretly obtaining "evidential" data on their clients and by resorting to trickery to produce sensational physical phenomena.

The same strange amalgam is found in the lives of many perpetual-motionists of the past two centuries. They begin by truly believing they have invented a workable machine. When their model fails to perform— such gadgetry often proves extremely difficult even to turn by hand—the naive inventors delude themselves that the difficulty will disappear once they have eliminated enough friction, or removed some other defect by building an improved model. All they need is money. But to get the funding they have to persuade investors that their machines will work. And what better way to do this than by running their device with a secret power source? After all, they rationalize, it's only a harmless ploy to aid a worthy cause. Will not their machine ultimately benefit humanity by providing unlimited sources of free energy?

Oddly enough, the two most celebrated cases of perpetual-motion flim-flam occurred in Philadelphia. When, in 1812, one Charles Redheffer (or Redheifer) began exhibiting a perpetual-motion machine for which he sought financing, the press gave him oodles of space. Each day hundreds of Philadelphians paid admission to his home to watch the amazing machine in action.

One of them, Samuel Emlen, writing to his cousin, expressed an opinion that was probably shared by many: "I heard of Redheifer's supposed discovery when I was last in the City. What an era of invention this is; should this man prove to have made the discovery he claims, what a change will be produced by it—away go steam engines, water mills, horses, etc." (November 9, 1812).

No less a distinguished inventor than Robert Fulton finally unmasked the fraud. As soon as Fulton saw the machine, he guessed, by the irregular motion of its main wheel, that it was being operated by a hidden person. After knocking away portions of the supporting framework, he discovered, to the dismay of Redheffer and the cheers of the crowd, a catgut-belt drive that went through a wall, along a floor, and up to an attic room. In the room sat an aged man with a long beard, nibbling at a piece of bread in one hand and turning a crank with the other.

According to Cadwallader David Colden (1769–1834), in his *Life of Robert Fulton* (1817), the enraged spectators demolished the machine; and Redheffer, red of face, was forced to flee. A surviving advertising circular discloses that the inventor charged $5 admission for men, but gallantly allowed all women to enter free.

At one time the Franklin Institute had on display a model of the Redheffer "Perpetual Motion" Machine. A placard bore the following legend:

> This model was made by Isaiah Lukens, first Chairman of the Committee on Science and the Arts. It was built for the purpose of exposing the fraudulent nature of the claim of Charles Reidheifer [*sic*] to have discovered a self-acting machine for the investigation of which the Legislature of Pennsylvania in December 1812 appointed a commission of experts. Oliver Evans (Delaware-born inventor, America's first steam-engine builder and "one of the most ingenious mechanics that America ever produced") was a member of this commission. The original Reidheifer machine was operated by means of a crank. The model illustrated is operated by clockwork concealed in the base.

Most perpetual-motion swindlers have powered their devices with subtler methods. The greatest of all such mountebanks was John Worrell Keely, a Philadelphia carpenter, who in the 1870s announced his discovery of a way to tap the enormous energy contained in ordinary water. Even then, there was a considerable basis for the belief that a drop of water did indeed contain awesome amounts of energy.

When Keely exhibited his apparatus, first in Philadelphia and later in New York and Boston, his claims were widely accepted. What if scientists were skeptical? As usual, they hesitated to waste time trying to counter claims so obviously preposterous. Small wonder, then, that with newspapers routinely whipping up enthusiasm, Keely had no trouble raising tens of thousands of dollars from credulous investors. The Keely Motor Company was formed to support his "research," promote his discoveries, and probably impart an aura of respectability to a phony enterprise.

Nobody seemed troubled by Keely's lack of education, least of all Keely himself. He seems to have been a virtuoso con artist. Large and muscular, imposing in appearance, he talked rapidly and with unbounded confidence about the "etheric force" that could be extracted from one thimbleful of water and used to drive trains, fire bullets, and do just about anything else that required power.* He gave the impression of being totally honest and eager to benefit humanity although nobody knew what he meant when he rattled on about his "hydro-pneumatic-pulsating-vacue-engine" with its "quadruple negative harmonics."[6]

No matter that top physicists called him a fraud—his immunity to such imputations has its parallel today. Admirers of Immanuel Velikovsky, the *Worlds in Collision* man, are not in the least dismayed by astronomers who call Velikovsky's cosmology hogwash. Thousands of people, many of them poor, bought stock in Keely's company believing it would soon make them rich.

When the principal stockholders of the Keely Motor Company became disillusioned by the perpetual-motionist's perpetual delays in producing a practical machine, they withdrew support. Keely then found a wealthy benefactor in Mrs. Clara Bloomfield Moore, the widow of a Philadelphia paper manufacturer. She not only subsidized his harebrained "experiments" and projects (allowing him a yearly salary of $2,500 and advancing him well over $100,000 to meet the expenses of his research programs) but wrote articles in his defense for publication in journals and books and tirelessly sought out scientists who would validate Keely's claims. One British physicist, Professor W. Lascelles-Scott, went on record with: "Keely has demonstrated

---

*Keely, whom the *Dictionary of American Biography* describes as an "inventor and impostor," evidently dazzled his customers with his fancy footwork. In speaking of the vast reservoir of energy waiting to be tapped by his state-of-the-art equipment, he would, for example, mesmerize the public with such gobbledygook as follows: "With our present knowledge no definition can be given of the latent force, which, possessing all the conditions of attraction and repulsion associated with it, is free of magnetism. If it is a condition of electricity, robbed of all electrical phenomena, or a magnetic force, rebellant to the phenomena associated with magnetic development, the only philosophical conclusion I can arrive at is that this indefinable element is the soul of matter." Keely's expertise consisted of, as one commentator explained, "drawing the unknown energy from the medium in motion around us, made available at any point by his operating instrument."

to me, in a way which is absolutely unquestionable, the existence of a force hitherto unknown."

Keely died in Philadelphia on November 18, 1898, his great work still unfinished. Mrs. Bloomfield Moore's son, Clarence, understandably miffed over having been deprived by Keely of a substantial share of his inheritance, rented the late inventor's house. He and several others dismantled Keely's machines and explored the building.

What appeared to be solid supporting rods of metal—Keely frequently proved they were solid by pretending to pick one at random and filing through it—turned out to have microbore tubes inside for transmitting compressed air. The tubes ran to a tank in the basement where a motor compressed the air. Keely also used concealed springs, magnets, and other devices. There was nothing simple about his techniques! "An unadulterated rascal" was how Clarence described his mother's friend.

FIGURE 13. The cover of *Science and Invention* for March 1925, which announced a $5,000 award to anyone demonstrating a working gravity machine in the presence of the magazine's editorial staff. During the twenties, *Science and Invention*'s covers were printed on simulated gold paper to symbolize the golden age of science that the editor and publisher, Hugo Gernsback, believed was just beginning. Sad to relate, even the incentive of a handsome monetary reward failed to attract to Gernsback's brave new world even one genuine perpetual motion machine.

When Mrs. Bloomfield Moore died a few months after Keely's demise, she was still persuaded he was a genius, which in a way he really was. It is a tribute to Keely's consummate skill as a bamboozler that for a quarter of a century, until his death in 1898, no one had been able to expose his manipulation of his pseudoscientific apparatus.

In 1928, not to be outdone by Philadelphia, Pittsburgh produced a new perpetual-motion scamp named Lester J. Hendershot. Hendershot announced in New York City that he had perfected a device that would run forever on force from the earth's magnetic field. The commandant of the U.S. Army's Selfridge Field, in Detroit, personally endorsed the machine and spoke glowingly of its future. But the head of the Hockstetter Research Laboratory in Pittsburgh called a press conference in New York to tell a different story. He had investigated Hendershot's machine, he said, and found a tiny battery cleverly hidden inside one of the motors.

Hendershot did not deny he had put the battery there. He did this, he insisted, just to steer scientists away from his machine's true secret. Charles Fort, who tells the story in his book, *Wild Talents,* writes that a few weeks later a New York paper reported that Hendershot had checked into a hospital in Washington, D.C.

It seems he had been demonstrating his fuelless motor to a patent attorney when a bolt of electricity shot from it and temporarily paralyzed him. Apparently that was the last anyone heard of Hendershot. Fort speculates on the possibility that his motor, as well as Keely's, was a psychic motor "fueled with zeal"—operated by a wild talent, the unconscious psychokinetic power of the inventor's mind.

During the nineteen-twenties there were so many advertisements in papers and magazines for perpetual-motion machines, placed by inventors seeking investors, that *Science and Invention,* a colorful magazine edited by Hugo Gernsback (Gernsback is known as the "father of science fiction" because he was the first to publish such fiction in his magazines), offered a $5,000 prize to the inventor of any workable gravity machine. The cover of the March 1925 issue, in which this contest was announced, is shown in Figure 13, minus its original gold color. Gernsback explained the contest in plain terms:

> The reason that *Science and Invention Magazine* is offering an award of $5,000.00 for a working model of a perpetual motion machine may be given in a few words. Throughout the country we see advertisements, placards and postal cards advising the public to invest in means of developing perpetual power. Some of these advertisements are reproduced on these pages. Always the inventor claims to be the proud possessor of the one and only working

perpetual motion machine. Invariably the inventor claims to be looking out for the investor's individual welfare. He does not want to give the system to the "crooked politicians" who are anxiously waiting to give him several hundred thousand dollars for his rights to the invention. He glibly paints a wonderful picture of the earning capacities of such an invention and zealously and covetously guards his secret. If he gets your ten cents or a hundred dollars for a share in the invention, he gloats over his success. The next time one of these inventors calls to see you, show him a copy of this publication, tell him there are no strings tied to the offer. Tell him *Science and Invention* does not want the rights to his invention. *They merely want to see it working,* and if it does so, they will praise it from the housetops and give it not $100.00 but $5,000.00.

No one claimed the prize. Of course this no more deterred perpetual-motionists than proofs of the impossibility of trisecting the angle have inhibited angle trisectors. Today, as always, leading scientists are constantly besieged by ignorant cranks who demand validation of their simple-minded theories.

Most scientists never answer crackpot letters or phone calls, having learned from bitter experience that the slightest criticism often triggers a flood of abusive letters or vituperative attacks via the telephone. Sometimes the crank himself turns up uninvited on one's doorstep (this once happened to me, a mere science writer). In another context, Sir John Falstaff neatly expressed the sentiments of all of us who have been thus pestered: "I were better to be eaten to death with rust than to be scoured to nothing with perpetual motion *(Henry IV;* I, ii, 218).

I recommend a marvelous stratagem discovered by Arthur C. Hardy, a physicist at MIT. This is how Francis Sears described it in a letter to *Physics Today.*[7]

> Your remarks on inventors of perpetual-motion machines (*Physics Today,* July, page 15) bring to mind the following story told me by Professor A. C. Hardy. It seems that Hardy received a letter from such an inventor, describing his machine and demanding, as is customary, to be told why it wouldn't work. Before he had replied to this letter, Hardy received a second letter from another inventor, making exactly the same demand.
>
> Hardy then wrote to both inventors, saying that although he himself was not an authority on perpetual-motion machines, he knew someone who was, and sent each inventor the name and address of the other.

Notes

1. Dircks's history has been reprinted several times. The latest was an Amsterdam edition in 1968. A shorter work, *Perpetual Motion: The History of an Obsession,* by Arthur W. J. Ord-Hume (Allen & Unwin, 1977) is currently available in the United States as a St. Martin's Press paperback. It contains a bibliography of other references.

2. Schadewald, " 'What Goes Up' Is Basis for a Breakthrough," *Science Digest,* April 1978.

3. "Mathematical Games," *Scientific American,* February 1972. The article is reprinted in my book, *The Magic Numbers of Dr. Matrix* (Prometheus Books, 1985).

4. "Last Word," by James Randi, *Omni,* January 1981, p. 118.

5. "Mr. Newman's Fantastic Machine," *Discover,* April 1984, p. 6; "Newman's Impossible Motor," by Eliot Marshall, *Science,* vol. 223 (Feb. 10, 1984), pp. 571-572; "Newman's 'Energy Output' Machine Put to the Test," by Marjorie Sun, *Science,* July 11, 1986.

6. See Keely's incomprehensible article, "The Operation of the Vibratory Current," *New Science Review,* April 1895. (A sample: "The substance of the brain is molecular. The mind which permeates the brain is inter-etheric in substance; it is the element by which the brain is impregnated. This element, when excited into action, controls all physical motion as long as the necessary sympathetic conditions are maintained. These conditions are no more immaterial in their character than are light and heat. Electricity, magnetism, gravity, and heat are latent in all aggregations of matter. They are not obtained from terrestrial influences. Celestial radiation is the true impregnating medium in all these forces. The brain is the high resonating receptacle where the sympathetic celestial acts, and where molecular and atomic motion are induced, as according to the intensification brought to bear upon it by radiation.") In the annals of perpetual motion, Keely's prose must be the most turgid ever assembled. If there were a category of semantic protective camouflage, his stuff could be pigeonholed there as a classic example.

7. *Physics Today,* October 1968, p. 19.

Afterword

I have not tried to research the life of Mrs. Bloomfield Moore, Keely's wealthy patron, but it is surely a sad, fascinating tale. Mrs. Moore was born in England in 1824 and as a widow lived many years in London before her death in 1899. Clarence Bloomfield Moore, her son, became an archaeologist after graduating from Harvard and was best known for his exploration of U.S. Indian mounds. Apparently Mrs. Moore wrote poetry that was widely read in her day. At any rate, I found two poems by her in a multi-volumed anthology called *The Classic and the Beautiful* (see vol. 1, p. 49; vol 4, p. 442). Her relations with Keely are detailed in Ord-Hume's book, cited in Note 1 above.

I mentioned only in passing the fact that no convex polyhedron of uniform density can be unstable on all its faces, otherwise it would flop around forever on a horizontal plane. Can such a polyhedron be unstable on all faces but one? Yes, but determining the least number of faces is still an intriguing unsolved problem. The record is held by Richard K.

Guy, who reported his discovery of a "unistable" (or "monostatic") convex polyhedron of 19 faces in "A Unistable Polyhedron" (Research Paper No. 62, University of Calgary, Alberta, Canada, October 1968). The polyhedron has since been rediscovered by others. It is a 17-sided cylindrical prism, truncated at both ends at oblique angles.

My chapter has only a paragraph about Joe Newman and his machines, but since I wrote that article Newman has become the most famous perpetual-motion machine inventor since Keely. I hasten to add that Newman vigorously denies that his generators are perpetual-motion devices. Instead of creating energy, they release energy from gyroscopic particles that he believes are the fundamental particles of the universe and the key to a unified-field theory that has so far eluded all particle experts. For some curious reason he hasn't named his particles (one science writer proposed calling them "putons"), although he *has* named his son (born in 1983) "Gyromas" to honor the particles. I should also add that Newman, in my opinion, is not (like Keely) a charlatan; he's a true believer in his own genius.

Newman is also a high-school dropout, but he has read just enough to talk like a physicist. In his theory, movement of the gyroscopic particles creates electric and magnetic fields. As they stream through a magnetic field, from north to south poles, his generators supposedly convert part of the mass of each particle into kinetic energy. The law of mass-energy conservation is not violated. Joe likens his machine to a paddle wheel. How long did men sit beside a stream, he asks, before they thought of putting a paddle into it? How long will men sit beside a magnetic field before putting a paddle in it? In brief, Newman claims that his machines release subatomic energy. "The ingenious principle is so simple," he says, "it befuddles the mind." It is so simple that the world's greatest physicists are incapable of understanding it.

When a science writer (see *Omni,* December 1985) asked Newman how much mass one of his particles has, Newman replied: "I haven't concerned myself with that. I don't give a hoot about mathematics."

In spite of Joe's near-total ignorance of modern physics, his evangelistic fervor and passionate rhetoric have generated vast clouds of favorable publicity in the media and huge sums from naive investors. A corporation called Energy Resources Unlimited, based in Sacramento, California, gave him half a million dollars. Dan Benvenuti, a Sacramento real-estate broker, gave a similar amount. Benvenuti says God spoke in his heart three times saying, "You must meet Joe Newman." After signing an investment deal with him in 1984, Benvenuti tried to get Newman on Pat Robertson's "700 Club" television show. Newman was turned down (according to *Discover,*

May 1987) because he said that, although he believed in God, he was not a follower of Jesus. This frank statement probably cost him millions of investment dollars from "700 Club" viewers.

Two years later Benvenuti became disenchanted by Newman's continual failure to demonstrate the efficiency of his machines. He was also put off, he says, by Joe's increasing arrogance. *Discover* reported (in the article cited above) that Benvenuti has filed suit against Newman for making misleading claims to obtain funds.

Among a tiny group of Newman enthusiasts who have scientific credentials—most of them are engineers—none has been more vocal than Roger Hastings, formerly a physicist with Sperry Univac, in Minneapolis, now with the Superconductive Electronics Center for Unisys, in St. Paul. After many tests of Joe's generators, Hastings became convinced they work. When Stephen Ullman, an MIT electrical engineer, read one of Hastings's papers about Newman's particle theory, he commented: "It's like reading bad science fiction."

Newman's application for a U.S. patent was turned down by the Patent Office in 1981. Responding to a lawsuit to force the government to grant a patent, a Federal District Court ordered Newman to allow the National Bureau of Standards to test one of his machines. Its 1986 report found the machine to be nothing more than a crudely constructed generator. "In all conditions tested," the report said, "the input power exceeded the output power." Newman claims 800-percent efficiency, but the NBS found the efficiency to range from 27 to 67 percent. (See "Newman's 'Energy Output Machine' Put to the Test," by Marjorie Sun, in *Science,* July 11, 1986).

Predictably, Newman and his lawyer blasted the report as "just another example of the injustice I'm fighting against." No one waxes more eloquent than Joe when he is describing the tremendous benefits his discovery will give to the world if he can only get his generator patented and obtain enough funds to build a machine that will convince everybody. He constantly attacks the nation's education system for producing scientists who are not open to new ideas. "My machine will do more for world peace," he told *Discover,* "than all the kings, queens, and politicians that ever lived. Men the world over will see joy in their children's eyes again."

Newman is easy to understand, but it is astonishing how many intelligent people have been taken in by his preaching. When he appeared on the "Tonight Show," Johnny Carson treated him as if he were a great scientist who is being persecuted by an establishment—men with vested interests in present-day energy sources that Newman's generators threaten to make obsolete. My respect for syndicated columnist James Kilpatrick sank to a new low when he devoted an entire column (June 1986) to praising Newman.

"My own guess, after reading a raft of material," Kilpatrick wrote, "is that Newman is probably a genius. His name one day may rank with such familiar names as Faraday, Watt and Ampere."

In 1985 Newman privately published a 287-page book titled *The Energy Machine of Joseph Newman.* I was tempted to buy it until I learned it would cost me $38.45 to obtain it by mail. For a good coverage of recent developments in Newman's battles with the scientific community, see David Noland's "A Man Who Defies Laws," in *Discover,* May 1987, and follow-up letters in the June issue. Although written by a skeptic, the article probably generated large amounts of funding. For an amusing article on the unshakable mind-sets of perpetual-motion cranks, see "Wheels Go Round and Round, But Always Run Down," by Doug Stewart, in *Smithsonian,* November 1986.

On November 28, 1987, an Associated Press story reported that Newman had plans to run for president as an independent in his own Truth and Action Party. God directed him to seek the presidency, he said, and he has "clear scientific facts" showing that the human race is headed for catastrophe unless people listen to him. If people "stick their heads in the sand," he warned, "great destruction across the world" will begin in six months, and by 1999 "most life on earth will be gone."

Newman denied being a religious person. He refused to give details about his revelations, saying only that "God is angry with the world and God is going to get the world's attention." It will be interesting to see how this turn in Newman's career will play in the minds of his admirers and financial backers.

22 | Psychic Surgery

Andy Kaufman, known to television viewers as Latka Gravas, a zany mechanic on the hit show "Taxi," died of lung cancer on May 16, 1984. He was 35. Two months earlier he had gone to the Philippines in a sad, futile effort to be cured by a "psychic surgeon."

For many decades "psychic surgery" has flourished in the Philippines and Brazil. While a patient is fully awake, the surgeon pretends to enter the body with his bare hands, sometimes with a knife as a prop, to remove tissues that are said to cause the ailment. The skin is never punctured. There are no scars, though usually there is plenty of blood.

According to the *Star* (June 5), Kaufman was "operated" on twice daily, for a fee of $25 per treatment, by Ramon "Jun" (for Junior) Labo, one of some 50 charlatans who operate in "clinics" in the Philippines. After Kaufman's death the *National Enquirer* (June 5) printed three grisly photographs showing Labo's healing session, in which he seemed to pull bloody tissue out of Kaufman's chest. In the first picture Labo's fingers seem to be penetrating the skin. This illusion is produced by bending the fingertips so that the middle knuckles of the fingers press firmly on a patient's body. The tissues and blood, which usually come from animals, are concealed before the operation and produced at the appropriate time by the surgeon, who uses standard magician's sleight of hand to make them appear.

Kaufman's girlfriend, who accompanied him on the trip, was quoted by the *Star* as saying there was no possibility that Labo had used deception, because she stood "not a foot away." "We saw Jun cure a man with an eye problem. He actually removed the eye, and you could see the empty socket. And then he put the eye back in." What Jun really did is described in detail by surgeon William Nolen in the chapters on psychic surgery in his popular book, *Healing: A Doctor in Search of a Miracle*. The surgeon conceals an animal eye in his closed hand, which he adroitly opens several inches in front of the patient's face after he has pretended to take out

---

This originally appeared in *Discover,* August 1984, and is reprinted with permission.

an eye. According to the *Enquirer,* Kaufman was as impressed by Labo as was his girlfriend. "The doctors don't know everything," he said in a state of high elation when he returned to California. A few weeks later he was dead in a Los Angeles hospital.

One reason Kaufman went to the Philippines, the *Star* reported, was that he had seen a film about the Filipino surgeons, narrated by that eminent authority on medical science, Burt Lancaster. "We saw the film, and it showed that the cures could work," said Kaufman's girlfriend. What they saw was part of a longer film called "Psychic Phenomena: Exploring the Unknown," which was aired in 1977 by NBC on Sunday night prime time. The lurid segment on the Filipino surgeons was so effective that promoters of psychic surgeons have been showing it ever since. NBC replied to the protests of scientists over the show by insisting that it had been produced solely for entertainment. "We can't imagine anybody taking it seriously," one spokesman declared.

Publishers, too, must share the blame for keeping psychic surgeons busy. On the jacket of the book *Psychic Surgery* by Tom Valentine (Henry Regnery, 1973) is this blurb: "The study of Antonio C. Agpaoa, Spiritualist healer of the Philippines, and the astounding facts about successful surgery without instruments, anaesthesia, or pain." Another offender, *Arigo: Surgeon of the Rusty Knife* by John G. Fuller (Thomas Y. Crowell, 1974), is a Fullersome account of the miracles performed by one of the many Brazilian psychic surgeons. Pocket Books has published both in paperback.

In 1975 the Federal Trade Commission ordered four West Coast travel agencies to stop promoting tours of patients to the Philippines, declaring: "Because we are dealing here with desperate consumers with terminal illnesses who want to believe psychic surgery will cure them, no amount of disclosure will suffice to drive home to all the point that psychic surgery is nothing but a total hoax."

Still, the gullible sick keep coming. Business slackened a bit in 1982 after the most famous of the Filipino "surgeons," Tony Agpaoa, age 43, died of a heart attack. Now the customers are back by the thousands. Every day that Kaufman was at Labo's clinic, as many as a hundred waited in line for his quickie operations.

Perhaps someday the television networks and major publishers, in a fit of moral courage, will realize that when they give invaluable free publicity to medical quacks they are playing with the lives of the innocent and poorly informed. The tragedies occur when the seriously ill, swayed by the glowing testimonials of famous personalities and irresponsible journalists, forgo reputable medical aid until it is too late.

Afterword

For details about Arigo, the Brazilian psychic surgeon, see my review of John Fuller's book about Arigo, in *Science: Good, Bad and Bogus,* Chapter 25.

James Randi, the magician who won a MacArthur Fellowship award in 1986 for his tireless efforts to expose psychic charlatans, medical quacks, and phony faith-healers, routinely demonstrates psychic surgery in one of his lectures. The "operation" is performed on a volunteer from the audience. It is so miraculous and bloody that when he operated on a young man on Johnny Carson's "Tonight Show," early in 1986, a lady in the audience fainted. Even magicians have difficulty following the numerous secret "moves" in Randi's surgery routine. That any intelligent person today could take psychic surgery seriously, in either its Brazilian or Philippine varieties, is beyond belief, yet such is the scientific illiteracy of our times.

23 | 666 and All That

Here is the wisdom. Let him that hath understanding count the number of the beast: for it is the number of a man; and his number is six hundred threescore and six.

Revelation 13:18

No verse of biblical prophecy has been subjected to more bizarre and futile speculation than this verse from the Book of Revelation, the last book of the New Testament. Most fundamentalists believe that the passage refers to the Antichrist (described more explicitly in the epistles of John), who it is said will acquire a vast following just before the Second Coming of Christ. The beast in this biblical scenario will be Satan's earthly agent. Before the Battle of Armageddon, the great conflict between the forces of good and evil, the faithful will be "raptured," lifted into the skies. There will be mass conversions of Jews to Christianity (the unconverted, according to this apocalyptic account, are destined for eternal damnation). Ultimately, Satan will be banished and held chained in an abyss, and a millennium of peace will begin on earth.

As Revelation (13:16-17) foretells, the Antichrist "causeth all, both small and great, rich and poor, free and bond, to receive a mark in their right hand, or in their foreheads; and that no man might buy or sell, save he that had the mark, or the name of the beast, or the number of his name." The number will be 666.

Many biblical scholars have attempted to unravel the mysterious number. Most think it is a cipher that stands for a name. This kind of mathematical game-playing was popular among the Greeks and Hebrews, who used letters of the alphabet as numbers at the time Revelation was written in the first century A.D. The likeliest name is that of the tyrannical emperor Nero (37-68). As the name is transliterated from Greek, Neron Caesar is represented in Hebrew as Nron Ksr, whose letters have these

This article originally appeared in *Discover*, February 1985, and is reprinted with permission.

A watercolor by William Blake that depicts the two beasts of Revelation 17. The main beast, coming out of the sea, is the incarnation of Satan as the Antichrist. The lower beast, who comes out of the earth, is a second Antichrist, loyal to Satan, who becomes the world leader. Sixes are hidden all over the painting, in both normal and mirror-image form. You see them around the head of the larger beast, under the left hand of the smaller beast, in the horns of both beasts, and in many other spots.

numerical values: N = 50, r = 200, o = 6, n = 50, k = 100, s = 60. Added up they total 666.

Not surprisingly in light of their Semitic heritage, the early Christians were finding 666 in the names of many persecutors of their young faith, including the Roman emperor Domitian (51-96), who tried to restore paganism. Among other things, he exiled John, the author of Revelation, to a lonely island off Asia Minor. Later they uncovered John's mystical number in the names of Muhammad and other leaders of rival religions. And during the Reformation, Protestants devised all sorts of ways to extract 666 from the names of the popes. Catholics retaliated by discovering 666 in the names of Luther, Calvin, and other leading reformers. More recently, numerologists have easily obtained 666 from the names of the likes of

Napoleon, Hitler, Mussolini, and Stalin.

Biblical numerology has flourished especially among four religions born in the New World, all of which believe Armageddon is around the corner: the Church of Jesus Christ of Latter-day Saints (Mormons), Seventh-Day Adventists, Jehovah's Witnesses, and Herbert Armstrong's Worldwide Church of God. For many decades the Adventists made clear their feeling about the Roman Catholic church with their numerical analysis of the Latin phrase often used to describe a pope, *vicarius filii dei* ("in place of the Son of God"), from which comes the title Vicar of Christ. By adding the letters that are Roman Numerals—V and U = 5 (the Romans used V for U), I = 1, C = 100, L = 50, and D = 500—they get 666. Eventually, to their great embarrassment, the Adventists learned that the same method yields 666 when it is applied to Ellen Gould White, the name of their church's nineteenth-century prophetess (if W, or double U, is taken as two Vs).

Today most leading fundamentalist scholars avoid linking 666 to any person or institution. Billy Graham, in his many sermons on the Antichrist, invokes the popular view that because 7 is a symbol of perfection, 6 indicates a falling from perfection. But he allows there is a deeper mystery about 666 that has yet to be revealed.

Some fundamentalists are less cautious. In her 1981 prophetic book, *When Your Money Fails,* Mary Stewart Relfe argued that 666 is already deeply embedded in the practices of big business: in production codes, computer programs, credit-card numbers, the code lines on supermarket items, including such magazines as *Discover,* not to mention its use by the IRS and the Common Market. She suggested that soon the number would be branded with laser beams on the foreheads or hands of everybody except the faithful. There was nothing beastly about the book's numbers. It sold 300,000 copies in only the first six months after publication.

With many Americans, including President Reagan,* now taking the possibility of a biblical Armageddon seriously, it is not surprising that many frightened fundamentalists fancied they could discern 666 in the beard of a face in the tiny logo of Proctor & Gamble, the giant soap-maker, and traced the dreaded number by joining the logo's 13 stars. (See Figure 1.) Fundamentalist clamoring for a boycott of company products was so shrill that P & G spent a fortune trying to combat fears of a satanic connection. In 1982 the company filed half a dozen lawsuits for slander, including one against Guy Sharpe, a Methodist lay preacher and Atlanta television weather-

---

*Who acknowledged during a presidential debate that he had had "philosophical discussions with people who are interested," but added soothingly: "No one knows whether those prophecies mean that Armageddon is a thousand years away or the day after tomorrow."

The P and G logo.

man, who allegedly spread rumors in at least one talk about P & G's link to Satan. After Sharpe apologized publicly, the company dropped the suit. The other lawsuits have been settled in a similar fashion.

There has been other legal action. In 1980 Tonya Turnbull, a Kansas City fundamentalist, went to court to get her license plate changed from CPG-666 (note the P & G) on the grounds that church members were shunning her. In the movie version of Hal Lindsey's phenomenal best seller *The Late Great Planet Earth* (narrated by, of all people, Orson Welles), there is a scene showing computers analyzing the names of world leaders to see if any of them yields 666. *The Omen,* an occult film, had the Antichrist born on the sixth day of the sixth month at six in the morning, with 666 as a birthmark on his scalp.

The fact is that the digits 666 can be uncovered in almost anybody's name, if you're willing to work a little at such mischief-making. Using the code A = 100, B = 101, and so on, Hitler adds up to 666. With a simpler code of A = 1, B = 2, and multiplying each letter-value by six, Sun Moon adds to 666. The same technique works on Kissinger, as well as the word *computer,* which suggests to those so inclined that the Antichrist will appear in the computer age, perhaps even in the guise of an especially diabolical machine.

Another clever way to derive the mystical number is to append six to each letter-value instead of multiplying by six. Thus A = 16, B = 26, and so on. This device was used in Allied countries during World War I to get 666 from "Kaiser." It also yields 666 when applied to the first name of Garner Ted Armstrong, Herbert's excommunicated son who runs the rival Church of God, International, headquartered in Tyler, Texas.

It is possible to uncover 666 in the names of other leading fundamentalist preachers. By adopting the so-called Devil's code (a favorite ploy of numerologists, whereby the alphabet is numbered backward from zero; Z = 0, Y = 1, X = 2 . . .) and multiplying each letter-value by 6, Moral Majority founder Jerry Falwell's last name adds up to 666. Billy Graham requires more elaborate numerical treatment. His initials are W. F. G. (William Franklin Graham). Using the A = 1 code, the letters add up to 36. The sum of the counting numbers from 1 through 36 is 666, and 36 = 6 × 6.

Mischievous Democratic numerologists, stung by the recent election, point out that each of the president's names, Ronald Wilson Reagan, has six letters. That's not all: using the A = 100 code, the letters of the three names total

1984, the year of the president's landslide re-election. And what about Walter Mondale? In the A = 1 code, W = 23 and M = 13, adding up to 36, from which 666 is obtained by the method applied to Billy Graham.

34	35	36	37	38	39	40	41	42
43	44	45	46	47	48	49	50	51
52	53	54	55	56	57	58	59	60
61	62	63	64	65	66	67	68	69
70	71	72	73	74	75	76	77	78
79	80	81	82	83	84	85	86	87
88	89	90	91	92	93	94	95	96
97	98	99	100	101	102	103	104	105
106	107	108	109	110	111	112	113	114

A "beastly" magic square.

And now, students of numerology, here's a devilish way to relate 666 to the name of Pat Robertson, the host of television's popular "700 Club," a fundamentalist program. Start by evaluating his initials in the A = 1 code. P = 16, R = 18, for a total of 34. There are nine letters in Robertson, so we draw a 9-by-9 matrix as shown in Figure 2. Put 34 in the first cell, then continue with consecutive numbers until the matrix is filled.

Select any number you like. Circle it, then cross out its row and column. Choose another number not crossed out, and repeat what you did before. Keep doing this, always picking a number not previously circled or crossed out, until no numbers remain. Nine numbers, all chosen at random, will be circled. Add them up and hold onto your hat!

Afterword

If you think my way of getting 666 from Pat Robertson's name is too contrived, consider this simpler method. Using the A = 1, B = 2, . . . cipher, PAT adds to 37. R = 18. The product of 37 and 18 is 666.

How about Jimmy Swaggart, another Pentecostal Bible walloper? SWAGGART (A = 1, B = 2, . . .) adds to 96. JIMMY (A = 101, B = 102, . . .) adds to 570. The sum of the two numbers is 666.

As Scott Frank pointed out in a letter (*Discover,* March 1985), applying to GARDNER the code A = (1 × 9) + 9, B = (2 × 9) + 9, C = (3 × 9) + 9, and so on, you get 666. Nine of course is 6 upside down.

If you are curious about why that magic matrix works, and how to construct such squares for forcing any desired number, see Chapter 2 of my *Scientific American Book of Mathematical Puzzles and Diversions.*

24 | D. D. Home-Sweet-Home

Thousands of books about spiritualism have been written by believers, skeptics, and fence-sitters, but none demonstrates as convincingly as *The Spiritualists* (Knopf, 1983; paper ed., Prometheus, 1985) the unbelievable ease with which persons of the highest intelligence can be flimflammed by the crudest of psychic frauds. Drawing on rare volumes and obscure articles, Ruth Brandon has skillfully interlaced the highlights of a history so sordid and fantastic that one finishes her book with an overwhelming sense of the futility of all efforts to expose fraud. "It is like punching a feather pillow," she writes, "an indentation is made, but soon refills, and the whole soft, spongy mass continues as before."

The book opens, as all such histories must, with the sad saga of the three Fox sisters. Leah, the oldest, was the "tigress" who dominated the others, ran the show, and died wealthy. Kate and Maggie ended their lives as miserable alcoholics whose bodies now molder in paupers' graves in Brooklyn. Before they died, both Kate and Maggie declared themselves charlatans. To a packed house at the Brooklyn Academy of Music, Maggie demonstrated how easily she produced spirit raps by cracking an abnormal joint of her toe. Later, she wrote an incoherent recantation.

Maggie's lover was a wealthy Arctic explorer and physician, Dr. Elisha Kane. After his death, Maggie published a book of his love letters and described their "secret marriage." Kane, who knew the sisters were cheats, constantly urged Maggie to abandon her detestable trade. Brandon reprints part of a prophetic letter from Kane to Kate, expressing his disgust:

> Now, Katy, although you and Maggie never go so far as this, yet circumstances must occur where you have to lacerate the feelings of other people. . . . You do things now which you would never have dreamed of doing years ago; and there will come a time when you will be worse than Mrs. Fish [Leah], a hardened woman, gathering around you victims of a delusion.

Alas, as Brandon makes clear, deceiving the gullible was the only way poor Kate and Maggie knew how to make a living.

D. D. Home

Brandon's next chapter, about the greatest of all mediums, D. D. Home, contains a marvelous account of how Home captured the mind of Elizabeth Browning—though not the mind of Robert—and almost destroyed their marriage. From the archives of Yale, Brandon has unearthed a remarkable letter in which Browning describes a séance with the Scottish medium that he and his wife attended. First came the rappings and table-wobbling, then the lamp was extinguished and, in Browning's words, one could see "nothing of what was done at the table—the night being cloudy." It was Home's practice to begin his séances in a lit room, then darken the room for the more startling phenomena. Why spirits prefer to operate in darkness has always been difficult for spiritualists to explain, though magicians understand it quite well!

Sitters were touched by spirit fingers. A snow-white hand lifted a wreath of flowers from the table and put it on Elizabeth's head. Home picked up what today is called a concertina, holding it below the table with one hand at the end opposite the keys, while it wheezed some simple tunes. Browning noticed Home's loose clothes, sacklike overcoat, and "inordinate sleeves." "On the whole," he wrote,"I thought the whole performance most clumsy." After speculating on how the hands could have operated, he sensibly adds: "There are probably fifty more ingenious methods at the service of every prestidigitateur."

Home's accordion bit was one of his specialties. Brandon considers the possibility of an accomplice playing another concertina, or the use of a concealed music box, but I think James Randi has hit on the most likely method. Among Home's effects were found several miniature mouth organs of the sort vaudevillians often put inside their mouths and play. Home's two favorite tunes were *Home Sweet Home* and *The Last Rose of Summer* (his spirits had a limited repertoire), both easily rendered on the eight notes of these tiny instruments.

Home was exceedingly vain, but lovable, good-looking, charming, and muscular, though he professed to have "no strength at all." He affected the manners of a child, bewildered by the source of his strange powers. It is easy to understand why he was never caught cheating. No medium was ever more cautious in refusing to produce phenomena unless certain that no "sitter" knew anything about methods of deception. During the séance Browning attended, five sitters were ejected from the circle at the request of spirit rappings. As always, the fact that nothing whatever occurred at numerous séances was taken by believers to be proof of Home's genuineness.

Although many books have been written about Home's life, including one by himself and another by his second wife, he remains, in Brandon's words, a "mysterious and shadowy figure," like the protagonist of "a badly-written novel." Episodes in this novel include his abrupt conversion to Catholicism, his quickly abandoned decision to enter a monastery, efforts to gain recognition as a sculptor, a brief career as a stage reciter, his expulsion from Rome as a "sorcerer," and his sudden departure from Paris for reasons still unclear. He was admired by Napoleon and the czar of Russia. His first marriage was to a wealthy Russian aristocrat who died a few years later.

In London, Home met a rich, childless, addlepated widow who was crackers about spiritualism. Home's discarnates instructed her to adopt him as a son and give him 60,000 pounds. She later decided the young man was trying to fleece her. He was arrested, and after a bitter court-battle the judge ruled in the old lady's favor, describing her as "saturated with delusion." It is amusing to read in Conan Doyle's account of Home that he believed Home to have acted throughout this sleazy episode with exemplary morality. Home's second wife was another Russian aristocrat, even wealthier than the first. Little is known about the last ten years of his life before he died in France in 1886.

Brandon is devastating in picturing the boundless gullibility of such distinguished scientists as Sir William Crookes, Alfred Russel Wallace, Oliver Lodge, and Charles Richet. There is a splendid account of the friendship between Doyle and Houdini, and how it fell apart when Houdini refused to accept as genuine a sentimental message that his dead mother supposedly dictated to Mrs. Doyle. Other colorful sections tell of such famous mountebanks as Eusapia Palladino, the uncouth little Italian woman who was once married to a magician, and Eva C., a famous lesbian sensitive who liked to work naked and exude ectoplasm from her vagina. When some spirit faces on photographs of Eva's séances were found to be identical with those in a French magazine, believers were no more dismayed than was Jule Eisenbud when some "thoughtographs" of psychic Ted Serios proved to be copies of *National Geographic* illustrations. Eva's faces were "idoplasts," claimed one prominent psi researcher, projected onto the film by Eva's memory of what she had seen in the magazine.

Such imbecilic rationalizations are still with us. Brian Inglis, a British paranormalist who blasted Brandon's book in the *Journal of the Society for Psychical Research* and in recent interviews with British reporters, once considered the charge by two scientists that they had seen Palladino using her feet, rather than psychic "pseudopods," to produce manifestations. "It was far from certain," Brandon quotes from a book by Inglis, "that what had been described as 'feet' were Eusapia's feet . . . given the possibility that she could produce psychic elongations, the experiments were simply not designed to distinguish between them and her arms and feet." In brief, the scientists may have only thought they saw her feet!

It is all so dreary and infantile. Brandon quotes a famous remark by T. H. Huxley that says it all: "The only good I can see in the demonstration of the 'Truth of Spiritualism' is to furnish an additional argument against suicide. Better live a crossing-sweeper, than die and be made to talk twaddle by a medium hired at a guinea a séance."

25 | PK (Psycho-Krap)

Many worthless books by writers who call themselves parapsychologists have been published in recent years, but *Psychokinesis* (Souvenir Press, 1982), by John Randall, a biology teacher at Coventry School, tops them all. It is not just that he rakes over stale ground but that his book is hopelessly out of date.

Consider, for example, his enthusiastic endorsement of the psychokinetic (PK) powers of Uri Geller, the Israeli magician turned flimflam artist. Randall makes much of John Taylor's high praise of Geller, and of the spoon-bending children featured in Taylor's book *Superminds* (Macmillan, 1973). He never informs his readers that in 1980 Taylor wrote a book called *Science and the Supernatural,* in which he repudiated his earlier book and denounced all psychic metal-bending as fraud.

Consider the pages in which Randall rhapsodizes over Geller's alleged alteration of the chemical structure of a piece of nitinol wire, giving it a new "memory" that experts could not remove. That is totally false. Eldon Byrd was in error when he made this sensational claim, reporting on his nitinol tests with Geller in Charles Panati's now discredited anthology, *The Geller Papers* (Houghton Mifflin, 1976). Experts at the Lawrence Livermore Laboratory, in California, removed the wire's memory easily. This was carefully detailed in my paper, "Geller, Gulls and Nitinol" (1977; reprinted in *Science: Good, Bad and Bogus*), but either Randall never read it, or what is worse, read it but did not want to mention it.

Consider too the section in which Randall extols the "thoughtography" of Ted Serios, a Chicago bellhop, who for a short time was apparently able to project onto Polaroid film his memory of photographs he had seen earlier in magazines. No one, says Randall, ever found evidence of trickery. Nonsense. In 1967 Charles Reynolds and David Eisendrath published in *Popular Photography* a complete exposé of how Serios. performed his whimsical trick. Ted has been unable to replicate it since,

This review originally appeared in *Nature,* November 11, 1982, and is reprinted with permission.

although magician James Randi demonstrates it regularly and with more skill. Did Randall know of this exposé? If not, his research was amateurish. If he did, his failure to discuss it is reprehensible.

The sad fact is that Randall buys almost everything on the psi scene no matter how flimsy the evidence. He believes that PK is behind the spirit rappings and the table liftings produced by great mediums of the past. Many pages describe the levitations of human bodies, from early Christian saints to meditating yogis; Randall suspects that PK helped Nijinsky make his high leaps on the ballet stage! He is persuaded that PK can hurl heavy objects across a room, move the hands of a clock, and cause light objects, such as matches and pillboxes, to "walk" across a table.

A postscript summarizes the 1981 "minilab" phenomena recently disclosed by W. E. Cox, a former associate of J. B. Rhine and a confirmed Gellerite. Leather rings link and unlink. A pencil rises in the air and writes on a notepad. Randall assures us that Cox captured all these wonders on film, but he doesn't reveal that the films are peppered with time breaks, and that Cox's efforts to prevent fraud were so minimal that when he presented his stop-action films at the 1981 parapsychology conclave in Syracuse, New York, they were greeted with derision.

Randall even thinks PK is behind an old parlor trick in which four people use extended little fingers to hoist a heavy person from a chair. Samuel Pepys described it in his *Diary* as a pastime of French schoolgirls. Geller does this stunt often in his stage act, using a fat man from the audience and three volunteers to assist him in the lifting. (By including himself among the lifters Geller can make sure the lift fails on the first attempt when PK forces are not invoked.) Hilarious photographs of Colin Wilson being "levitated" in this manner are in Wilson's preposterous book, *The Geller Phenomenon* (Aldus Books, 1976). "As far as I know," says Randall, "no physicist has ever given a 'normal' explanation of this phenomenon."

What is there to explain? The first lift is uncoordinated. When it is repeated, after a preliminary ritual of some sort, the four lifts are synchronized, the weight is thereby evenly distributed four ways, everybody tries harder, and up goes the fat man.

Randall believes everything. Well, not quite. He is surprisingly skeptical about what parapsychologists call "animal psi." When Helmut Schmidt's cockroaches seemed to use their PK to bias an electronic randomizer, Randall suspects it was not cockroach PK that did it, but PK from Schmidt or one of his assistants. Randall himself has published papers on how an experimenter's PK can influence animal life: In one case it modified the paths taken by crawling wood lice; in another test, the direction in which gerbils jumped. He was unable to replicate the positive results of a 1952 experiment by Nigel Richmond in which Richmond's PK influenced the paths of swimming paramecia.

To explain PK, Randall dredges up an old theory, popular with spiritualists a hundred years ago, that psychics somehow have the power to shift matter in and out of hyperspace. This was the opinion of German physicist Johann Zöllner, to whom Randall devotes an entire chapter. Zöllner used the theory to account for the sensational results of his experiments with the famous American slate-writing medium, Henry Slade. His book about Slade, *Transcendental Physics* (English translation, 1880), is almost as funny as Jule Eisenbud's *The World of Ted Serios* (Morrow, 1967). Randall thinks I was unfair to Zöllner when I once called him "a remarkably stupid fellow." On the contrary, Randall is convinced that Zöllner was an astute investigator of Slade's genuine powers.

Randall's bibliography of 193 references is notable only for its omissions. Where, for example, is Edward Girden's classic paper, "A Review of Psychokinesis" (*Psychological Bulletin* 59, 353-388; 1962)? In view of Randall's claim that magicians have no idea how Geller does his tiresome tricks, why does he neglect to list two books on sale in magic shops, *Confessions of a Psychic* (Karl Fulves, 1975) and *Further Confessions of a Psychic* (Karl Fulves, 1980), both by Uriah Fuller, which give Geller's techniques in full detail?

Uninformed readers may find Randall's book persuasive, but most professional parapsychologists will be as embarrassed by it as they are by the scribblings of such irresponsible journalists of the occult as Colin Wilson, Lyall Watson, and D. Scott Rogo. *Psychokinesis* is only the latest, but surely not the last, of a seemingly endless line of lurid books about the paranormal, hacked out by gullible believers who are incapable of distinguishing competent investigations from shabby research and anecdotal poppycock.

26 | Chicanery in Science

What to do about scientific fraud? The recent disclosure that a researcher at New York City's Mount Sinai School of Medicine had faked data on a patent application for hemophilia drugs was only the latest such scandal. Considering the explosive growth in research, it is no surprise that chicanery is also rising.

Science writers William J. Broad and Nicholas Wade have put together a valuable, entertaining account of science fraud, not so much by obvious cranks and charlatans as by respected scientists who betrayed their calling from within the mainstream. Their book, titled *Betrayers of the Truth* (Simon and Schuster, 1982), contains fresh accounts of René Blondlot and his imaginary N-rays, Charles Dawson and his Piltdown man, Paul Kammerer and his phony midwife toads, and other classic frauds. Most of the book, however, concentrates on more recent examples of deception—deliberate, unconscious, or half-intended—especially in medical research, where human lives and lots of money are at stake.

Why do they do it? Why do bright young men like John Long, investigating Hodgkin's disease, and William Summerlin, working on tissue transplants, shatter their medical careers by faking results? Why did Elias Alsabti shamelessly plagiarize the work of others? What motivated Cyril Burt, England's distinguished psychologist, to fabricate his data on identical twins? In most cases the answer is obvious: There are enormous academic and financial pressures to produce.

The authors' recommendations are hard to fault. Published papers should be fewer in number and better refereed, peer reviewing of applications for financial support should be improved, top scientists should stop seeking credit for work by underlings, and so on. But Broad and Wade move to shakier ground when they attack philosophers and scientists for holding views that the authors believe encourage fraud.

There is a pernicious myth, they are persuaded, that just about everyone

---

This review originally appeared in *Discover*, April 1983, and is reprinted with permission.

in the science community believes: the myth that science is totally rational, free of all human passions. No motives of greed, ambition, envy. No awareness of how disheveled science really is. Its history, so goes the myth, is strictly logical, a clean, linear progression from darkness to higher truth. The existence of such a myth is a myth. Almost no scientists think this way, and very few philosophers think they think this way.

No one can quarrel with the book's stress on the rationality of science as a long-run social process with an "invisible boot" that sooner or later kicks out the scoundrels. Broad and Wade are distressed by how slowly the boot operates today. Others, however, are impressed by its speed. A few hustlers may get by with trivial flimflams for years, especially in medicine and the behavioral sciences, where so much is fog; but any astronomer who faked the observation of a new pulsar, or any geneticist who faked the cloning of a cat, would quickly feel the kick in the pants.

Broad and Wade belabor scientists unmercifully for their reluctance to repeat experiments, but they seldom distinguish between important and unimportant claims. Scientists have neither the time, funds, nor desire to repeat more than a tiny fraction of the hundreds of thousands of experiments reported annually. The authors dwell on failures to replicate, but say nothing about the extraordinary efficiency with which the science community tested and abandoned such "revolutionary" claims as the detection of gravity waves, the existence of polywater, the transference of memory by cannibal flatworms, the value of laetrile, the emotions of plants, and other loudly proclaimed wonders.

There are other mystifying gaps. Several paragraphs tell of the cheating of Walter Levy, an obscure parapsychologist, but there is no reference to the far greater scandal over the skulduggery of England's most eminent parapsychologist, S. G. Soal. There are examples of how a strong desire can cause a scientist to "see" what is not there, but the outstanding case of this in modern times, Percival Lowell's detailed maps of Martian canals, is not mentioned. Lysenko's destruction of Soviet genetics is well described. Not a word about the humbug Nazi anthropologists who did so much greater harm to humanity.

Enjoy the book for its colorful, sad accounts of how some foolish scientists, small in number compared to their counterparts in other enterprises, tried to hoodwink their peers. Don't look for deeper insights into why science, for all its human frailties and its shaggy history, is so successful.

27 | Fools' Paradigms

Frames of Meaning: The Social Construction of Extraordinary Science (London: Routledge, 1982) is the most peculiar book about the sociology of knowledge to come along since Paul Feyerabend's *Science in a Free Society*. The authors, H. M. Collins and T. J. Pinch, are sociologists at the University of Bath. Pinch, who was trained as a physicist, is mainly responsible for the book's excellent chapter about rival interpretations of quantum mechanics and the possibility that quantum laws underlie psi phenomena. Collins was in the news in 1975 when he and Brian Pamplin, a physicist, conducted an experiment with British children who pretended they could bend cutlery by PK (psychokinesis). Watching through a secret one-way mirror, Collins and Pamplin were amazed by how crudely the children cheated.

The authors view themselves as radical Kuhnians. Although Thomas Kuhn has made clear that in his famous book *The Structure of Scientific Revolutions* he did not mean to deny that science is a rational enterprise, Collins and Pinch prefer to believe what they thought Kuhn originally intended. Their approach is a relativism as extreme as Feyerabend's. No methods exist for the overall evaluation of competing scientific theories. Such theories are like disparate cultures—incommensurable ways of seeing reality. As the authors put it, "Rationality is discontinuous across cultures, and across time."

Instead of orderly progression toward better pragmatic truth, the history of science, in their view, exhibits a perpetual shifting of equally admirable paradigms. Although one can only guess what new paradigms will dominate future science, sociologists may profitably investigate how the culture of science operates while undergoing a revolutionary paradigm shift. Indeed, the authors claim that their book is the first attempt at just such an empirical study.

In choosing their potential paradigm, the authors agreed that it must be one in radical conflict with orthodoxy, as well as a challenge originating

This review originally appeared in *Free Inquiry,* Fall 1983, and is reprinted with permission.

from within the science community. It should not be an outlandish proposal by an "outsider" like Velikovsky or Wilhelm Reich. Moreover, it must have a potential for change comparable to the great paradigm shifts of the past: Copernican cosmology, Newtonian physics, relativity, quantum mechanics, the germ theory of disease, evolution, and so on. So what did they pick? Spoon-bending! The book's jacket shows the bowl of a spoon in which you see a distorted reflection of the word *nature*. It is a symbol of how paranormal metal-bending, or PMB, as the authors shorten it, may bend and reshape the way science looks at the world.

Collins and Pinch give a detailed account of how PMB was introduced into parapsychology by the Israeli magician Uri Geller and how it produced in England a horde of children who claimed the same psychic ability. They tell again the sad story of how John Taylor became an enthusiastic convert to the new paradigm and wrote a glossy book about its wonders, only later to become totally disenchanted. They tell how John Hasted, a physicist at Birkbeck College, became and still is the world's most passionate defender of PMB. They devote two chapters to the historic Bath experiment with "mini-Gellers" and explain why they believe it decided nothing. After all, the experiment may have attracted only liars to the laboratory. Besides, the children may have cheated because under the circumstances they were unable to generate genuine PK.

In line with their radical relativism, the authors maintain that, at present, the believers in PMB and the disbelievers are two hostile subcultures of science, incapable of cross-communication. Seemingly authentic cases of PMB can always be explained as fraud, and exposures of fraud do not prove *all* is fraud. Sheep and goats "talk through each other." No yardstick is available for measuring the worth of the two incommensurable perspectives.

The book's funniest chapter describes how science is likely to be altered if PMB is genuine. During the confused period of transition, which possibly is now, there will be strident antagonism between believers and skeptics. Slowly, as the new paradigm forges ahead, the style of scientific investigation will be profoundly transformed. Skeptics will have to be excluded from laboratories because their hostility inhibits the operation of PK. Only believers will be included in the testing areas because their very presence amplifies the effects being investigated. The cool, impersonal detachment of today's researchers will give way to extroverted bonhomie, to enthusiasm, because such emotions clearly encourage the results.

The most radical change will be the recognition that PK can influence all pointer readings. Perhaps instead of measuring gravity waves, as Joseph Weber claims he did, he was actually measuring his own mind's influence on his apparatus. Elaborate precautions obviously will have to be taken to rule out this "experimenter effect" in all fields of science, not just parapsychology. It is worse than that:

> Certain theories . . . suggest that the participants in a parapsychological experiment are not restricted to those individuals within the four walls of the laboratory, but include all potential observers of the experimental results. That is, they include all the potential readers of the journal in which the results are published. That means that the numbers of believers and skeptics among the eventual readership determine the outcome perceived by the experimenters themselves.

As the authors sensibly observe, if experiments can be influenced by backward causality from the PK powers of those who later read about the testing, "then a part of experimental life would come to be involved with persuading the public at large of the possibility of these phenomena."

While one's mind is still staggering from such possibilities, Collins and Pinch uncork a great surprise. On the book's last page but one they write: "The authors do not know whether paranormal metal bending is 'real' or not—nor, as sociologists, do they care. It would make not one jot of difference to the analysis. Doubtless, however, the scientific fate of the phenomenon will affect what will be looked for in this work. If, as seems almost certain, it is to fade away as just another fad, the authors will probably be accused of missing the whole point."

Yes, rationalists will accuse Collins and Pinch of having missed the whole point of science. It simply is not the case that there are no rational ways to evaluate the empirical worth of radical new claims. That there are cross-cultural methods of deciding, with high probabilty, between conflicting theories is readily seen by considering scores of recent claims that have been shot down by carefully controlled testing. The story of polywater, for example. Did polywater evaporate for sociological reasons or for reasons independent of cultural conflicts?

This brings us to the basic blunder of the authors. At the time Geller was riding high and spoon bending was a craze in England, Collins and Pinch should have taken a year off from academia to study conjuring. Collins in particular, instead of devoting vast amounts of energy trying to understand quantum theory, should have spent the time studying magic. Had he done so, the flimflammery of PMB would have at once been apparent. He would not have wasted time on a book that now is as quaint and irrelevant as Johann Zöllner's *Transcendental Physics,* a book that investigated the possible paradigm of explaining the physical phenomena of spiritualism by invoking hyperspace.

Let me conclude with a fable. A London club is owned by a group of sociologists who call themselves the "Radical Incommensurables." They are fond of gambling, and so poker games are constantly under way in the club's basement. One member of the club, Uriah Fuller, has been consistently winning. Some members suspect him of cheating, but Fuller insists he is merely using PK to influence card shuffling and that this does not violate any club rules.

"Why don't we hire Mr. D?" a member suggests. "He's considered the best card mechanic in England. For years he earned his living as a card hustler. We can let him sit in on a few games."

"Out of the question," replies Carey Hollins, the club president. "If Fuller is a true psychic, D's presence would so upset him that he'd be unable to use his PK. We would learn nothing."

"But Fuller has never seen D. We can pretend D is a new member."

"No, no! That would be unethical. We would be behaving no better than Randi."

Ten years go by and Fuller is still winning. Hollins has published six learned papers on Fuller's amazing psi powers. John Hasted has been called in to monitor Fuller's card playing by attaching electrodes to his skull and strain gauges to the deck. Results have been inconclusive. E. H. Walker is seeking a grant from the James McDonnell Foundation for a thorough investigation of how Fuller's brain collapses the deck's quantum wave functions so that winning hands are more likely to go to him than to other players.

Hollins stoutly maintains he has no idea whether Fuller cheats or not. Asked why he doesn't study some books on card cheating, he replies that he hasn't the time. He is deeply in debt as a result of losses to Fuller, but he hopes to pay off his debts with royalties from a book he is writing. It will be, he declares, the first empirical study of how the culture of gambling will radically alter if PK can indeed influence card shuffling, dice tossing, roulette-wheel spinning, and other randomizing techniques commonly used in betting games.

28 | Look, Shirl, No Hands!

"Rain in the Northeast, clear skies to the South, while large portions of the Midwest continue to be blanketed by Shirley MacLaine's aura."
                                    Caption of a *New Yorker* cartoon (March 30, 1987)
                                    showing a television weather broadcast.

In the halcyon days of spiritualism, a psychic whose vocal cords were seized by a discarnate, or in whose presence the dead were able to speak without using a live mouth—often by talking through a floating trumpet—was called a "direct-voice" medium. In the United States the most gifted direct-voicer was George Valiantine, of Williamsport, Pennsylvania. His entities had more than a hundred different accents and spoke in half a dozen languages. One of his controls was Confucius. Valiantine's followers were typically undismayed whenever he was caught in fraud. After a luminous trumpet was found warm on the side and moist at the mouthpiece, doubters were told that spirits couldn't use it without materializing warm hands and wet lips. A thumb print of Conan Doyle, produced in a séance, proved to be a print of Valiantine's big toe.

Today's direct-voice mediums, now called "trance channelers," no longer float trumpets or materialize fingerprints of the dead. Some even speak in their own voices without troubling to acquire strange accents or personality changes. For decades the occult shelves of bookstores have been crammed with volumes supposedly dictated through channelers, notably the popular Seth books of the late Jane Roberts, of Elmira, New York. Roberts liked to fling her thick glasses on the table when Seth, in a deep, booming voice, took over her body. Tam Mossman, formerly her editor at Prentice-Hall, edits a quarterly journal called *Metapsychology: The Journal of Discarnate Intelligence,* out of Charlottesville, Virginia. (Another channeling journal, *Spirit Speaks,* is edited in Los Angeles by Mollie Nickell.)

Among those who are into New Age trends, searching for occult

This review, in a slightly cut version, originally appeared in the *New York Review of Books,* April 9, 1987, and is reprinted with permission.

alternatives to Judeo-Christian faiths, there is a growing hunger for evidence of reincarnation. In response to this demand, all over the nation, especially on the West Coast, channelers are popping up like weeds. In California, a former country-western singer, Jamie Sams, channels the entity "Leah," who lives on Venus 600 years in the future. In Malibu, Ron Scolastico channels a group called the "Guides." In North Hollywood, Darryl Anka channels Bashar, from the planet Essassani, 500 light-years from Earth. Jack Pursel, another California medium, channels Lazaris. Hosca Harrison, in Boulder, Colorado, channels Jonah. Paul Tuttle, of Bellingham, Washington, channels Raj. Nobody knows how many hundreds of other mediums are now channeling here and there, some reaping enormous profits from their books, private sessions, seminars, and tapes.

Trance channeling got its biggest boost in 1983 when Shirley MacLaine's third autobiography, *Out on a Limb,* became a top seller. (Her first, *Don't Fall Off the Mountain,* was about travels abroad and early life in Hollywood; her second, *You Can Get There From Here,* concerned her work for the presidential campaign of George McGovern and the making of her documentary film on Mao's China.) *Out on a Limb* has two startling main themes: the author's undercover romance with a married member of the British Parliament—she calls him Gerry Stamford—and her rapidly exploding enthusiasm for reincarnation and the paranormal.

Among dozens of eminent thinkers and writers cited by MacLaine as believing that we have lived before on Earth, many actually opposed this view—Kant and Milton for instance. John Dewey would have been amazed to find himself among those who "deeply believed in metaphysical dimensions that would ultimately explain the mystery of life." At the same time, MacLaine missed philosophers who really did believe, such as F. C. S. Schiller and C. J. Ducasse, and writers like William Butler Yeats. Somehow she did discover Cambridge University's great eccentric John McTaggart Ellis McTaggart, an Hegelian of sorts who managed the extraordinary trick of combining reincarnation with outright atheism.

"Profound McTaggart," as Yeats called him in a poem, deserves a digression. Bertrand Russell recalls attending student breakfasts at McTaggart's gay bachelor lodgings where the food was so meager that guests took to bringing their own eggs. When Russell decided that stars existed even when no one looked at them, McTaggart asked him to stop coming. MacLaine has a long quote from McTaggart, rightly calling him the greatest philosopher of this century who defended reincarnation. If you're interested, there's a good section in Paul Levy's book *Moore* about McTaggart's curious crablike walk, his penchant for riding a large tricycle, his Tory opinions, and his inexplicable influence on the early views of

G. E. Moore. It's hard to believe that this now-forgotten sage was once so respected that his colleague C. D. Broad actually devoted two volumes (1,250 pages!) to refuting McTaggart's bizarre metaphysics.

In *Out on a Limb* it is David Manning, a young occultist, who initiates MacLaine into a smorgasbord of fashionable paranormal beliefs. She later disclosed that David is a composite of "four spiritual men," each claiming to have known extraterrestrials from the Pleiades. Her psychic heroes range from the great mediums of the past to such living miracle-mongers as India's Sai Baba, who materializes jewelry in his fists. The book swarms with occult shibboleths: energy vibrations (of which love is the highest), karma, other dimensions, auras, OBEs (out-of-body experiences), synchronicity, ESP, precognition, holism, Atlantis, Lemuria, UFOs, the Shroud of Turin, and a hundred others. Discarnates who tell MacLaine about her past lives get their data from the Akashik records. These are archives, theosophists maintain, on which are stored the vibrations of every event that has occurred since the universe began. "Akasic records of all that ever anywhere wherever was," is how Stephen puts it in Joyce's *Ulysses*.

Channeled entities, consulting the Akashik records, inform Shirley that she and Gerry had been married in a previous incarnation—a stormy marriage because Gerry was too preoccupied with "important work involving cultural exchanges with extraterrestrials." In his present body, Gerry is a socialist who wants to be England's prime minister. After the book was published, MacLaine revealed that he too is composite, a blend of two political leaders now widely assumed to be the Australian Andrew Peacock and the recently assassinated prime minister of Sweden, Olof Palme. At one press conference, after MacLaine said, "I guarantee you Gerry is not Margaret Thatcher," a voice from the rear shouted, "That's one down!"

A film dramatization of *Out on a Limb,* in which the author plays herself, was aired by ABC-TV on January 18 and 19, 1987, as a two-part miniseries. Charles Dance took the role of Gerry, John Heard played David, and Anne Jackson was Shirley's longtime friend, the big-hatted Bella Abzug.

Apart from the film's pervasive paranormal poppycock, its dialogue is unbearably banal. Over and over again Shirley murmurs "I love you" or "I missed you" to Gerry, and he comes back with "I love you too" or "I missed you too." Twice Shirley says "I love you" to Bella. Bella cleverly responds with "I love you too."

More cornball highlights:

Shirley: "Intelligence has become my new erogenous zone."
Shirley: "Those stars. They're like zircon plums close enough to pluck."

In an occult bookstore a volume titled *Dwellers on Two Planets* magically hops off a shelf into Shirley's hands.

Shirley to Gerry: "There is much more going on on this planet than meets, the eye."

Shirley and David face the surf on a Malibu beach, arms outstretched like Jesus on the cross. They repeatedly shout in unison "I am God!"

In a Stockholm restaurant, Gerry struggles to break the news to Shirley that he intends to dump her. He starts with "I love you deeply," then works up a sequence of sniffles. Is it bad acting, or is Dance subtly portraying a man pretending to have the sniffles?

Sturé Johannsen, a Swedish channeler, plays himself in a roomful of devotees. Creativity is inside each of us, his entity, Ambres, explains. God loves us all, and we must love ourselves. Atlantis was destroyed because its technology exceeded its wisdom. The Great Pyramid of Egypt is a library in stone we will soon be able to decipher. Shirley's mind reels as she absorbs these gems.

Back in the United States, Miss MacLaine has her first session with channeler Kevin Ryerson. As a youth in Sandusky, Ohio, Kevin steeped himself in occult literature, and later studied at the Edgar Cayce Institute, in Virginia Beach, Virginia. He became a medium after he discovered that, while meditating, entities from the astral plane would grab his body.

Like the Swedish channeler, Kevin plays himself in Shirley's miniseries. Both he and MacLaine have since insisted that on the set he went into a genuine trance. Young, tall, with dark hair and blue eyes, handsomer than Uri Geller and twice as smart, Kevin shows up at Shirley's Malibu home wearing a slouched hat that makes him look like Humphrey Bogart. On the Oprah Winfrey television show, Shirley called Kevin "a fantastically wonderful intelligent man." Although *he* couldn't remember his lines, she said, his spirit controls recalled them perfectly.

First Kevin removes his jacket, loosens his tie, seats himself, and says, "I'll see you later." After several deep breaths and a few coughs he goes into a trance. John, a contemporary of Jesus, takes over. He speaks English, not Aramaic, in a slow scholarly fashion, with lots of biblical ye's and thou's. "Ye are co-creator with God," he tells a wide-eyed Shirley, reminding her of the time on the beach when she shouted, "I am God!" MacLaine is floored by this revelation. How could John possibly know? It never occurs to her that, since Kevin is acquainted with many of her friends, he easily could have obtained this information.

After more coughing, John is replaced by Tom McPherson, an earthy Irish pickpocket from Elizabethan England. The light bothers Tom, so he asks Shirley for something to cover Ryerson's eyes. She finds a black cloth and Tom, or rather Kevin, ties it around his head like a blindfold. I could hardly believe it, but Kevin now goes into what magicians call an "eyeless vision" act. (If you want to know how they do it, see the relevant chapter in my *Science: Good, Bad and Bogus.*) Kevin stands up, gets a mug from a pantry, then returns to pour himself tea. Don't worry, he says in his Irish brogue, he won't spill any. Shirley is dumfounded. How can Kevin's body do these things when his eyes are covered?

After a brief return of John, who tells Shirley about her life with Gerry in Atlantis, Kevin wakes up and asks, "How did it go?" (Channelers profess not to recall anything said while channeling.) When Shirley tells him about the blindfold bit, he is amazed. He didn't know, he says, that Tom could manipulate his body like that. Shirley feels herself "vibrating with a strange magnetic energy."

David, who has been painting pictures of UFOs, invites Shirley to go with him to Peru to look for some real flying disks. Shirley accepts. Unfortunately, the cameras were never able to photograph a single UFO while on location in Peru, but the natives assure MacLaine that flying saucers constantly land in the area, plunging into a lake, later emerging to go back to the stars.

Although the relationship between David and Shirley is platonic, they constantly bathe nude together in icy mineral-water pools. During one such immersion, Shirley stares at a candle flame until she feels she and the universe are one. During another ablution, David slips into an OBE.

Observing Shirley's spiritual progress, Dave decides the time is ripe for some darker secrets. He tells about his "cosmic love affair" with Mayan, a small girl with big black eyes who was in Peru disguised as a geologist. The earth, she told him, is close to self-destruction. Because our planet is "important to the cosmos," her mission is to give David "scientific information" to pass on to Shirley. After much prodding, Dave finally reveals the stupendous truth. Mayan came from another planet.

A furious Shirley wants to go home. Has she been duped? The pair drive back to their lodgings in silence. Shirley leaves the truck without speaking while Dave smiles like the Sphinx. Next morning he tells how Mayan once asked him to go to a foothill and observe a certain peak. He went. A flying saucer emerged and landed near him. It was so beautiful— all white and iridescent. Then it shot upward and vanished.

"After that," David says, "I listened to Mayan."

The world awaits the truth, Dave rattles on, and you, Shirley, have been chosen to provide it. MacLaine is angry again. She calls it all "metaphysical mumbo-jumbo" and accuses David of setting her up to write a book just so he'll be in it. "I was wrong about you. You're a nut," she says.

David, who never gets mad, quotes Mayan as saying that, if you want to get to the fruit on a tree, you have to go out on a limb. Gerry once made the same remark when he and Shirley were lovers. Shirley weeps while David slips on her wrist a metal bracelet Mayan had given him. In the book he says it amplifies one's thoughts by drawing on what Mayan called a "third force."

Shirley, hopelessly confused, drives alone into the Andes Mountains to think. Is David crazy or for real? Night falls. It grows freezing cold. Birds and animals make weird sounds. Winds blow. The car won't start. On the verge of total panic, Miss MacLaine massages the magic bracelet and cries, "David, see me!"

Cut to a sleeping David. He suddenly awakes, rushes to his truck, and is there in a jiffy. He and Shirley embrace. How did he know where to find her? Mayan told him.

On the drive back, the film's most embarrassing episode now unrolls. Like Kevin's blindfold act, it's not in the book because, as Shirley has said on talk shows, her readers were not then prepared to believe it. Indeed, even now only the most mindless MacLainist will believe it. Did Shirley make it up, or blow up some trivial incident, to get into her film one of those wild car rides that audiences seem to love?

Here's what happens. David asks Shirley not to touch the truck's steering wheel. He starts deep breathing, closes his eyes, and takes his hands off the wheel. The car speeds along the perilous roads, making all the turns, while a frightened Shirley huddles on the seat.* After moments of sheer terror, she starts to laugh. Then, so help me, she bursts into her most famous song, "If you could see me now!" Next morning, in a bathing pool, Dave explains how the truck did it. Mayan put "an invisible force field" around it.

Suddenly Shirley sees an aura enveloping a plant, then a brighter aura around David. This is followed by her first OBE. A thin silver cord keeps her soul linked to her body as she soars above the mountains and travels to the moon. Beyond the moon she glimpses a spiral nebula, no doubt the very galaxy where Mayan lives. The cord draws her back. Shirley awakes,

---

*Philip Haldeman, writing about the miniseries in the *Northwest Skeptic* newsletter (April 1987), gave the most plausible explanation of David's eyeless-vision drive—assuming, of course, it really took place. It was pitch dark inside the truck. Shirley could see only David's profile. David could easily have closed only the eye on Shirley's side, raised his left leg, and guided the steering wheel with his knee.

kisses Dave's hand, says "Thank you." Dave kisses her hand and says "Thank yourself."

David has to stay in Peru to finish whatever mysterious thing he has to do, but Shirley must go home to write the book that may save our planet. She cries while she packs. "When will I see you again?" she asks. Dave doesn't answer. "Just remember that I love you," he says. Shirley: "I love you too."

Back in the Big Apple, in a taxi with big Bella, Shirley tells about asking Maria, a Peruvian psychic, whether Bella will get the democratic nomination for mayor she is seeking. No, said Maria, it will go to a "tall man with no hair and long fingers." Oy, vey! Could this be the dark horse Ed Koch? Up to now Bella has been a doubter, but now she phones her office to ask them to take another poll.

Gerry turns up in what Shirley, in the book, calls the "insane, sweet chaos that is Manhattan." She and Bella meet Gerry just before he is to give a speech. When Shirley tries to embrace him she is pushed away. Can they get together later? No, he has to catch a plane. The affair is at last kaput.

In 1984 Shirley won an Oscar for her brilliant portrayal of the mother in *Terms of Endearment*. A photo of her doing a high kick graced *Time*'s May 14 cover. Inside, in the feature essay, journalist Pete Hamill (with whom Shirley lived for almost seven years) calls her occult opinions ridiculous. That same year Hunter College gave MacLaine an honorary degree for, among other things, her "quest into philosophy and metaphysics."

The following year Shirley hit the jackpot again with her best-seller *Dancing in the Light*. This time the romantic centerpiece is her tempestuous love affair with a Russian film-maker. She calls him Vassily Okhlopkhov-Medvedjatnikov, but everyone in Hollywood knows his real name, Andrei Mikhalkov-Konchalovsky. In the book she addresses him as Vassy or Honeybear. He calls her his Nif-Nif, a Russian name for a small adorable pig.

Unlike Gerry, Vassy shares Shirley's views on reincarnation, but he has never escaped from his church's teachings about Satan and evil. He even thinks Shirley is influenced by Satan when she's angry. For Shirley, evil doesn't exist. It is nothing but "energy flying backward." Spell *live* backward, she writes, and you get *evil*.*

Shirley's spirit guides, speaking through channelers, tell of many occasions when she and Vassy were together in previous lives. They were pals in ancient

---

*In the first chapter of Lewis Carroll's *Sylvie and Bruno Concluded,* Bruno (a fairy) looks at the word EVIL on a black board and exclaims, "Why, it's LIVE backwards!" When his sister Sylvie asks how he managed to see that, he replies, "I just twiddled my eyes." More twiddling produces VEIL and VILE.

Greece—she a man, he a woman—studying to be oracles, the trance channelers of the time. In at least four incarnations Vassy was her son.

Tom, the whimsical Irishman, is back. We learn how he once mischievously dematerialized Shirley's purse while she was shopping. Later he sent it back in a manila envelope. When Steven Spielberg wanted her for the mother in *Poltergeist,* McPherson put down his astral foot. No, he said, the movie shows too much of the violent side of the paranormal. He predicted MacLaine would soon be offered a better mother role.

A new spirit guide called Ramtha, or the Ram, now enters Shirley's life. Ramtha is the control of J. Z. (for Judy Zebra) Knight, currently the most fashionable channeler in the United States. Knight is a handsome, husky-voiced blonde with an upturned nose, who lives in a multimillion-dollar brick palace in Yelm, a small farming town south of Seattle, Washington. My own opinion is that she's a reincarnation of Aimee Semple McPherson, in turn a descendant of Tom McPherson. Aimee died in 1944. That would be just right for her to be recycled as J.Z.

When J.Z. goes into a trance, Ramtha takes over. For hours she strides back and forth across the stage, speaking rapidly and with lots of finger-pointing gestures, to audiences of 300 or more who gather in hotel ballrooms. They pay $400 each for a lecture, and $1,500 for a weekend seminar. Satellite connections relay Ramtha to other cities. According to the *New York Times* (November 16, 1986) Knight admits she earns millions every year from her performances, from sales of Ramtha audiotapes and video cassettes, and from her book *Ramtha.*

According to *Ramtha,* based on tape recordings and edited by someone named Steven Lee Weinberg, Ph.D., the Ram was born 35,000 years ago in the slums of Onai, the major port city of Atlantis. Using a mammoth magic sword given to him by a "wondrous woman," he assembled a vast army, invented war, and became the world's first conqueror. Slowly he came to realize that he himself was part of the God he hated. After 63 OBEs, his body vibrating faster than light, he became one with the wind. On the side of Mount Indus, in Tibet, free of weight, he ascended into the Seventh Heaven, where he and God became one. He is now part of an "unseen brotherhood" of superbeings who love us and hear our prayers. Soon the brotherhood will usher in the "Age of God." Disease, suffering, and war will vanish. Death will be no more. "A new wind will blow."

Ramtha's God is not "out there" like the transcendent God of Christianity. He is the impersonal pantheist deity of such "process" philosophers as Samuel Alexander, Alfred North Whitehead, and Charles Hartshorne. He is the Absolute of Hegel, the Tao of Taoism, the Brahman of Hinduism. God is simply Everything. All he "knows how to do is be." The Ram

likes to tack "ness" on words, and his favorite word for God is *isness.*
God is "the isness of All That Is."* The word occurs hundreds of times
in *Ramtha,* often accompanied by God's ongoingness and foreverness. God
is the great I AM. He is pure thought, pure joy, and the "cosmic glue
called love" that holds everything together.

God is neither good nor bad. He is entirely without morals and
unjudgmental. There are no divine decrees. Isness is his only business. Hell
and Satan are the "vile inventions" of Christianity, a product of "your
insidious Book" which Ramtha advises his listeners *not* to read. There is
no such thing as evil. Nothing you can do, not even murder, is wrong.
The slain go on to better lives, but the slayers will endure remorse for
eons. To all this God is totally indifferent. I AM never weeps. He "does
not even have the *ability* to judge you." There is no forgiveness of sins
because there are no sins to forgive.

"Every vile and wretched thing you do," says the Ram, "broadens your
understanding." Everything we do is done because we needed to do it.
"If you want to do any one thing, *regardless* of what it is, it would not
be wise to go against that feeling; for there is an experience awaiting you
and a grand adventure that will make your life sweeter."

Regardless? Suppose a man feels the need to rape and kill a child.
You might expect Ramtha would invoke karma to explain how such crimes
are punished, but no—he is down on karma. It no more exists than hell
and Satan. Murder is not a sin to be expiated; it is a teaching experience.
You never have to *pay* for anything. Why the guilt a murderer feels is
not a payment, or how a deed can be called vile if there is no evil, are
questions that Ramtha, at least in this book, leaves unanswered. As someone
has said about the denial of evil by Christian Science, nothing is explained:
the problem of evil is merely redefined.

In light of the sentiments above, it is hardly surprising that the Ram
has nothing to say about helping the poor and suffering, the starving millions
in Africa, the wretched Untouchables in India. "Everyone . . . whether he
is starving, or crippled . . . has chosen his experience for the purpose of
gaining from it. . . . When you become a master, you can walk in the

---

*Did Ramtha steal this line from one of Robert Service's poems?

> God is the Iz-ness of the Is,
> The One-ness of our Cosmic Biz;
> The high, the low, the near, the far,
> The atom and the evening star;
> The lark, the shark, the cloud, the clod,
> The whole darned Universe—that's God.

And did the Ram steal the suffix "ness" from L. Ron Hubbard, who liked to write about
beingness, doingness, havingness, eatingness, sexingness, and so on, ad nauseamness?

murk and mire . . . and maintain your totality, because you understand the teeming masses and why they are the way they are. . . . You will allow them the *freedom* to be limited, which is true love, because you know that this is the only way they can learn. . . ." To love the masses "does not mean you must go out and teach them or succor unto them. Simply leave them alone and allow them to evolve according to their own needs and designs."

Leave them alone! This, together with belief in karma, is precisely how the rich and powerful, in countries where reincarnation flourishes, have tended to look upon the suffering masses.* And why not? If a child is starving because of bad karma, or (as the Ram teaches) because its soul has chosen starvation as a teaching experience, why interfere? Why condemn the Holocaust? Every murdered Jew *chose* to be killed, and Hitler was merely undergoing a learning experience.

Ramtha's main message is simple. You are God, and therefore capable of creating any reality you desire, if not now, then in a later incarnation. To support this crazy notion, Ramtha provides a mythology that comes straight out of the science-fiction fantasies of Scientology. God was originally a "void without form," but he wanted to experience all possible emotions and sensations. You can't smell a flower unless there is a flower and a nose. So what did the great Isness do? He "expanded himself into light," which in turn fractured into billions of "light beings" or gods. These spirits were all formed at the same time, and were endowed with free will so that through them God could create a universe in which he could play endless games that would continue his "expansion into forever."

We are those gods. *We* created the universe. *We* made the stars. It is through us that God experiences the joys of creativity and adventure. To play the games, we first had to make what Ramtha calls "electrum" (his neologism for electromagnetism). The electrum "coagulated" into matter, and the matter coagulated into the cells of living bodies. The great game of evolution was under way. The first humans, Ramtha tells us, were without sex organs. They propagated by cloning. Alas, they were so slow-footed they got eaten by animals. Superior men and women were finally fabricated, by us of course, and have been on Earth for 10.5 million years.

We now come to Ramtha's version of the Fall. After thousands and thousands of incarnations we, the great gods of light, have forgotten who we are! We no longer remember that we created the universe, that we

---

*The best discussion I know of this and other reasons for not believing in reincarnation is a four-part series of essays by philosopher Paul Edwards, "The Case Against Reincarnation," in *Free Inquiry*, Fall 1986, Winter 1986/87, Spring 1987, and Summer 1987.

invented all our adventures and dreams. The Ram's mission is to ram us into remembering.

Once we realize who we are, we must stop worrying about right and wrong, relax, go with the flow, and love God by loving ourselves. Even now we have the power to reverse aging and live forever in our present body. We have the power now to heal any disease, even to grow a new limb if one is cut off. What prevents us from doing these things? It is our "altered ego," the "Antichrist" within us who keeps telling us we are not God. In our present amnesiatic state, most of us will have to die and go on to adventures in other bodies, but many enlightened souls will conquer their altered egos and ascend like Ramtha, Jesus, Buddha, and Osiris. Omeka, Yukad, and Rackabia (whoever *they* are) also ascended, as well as thousands more we never heard about.

Because of impending natural disasters predicted by Ramtha—quakes, floods, and so on—he has recently recommended that everyone move to higher ground, especially to the mountains of the Pacific Northwest. According to the *New York Times* (cited above) up to 1,500 people have already moved to the Yelm region, something J. Z. Knight hadn't anticipated.* A "20/20" television show about J.Z. (January 22, 1987) interviewed a tearful housewife whose husband, smitten by Ramtha tapes, had abandoned her to live near J.Z.

Sandy Fallis, a good friend of J.Z. when she was Judy Hampton, a girl growing up in Artesia, New Mexico, told "20/20" about a prayer meeting in which Judy suddenly began speaking in a male voice that called himself a demon named Demias. (Knight denied that this ever happened.) Steven Bakker, formerly J.Z.'s advance man, told how devastated he became when during a desert hike he observed Knight smoking and practicing the Ram's gestures, slipping in and out of her Ramtha personality without bothering to have trances. Another disenchanted Ramster, Pamela Mc-Neeley, told *Newsweek* (December 15, 1986) about a similar incident. "We thought she did a better job of doing Ramtha than Ramtha. In fact, we couldn't tell the difference." Pamela became fed up with Ramtha's teachings after he began saying that the country should "get rid" of homosexuals.

Now married to her third husband, Knight continues the hobby she and a former husband had of raising Arabian horses on their 40-acre Messiah Arabian Stud Farm. According to "20/20," she began selling them to followers who were told that the Ram had recommended the purchases.

---

*"I don't want people moving to live near me," Mrs. Knight has been quoted as saying. "I love my small town the way it is. I'm not their leader. I'm not a guru. . . . I'm not somebody's savior. This is a business." According to Roy Burnside, a real-estate salesman in Yelm, 80 percent of his clients are Ramsters from other states.

One lady paid a quarter of a million dollars for a horse. Washington State issued a cease and desist order, which J.Z. accepted. Naturally she sees nothing wrong about such trance chiseling because she sees nothing wrong about anything.

Shirley MacLaine gives dramatic accounts of her many sessions with J. Z. Knight. When she first heard the name Ramtha, she writes, it aroused such a "strange soul-memory" that she broke down and sobbed. Using J.Z.'s arms, the Ram once picked her up bodily. On another occasion MacLaine says she saw "him" pick up a 200-pound man. Ramtha frequently laughs and weeps, and enjoys kissing the laughing-weeping women who sit transfixed in his audience. Sometimes he gets drunk on wine and poor J.Z. has to suffer the hangovers. The Ram told Shirley she had been his sister in Atlantis. In times of distress does MacLaine call for help on the Baptist God of her childhood in Virginia? No, she calls on Ramtha and McPherson!

Dancing in the Light climaxes in Galisteo, New Mexico, a village near Santa Fe where Shirley goes to see Chris Griscom. Chris uses acupuncture to help people remember past lives. Her long sharp needles jab into various "galactic points," especially into the third eye. The third eye is a term used by Theosophy and some Eastern religions for the pineal gland (occasionally for the nearby pituitary gland)—a small knob about the size of a cherry pit that lies behind the forehead between the eyebrows. In Hinduism the region is called the *ajna chakra.* The seven chakras are psychic centers associated with *kundalini,* a cosmic energy said to be responsible for sexual potency and higher awareness. It is often pictured in India as a serpent coiled asleep at the base of the spine, in the *muladhara chakra.* Some far-out parapsychologists believe the third eye is responsible for psi powers. The Hindu god Shiva uses his third eye to see the future.

While Chris waggles her needles in Shirley's chakras and gushes over the shifting colors of Shirley's auric field, MacLaine has kaleidoscopic visions of her past lives. Each night, to clean "negative energy" out of her body, she bathes in apple-cider vinegar.

There are hundreds of needle-induced memories. Shirley is a pirate with a wooden leg. She dances in a harem. She is a Buddhist monk. She lives in a jungle where she communicates with elephants by telepathy. She has a hand in framing the U.S. Constitution. In talk-show interviews MacLaine likes to recall her many incarnations as a prostitute. She thinks they gave her empathy for the hooker roles she has played. Louis XV had her beheaded because, as a court jester, she told improper jokes. Shirley's only child, her daughter Sachi, was her sister in one life, her mother in another. Shirley buys it all.

Her most hair-raising incarnation was as a Mongolian nomad. After being captured by a bandit, a jealous suitor slits her throat. Who was the murderer? Shirley recognized him as none other than her ex-husband Steve Parker! They were together for a year before Steve moved to Tokyo, where he still lives. Shirley divorced him in 1982, 30 years after their marriage.

During her sessions with Chris, Shirley has a momentous meeting with her Higher Self—a tall, imposing androgynous figure with high cheekbones and deep-blue eyes. He is more masculine than feminine, more Oriental than Western. The Higher Self—or H.S., as Shirley prefers to call him—reinforces what she has learned from the Ram. She is identical with her H.S. and he in turn is identical with God. To love God you must love yourself.

Well, there's no denying that in this sense Shirley has an overwhelming love for His Royal Isness. What a droll mixture of egoism and altruism, of intelligence and gullibility, of curiosity and willful ignorance, the dancing redhead is! I suppose most actors tend to be self-centered, but Shirley's obsession with herself tops them all. One of her fights with Vassy was triggered when Honeybear likened her chatter in bed to a radio you can't turn off. In an *Esquire* interview (December 1986), Debra Winger, who played Shirley's daughter in *Terms of Endearment,* had this to say:

> She gave me her book *Out on a Limb* to read, as if she had discovered reincarnation. I said, "Shirl, don't give me your book unless you want an honest opinion." And she said, "I do."
>
> When I finished it, I said, "My mom will like it very much. It's old news to me. I don't want to hear who you fuck, and I don't think they want to hear it either."
>
> At one point I told her, "Why don't you just strap a camera on your arm and photograph your life? That way you'll circumvent three steps: living the life, writing the book, and then doing the movie of the book." It's sick.
>
> I was actually forever grateful when she won [the Oscar] because I thought that would shut her up for a while. Imagine my dismay when she just kept having fiftieth birthdays and doing interviews.

All four of Shirley's autobiographies are available as a boxed set, and she is now working on a fifth. Who can guess what new astral adventures she will have to report? She is now on a tour of 16 cities, giving weekend seminars ($300 a person) on how to get in touch with your Higher Self. She is also teaching how to heal yourself by visualizing colors—blue for throat problems, orange for the genital area, green for the heart, yellow for the solar plexus, and so on.

A final observation about H.S. Give the letters a familiar scatological interpretation, closely related to J.Z.'s Arabian horses, and you have a good description of everything Shirley has learned from the Ram and other friendly spooks, from her mavens of metaphysical mysteries, from the occult junk books she keeps reading—above all from the effusions of her Higher Self while the Galisteo acupuncturist twirls those gold and silver needles in her chakras.

29 | The Channeling Mania

> The medium is the message.
>
> Marshall McLuhan

When I wrote the preceding chapter I had not read *Out on a Broken Limb* (Harvest House, 1986), by F. LaGard Smith, a professor of law at Pepperdine University, in Los Angeles. A neighbor of Shirley, in Malibu, Smith is a Protestant fundamentalist who believes in hell, Satan, the Second Coming, and creationism, and that paranormal phenomena associated with spiritualism is the work of demons. His flimsy book is not worth reading, but I mention it here because it has some amusing pages about Kevin Ryerson.

Smith attended some of Ryerson's trance sessions without revealing his skepticism. When he falsely told Tom McPherson that his mother was dead, Tom replied to questions as if she were. "Wouldn't the Akashik Records *know* whether or not my mother were still on the earth-plane?" Smith sensibly asks.

Smith also told Tom he had dreamed that he and Shirley were friends. Tom instantly revealed to Smith that yes, he and Shirley had been pals in eleventh-century China. Shirley was a puppeteer and Smith was a Taoist scholar. Smith found Kevin bright and likable, performing an act that "is simply one of the best road shows in America."

On a late-night radio show (January 17-18, 1987) I heard Ryerson talk and answer phone calls for several hours. He had high praise for trance-channeler Edgar Cayce, parapsychologist Thelma Moss, Jeffrey Mishlove's *Roots of Consciousness* (a monstrous addlepated book published by Random House), several books about OBEs and NDEs (near-death experiences), and the books *Mind-Reach,* by Russell Targ and Harold Puthoff, and *Mind Race,* by Russell Targ and Keith Harary (see Chapter 7), though he was a bit confused about the authors. He credited *Mind-Reach* to "Russell and Targ" and *Mind Race* to "Russell and Harary."

It is hard to keep up with the hundreds of new trance channelers who are popping out of the woodwork—the greatest concentration is in the Los Angeles area—but here are some more who have been in the news.

The *Cleveland Plain Dealer* (January 23, 1987) featured a local medium who calls herself Coyote Powhatan. Her entities include Alaric, a philosopher, and a vegetarian called Produce. Channeling sessions are free, but it costs $25 to have Coyote interpret your aura and give a tarot-card reading.

Penny Torres, a Los Angeles housewife, was featured in the *Globe* (March 24, 1987). Penny channels a 2,000-year-old man named Mafu. According to Mafu, extraterrestrials live among us and humanoid colonies flourish under the earth. (Ramtha also speaks of a hollow earth and underground races.) Mafu says a giant pyramid will soon rise from the ocean off Florida and cause many wonders. Someone named Tom Massarri is channeling Seth, but whether this is the Seth of Jane Roberts is not clear. A dozen other Seths are coming through other mediums. Richard Lavin, on the Phil Donahue show (February 24, 1987) went into a trance and channeled an entity called Exton, who spouted the usual platitudes and answered questions from the audience.

Still other channelers are mentioned in Kathleen Hughes's article on channeling in the *Wall Street Journal* (April Fools' Day, 1987). Hughes toured the Los Angeles area. In addition to performances by channelers already mentioned, she caught the following acts: Taryn Krive channeling Bell Bell, a giggling six-year-old from Atlantis, a Hopi Indian named Barking Tree, and an entity from Western Europe called Aeffra; David Swetland channeling Matea, a 35,000-year-old black female spice trader; Shawn Randall channeling Torah; Diana Hoerig channeling Merlin of Camelot. The funniest act of all is by Neville Rowe, who channels a group of dolphins. In the trance state he picks up their vibrations and translates them into English.

"I'm amazed," said a woman after one session, "that such wisdom and truth is coming from a dolphin. I didn't know they were so evolved."

"Very much so," said Rowe.

Here are some more channelers. William Rainan and his student Thomas Jacobson both channel Dr. Peebles. Vernon Yater channels Indira Latara, a nineteenth-century Hindu woman. Rhea Powers channels Sanat. Jessica Lansing channels Michael, a "recombined entity" who consists of more than a thousand souls. Pat Rodegast channels Emmanuel. Her *Emmanuel's Book* has a fulsome preface by Ram Dass. Scores of channelers—Virginia Essene, Elwood Babbitt, William Tenuto, and Annie Stebbins, to name a few—channel Jesus.

Fate magazine ran a series of three articles on channeling (May, June, and July 1987) by Craig Lee, reprinted from *L.A. Weekly*. J. Z. Knight, he tells us, first encountered Ramtha when she was experimenting with pyramid power. She put a model of the Great Pyramid on her head, and there in the doorway stood an apparition of the Ram. She has had the word *Ramtha* copyrighted, a fact that strikes Lee as like the Catholic church's copyrighting "Jesus." For a while Knight was telling her Ramsters that the money they spent on Ramtha was tax-deductible, but the IRS ruled it wasn't, since Ramtha was not a nonprofit organization.

Dozens of Ramsters have lately become disenchanted and are contemplating legal action against Knight. (According to Lee, Shirley MacLaine is among this group.) Pam McNeeley (mentioned earlier) spent more than $10,000 on Ramtha and is now one of his most vocal critics. Pam is single, 32, and works for a computer firm in Sausalito. She was horrified by what she heard the Ram say in 1985. He predicted that in three years there would be a great holocaust in which cities would be destroyed by disease before the coming of "Twelve Days of Light." A trio of gods— Yahweh, Ramtha, and Id (How did Freud's id get into J.Z.'s mind?) will then arrive in great ships of light to battle the evil Old Testament god Jehovah. AIDS, said Ramtha, is nature's way of eliminating gays. In addition to disease, there will be major earthquakes. "Don't live on a fault line," the Ram said, "It's a zipper." Ramsters were urged to buy pigs and chickens, move to the Northwest, and start farming. Ramtha warned his listeners that if they told anyone about all this he would destroy them.

Ram's predictions for the close of 1985 were wild. A great pyramid would be found in Turkey, with a shaft leading to the earth's center. Sabotage of the World Bank, by a high official, would plunge the United States into a major war. MacLaine, by the way, isn't much better as a prophet. In a *Playboy* interview (September 1984) she predicted that George Bush would get the '84 Republican nomination for president. Maybe she got the year wrong and really meant 1988.

Jack Pursel, a retired Florida insurance supervisor who channels Lazaris, seems to be the rising superstar of the mania. Like J. Z. Knight, he's getting rich from lectures, seminars, cassettes, and audiotapes. This rotund, bearded medium runs two New Age galleries in San Francisco, Illuminaria and Isis Unlimited, and heads a corporation called Concept: Synergy, Inc. He seems to have as many followers among movie and television celebrities as Knight has. Michael York and his wife brought him to the "Merv Griffin Show." When Sharon Gless (of the "Cagney and Lacey" show) accepted her Emmy award in September 1987, she included Lazaris among the people she thanked.

Like most channelers, when Pursel enters a trance state he first goes through a ritual of facial grimaces before Lazaris takes over. The entity, unlike most others who speak through mediums, has never lived on Earth— indeed, he is pure consciousness, an entity who has never had a physical body. This may explain why his accent is so hard to pin down. Fashionably dressed women in the audience, fondling quartz crystals, weep over the beauty of his messages. He tells them that many of them once lived in Atlantis. They were so frustrated over being unable to prevent the destruction of Atlantis that they have been reincarnated today to prevent the world from destroying itself in a nuclear holocaust. Like J. Z. Knight, he urges them to forget about the Judeo-Christian theology that says they can't create their own realities. They must stop thinking negatively and turn instead to "love, joy, and possibility," and so on.

Craig Lee was amused when Lazaris/Pursel, in the middle of a lecture, turned on a tape recorder that played "Theme from Lazaris." According to Lazaris, predictions found in the Great Pyramid and those made by Nostradamus and others, stop around the year 2000. That will not be the end of the world, but the beginning of the New Age, when everyone will cooperate to create a new reality. In an interview with Lee, Pursel warned against bad entities. They come through careless channelers to mislead the unwary. He admitted that some channelers—not him, of course—are out-and-out fakes.

Potboilers about channeling are starting to flood the New Age sections of bookstores. Jon Klimo, a California psychologist, has surveyed the scene in a book titled *Channeling,* published by Jeremy Tarcher, a specialist in occult literature. (I wonder if his wife, Shari Lewis, the ventriloquist, takes seriously the crap he publishes?) William Kautz's *Channeling: The Intuitive Connection* (Harper & Row) has a foreword by Kevin Ryerson. Warner Books is publishing the first of what may be several volumes of autobiography by J. Z. Knight. Titled *A State of Mind: Ramtha, the Adventure Begins,* it covers her career up to her meeting with her present husband, and I have no doubt that tens of thousands will be eager to pay for the cloth edition before Warner issues a paperback.

Shirley MacLaine's fifth and most boring autobiography, *It's All in the Playing* (Bantam), also published in 1987, is all about the making of her television miniseries. No new lovers are on the stage, but spooks Tom McPherson and John are back, spouting platitudes through the mouth of Ryerson. John reveals that he is none other than the John who wrote the Bible's Book of Revelation. It never occurs to MacLaine that theologians and Bible scholars can now, at long last, find out exactly what the prophecies in that book mean—just ask the author!

Chris Griscom returns with her acupuncture needles, and there is a new medium, Adele Tinning, of San Diego, who tips tables: one tip for *no,* three for *yes,* a wobble for *maybe.* J. Z. Knight, with whom MacLaine has had a falling out, is nowhere to be seen. In her place is her chief rival, Jack Pursel. MacLaine is now a great admirer of his entity, Lazaris. She likes to call Pursel on the phone to get advice from Lazaris.

Gerry, Shirley's composite lover in *Out on a Limb,* dies in a car accident in France, though how a composite character can die except in fiction is not explained. Shirley keeps feeling his presence. He appears to her in a vision to say how wrong his skepticism was, that the two of them are one, and that he'll always be with her in spirit.

Shirley has other visions. Tom McPherson told her she was developing "mediumistic potential," and so she is. Once when she sought vainly for a spot in the Bible where Jesus seems to refer to reincarnation, she went into a quick meditation, got in touch with her Higher Self, and asked for the reference. The answer came in "clear English" telling her she would find it in the Book of Matthew. She turned to Matthew, and the Bible opened on the very chapter she was looking for.

In another vision she saw a huge pack of cigarettes of the brand she smoked. When she climbed into it and found it empty, a voice said: "See to it that it stays empty." She hasn't had a puff since.

The book closes with Shirley's vision of a huge gray UFO that hovers over her head. The craft vanishes, replaced by a "spectacular ocean of liquid crystal shimmering in front of me." MacLaine dances on its waves— "It was glorious." She tells us that she had touched the "Christ consciousness" in herself. Jesus only walked on water; Shirley danced on it.

To me the most interesting aspect of the book is the disclosure that Shirley is teetering on the edge of solipsism, the ultimate in self-absorption. If each of us creates his or her own reality, she writes, then "objective reality simply does not exist." Could Gerry be nothing more than a creation in her dream? "Perhaps he didn't exist for anyone else at all!"

She seems serious. At a New Year's Eve party, a crystal was passed around, and everyone, when they held it, told what they wanted for the new year. Shirley began by saying she was the only person alive in her universe. Shock waves went around the table. Since everything is her dream, Shirley went on, the best way she can improve the world is to improve herself. When scandalized guests raised objections, Shirley felt she was "creating them to object . . . I hadn't resolved myself. In other words I *was* them. *They* were *me.*"

If so, someone asked, wouldn't it follow that everything you do for others you are doing for yourself? Here is Shirley's incredible reply:

And the answer is, essentially, yes. If I fed a starving child, and was honest about my motivation, I would have to say I did it for myself, because it made me feel better. Because the child was happier and more fulfilled, I would be. I was beginning to see that we each did whatever we did purely for self, and that was as it should be. Even if I had not created others in my reality and was therefore not responsible for them, I would feel responsible to my own feelings which desire to be positive and loving. Thus, in uplifting my own feelings I would uplift the feelings of my fellow human beings.

How do we change the world? By changing ourselves.

Later on she puts it this way:

If I created my own reality, then—on some level and dimension I didn't understand—I had created everything I saw, heard, touched, smelled, tasted; everything I loved, hated, revered, abhorred; everything I responded to or that responded to me. Then, I created everything I knew. I was therefore responsible for all there was in my reality. If that was true, than I *was* everything, as the ancient texts had taught. I was my own universe. Did that also mean I had created God and I had created life and death? Was that why I was all there was?

If Shirley really believes this, and the trend continues, she may be dangerously close to the mental snapping of the young cleric in a G. K. Chesterton story about which I wrote in the first chapter of my *Whys of a Philosophical Scrivener*. Perhaps if someone like Chesterton's poet-detective would pin MacLaine's neck to a tree, between the two prongs of a pitchfork, and leave her there for a few days, it might persuade her that *she* didn't create the universe. As Chesterton's cleric says, after his radical therapy, he stopped imagining he was God. It was too big a strain.

Shirley has purchased 800 acres of ranchland in the San Luiz Valley of southern Colorado on which she plans to build Uriel Village, a world center for teaching spiritualism, numerology, reincarnation, color therapy, and other wonderful things. "The seminars will be state-of-the-art metaphysics," said one of her spokeswomen, "with top metaphysicians from around the world to serve as teachers."

On August 20, 1987, the *Minneapolis Star and Tribune* reported that Charles Hurtado Silva, 43, who claims to have been Shirley's guide when she went to Peru, pleaded guilty to two charges of fourth-degree criminal sexual conduct. A native of Peru, Silva was in the city to conduct workshops on miracles and prophecies. Two local women charged him with "therapeutic deception" that forced them to sleep with him. Silva says he has lived in the United States for 26 years. A spokesperson for MacLaine told the paper that Silva was one of several men Shirley had in mind when she shaped the composite character of David for her book *Out on a Limb*. Was Silva the flimflam artist who performed the no-hands drive through the mountains? Silva wrote a book called *Date With the Gods,* published in 1977 by Living Waters. In December 1987 the publisher and Silva filed a million-dollar lawsuit against MacLaine claiming she stole material from this book.

Psychoanalysis is no longer chic. Encounter therapies and group grope have gone with the New Age winds. *Est* can rest in peace. The dead are alive and talking to us. The occult revolution shows no sign of abating.

30 | Who Was Ray Palmer?

Science-fiction fans have a long, dreary history of falling for outrageous quasi-religious, pseudoscientific cults that arise within the community of science-fiction writers and editors. L. Ron Hubbard's Scientology, first introduced as "dianetics" by John Campbell when he was editor of *Astounding Science Fiction,* is of course the prime example. This article will tell the story of an almost forgotten science-fiction editor, Ray Palmer, and the curious roles he played in the notorious "Shaver hoax" and, later, in promoting the cult of UFOlogy.

Although reports of mysterious unidentified flying objects go back to ancient times, and numerous UFO reports are scattered through the writings of Charles Fort, the UFOmania of the present century had an abrupt beginning. It was almost exactly 40 years ago, on June 24, 1947.

Kenneth Arnold, a manufacturer of fire-fighting equipment in Boise, Idaho, was flying his three-seat cabin plane from Chehalis to Yakima, in Washington. Arnold remembers it as a cloudless day with the air "as smooth as silk." At about 3 P.M. he spotted nine crescent-shaped disks bobbing up and down "like a tail of a Chinese kite" over the peaks of Washington's Cascade Mountains. They seemed headed for Mt. Rainier at a speed Arnold estimated to be more than 1,700 miles an hour. Later that afternoon in Pendleton, Oregon, Ken decided to report what he saw to the FBI. Finding its offices closed, he took his story to the editor of the *Eastern Oregonian.*

Whatever Arnold saw—some skeptics think it was a group of weather balloons—they seemed not to be circular. "They flew erratic," Arnold told a United Press reporter, "like a saucer if you skip it across water." In the story he sent over the wire, the reporter called the objects "flying saucers." Before a week had passed, newspapers throughout the nation were having a field day with reports of new sightings and wild speculations about what the mysterious "saucers" could be. Secret United States government aircraft? Soviet planes? Spaceships from Mars or Venus?

This article originally appeared in *Free Inquiry,* Summer 1987, and is reprinted with permission.

Amazing Stories warned its readers against the psychic forces of "evil deros."

The first issue of *Fate,* "the nation's top purveyor of psychic garbage."

The time was ripe for a new mythology. Traditional religions were declining, and the fundamentalist revival was yet to begin. Sea serpents had long ago retired to isolated spots like Loch Ness. Not many people were seeing visions of the Virgin Mary or conversing with angels the way Joan of Arc did. But out there, over our heads, was dark, endless space— a region teeming with mysteries far more exotic than any in Earth's ancient seas. Were aliens from other planets watching us? Could they be here to conquer us? To save us from self-destruction? Add to these fears and hopes the steady deterioration of science teaching, widespread resentment against technology for inventing the atom bomb and polluting the environment, the upsurge of enthusiasm for astrology and all things occult, and it is not hard to understand why the UFO craze spread so rapidly.

In our country's science-fiction subculture, Ray Palmer was the first editor to perceive the mythic potency of UFOlogy. "And who was Ray Palmer?" I can hear the young readers ask. We older readers remember him well.

Raymond A. Palmer (the "A" didn't stand for anything), born in Milwaukee in 1910, was a blue-eyed hunchback slightly more than four feet tall.* He always claimed that his deformed back had been caused by an accident when he was seven, but what sort of accident is not clear. In one version he was hit by a butcher's truck; in another, he was hit by a streetcar.

When Hugo Gernsback started *Amazing Stories* in 1926, Palmer became a lifelong fan. He edited what is said to be the first fanzine, *The Comet.* "The Time Ray of Jandra," in *Wonder Stories* (June 1930), was his first published story. According to Palmer, for the next ten years he sold hundreds of tales in such diverse fields as SF, mystery, western, romance, and even pornography. He used many pseudonyms.

Young Palmer belonged to a club called "The Milwaukee Fictioneers," which included Robert Bloch, Stanley Weinbaum, and Ralph Milne Farley. After Weinbaum died, Palmer edited a collection of his work, *Dawn of Flame and Other Stories.* When Weinbaum's widow objected to Ray's introduction, he substituted a new one, making the first edition of this book a rarity.

Amazing Stories was in the doldrums when Ziff-Davis took it over in 1938. It was being edited by Gernsback's friend T. O'Conor Sloane, then 86. Ziff-Davis replaced Sloane with Palmer, and the magazine's

---

*In the sixties, science-fiction writers Gardner Fox and Jule Schwartz wrote a comic book called *The Atom,* about a scientist who had the power to shrink himself to a height of six inches. They named the scientist Ray Palmer.

character altered overnight. The shift was away from hard science to action and adventure. Sales of *Amazing* leaped upward. The next year Palmer started *Fantastic Adventures,* featuring yarns on a level even more juvenile than that of *Amazing.*

At about this time Palmer's nose began to sniff the burning fuse of the coming occult explosion. Millions of young people, he correctly sensed, cared little about orthodox science. They were hungering for far-out science. Over the transom came some weird material of just the sort Palmer wanted. A Pennsylvania welder named Richard Sharpe Shaver claimed to be in telepathic communication with a race of evil humanoids who lived underground.

Let us try to encapsulate Shaver's vast, complex mythology. Long ago the earth had been the home of the Atlans and the Titans, godlike creatures who flourished on the now-sunken continents of Atlantis and Lemuria. To protect themselves from harmful solar radiation they constructed enormous caverns below the earth's surface. But the rays still damaged them, and they were forced to abandon the planet. An inferior race of humans discovered the caverns and the fantastic machines the superbeings had left behind. Alas, radiation from the machines turned the humans into midgetlike idiots whom Shaver called the "deros" (short for "detrimental robots"). The deros still live beneath us. All sorts of terrible disasters that occur above ground, including great wars, are caused by psychic forces coming from the evil deros.

Palmer printed Shaver's first short novel, *I Remember Lemuria,* in the March 1945 issue of *Amazing.* The response from simple-minded readers was indeed amazing. After thousands of letters, many from persons reporting their own encounters with deros, Palmer realized he had on his hands the making of a monstrous swindle. For the next few years he rewrote all of Shaver's demented submissions, presenting them not as fiction but as sober fact. Only older SF fans can comprehend the furor that resulted.

Little is known about Shaver, but some evidence suggests he may really have believed he was in psychic contact with creatures of the caverns. In the July 1971 issue of *Forum,* Palmer revealed that for eight years, while Shaver was feeding him raw data, Shaver was in a mental hospital. "He suffered from being a tremendous psychic person," Ray wrote, "and this in my belief makes him superior, mentally, to those people unable to perceive the ordinarily unseen aspects of our total existence." A few months later Palmer reported that Shaver had years earlier escaped from the mental hospital and "is at present a fugitive."

It was a period in which the two men seemed not on good terms. Palmer published a letter from Shaver that vigorously denied Palmer's disclosures. He had, Shaver said, been in a sanitorium for only two weeks, and only to recover from a heat stroke. The two men also clashed over the nature and location of the deros. Palmer put forth the theory that they could be spiritual beings *above* the earth, on a higher astral plane. Shaver responded with anger: "I was in the caves. Not in the clouds overhead or in any mental world of the liar's imagination, but in actuality." How much of this debate, in the few years preceding Shaver's death in 1975, is accurate and how much was cooked up by the pair to keep the Shaver mystery alive is impossible to say at this time.

Did Palmer ever believe in the deros? Some think he did, or maybe half-did, but I can't buy it. Jim Wentworth, in a history of the Shaver flap that I'll return to later, tells us that neither Palmer's wife, Marjorie, nor Shaver's third wife, Dorothy, took the deros seriously. I met Ray on several occasions in the forties, when I lived in Chicago, and I have talked to many people who knew him well. He impressed us all as a shy, kind, good-natured, gentle, energetic little man with the personality of a professional con artist. He may have been slightly paranoid in the pleasure he got from his endless flimflams, but I think his primary motive was simply to create uproars that would sell magazines.

Sell they did. It is said that at the beginning of the Shaver flap *Amazing* reached a circulation higher than any other SF magazine up to that time. Mature readers, however, were strongly disturbed by what came to be called the Great Shaver Hoax. It was immoral, they thought, to deceive gullible readers into thinking Shaver's delusions were true. The hoax was giving SF a bad name. The management of Ziff-Davis stood it as long as they could. Eventually, smitten by an attack of conscience, they asked Palmer to go.

The time was the late forties and the occult revolution was running full blast. Why not, Palmer decided, start a new pulp devoted entirely to the occult? His friend Curtis Fuller, then editing the Ziff-Davis periodical *Flying,* agreed that this was an idea whose time had come. The pair formed Clark Publishing Company—the name was taken from Chicago's North Clark Street where the firm had its first office—and in early 1948 *Fate* was born. (Palmer has written that he suggested the name, but Fuller recently claimed *he* thought of it first.)

Many years later Fuller bought the magazine from Palmer and has been its publisher ever since. With a current circulation of about 150,000, *Fate* is the nation's top purveyor of psychic garbage. Fuller's wife, Mary, is editor. The pair, both in their seventies, are Unitarians who have almost as little belief in what they publish as Palmer did. "The Bermuda Triangle," Mary told a reporter a few years ago, "is for the birds."

When Palmer saw the newspaper accounts of Ken Arnold's famous sighting, he lost no time getting in touch with Arnold and requesting an article for *Fate*. The first issue (Spring 1948) led off with "I *Did* See the Flying Disks!" in which Arnold gave more details about his sighting. In the same issue he reported his investigation of a later UFO sighting in Tacoma. "What Were the Doughnuts?"—another UFO piece in the issue—was written by Fuller under the pseudonym John C. Ross, a name he used for later articles in *Fate* and other magazines. Palmer wrote *Fate's* editorials, as well as many of its articles, under the byline of Robert N. Webster. Several years later, when I sold *Fate* a manuscript, my correspondence was entirely with "Robert Webster."

The first issue of *Fate* marked the beginning of a long collaboration between Arnold and Palmer. The second issue featured Arnold's "Are Space Visitors Here?" This was possibly the first magazine piece to argue that UFOs were extraterrestrial. In 1950 Palmer advertised and distributed Arnold's pamphlet *The Flying Saucer as I Saw It*. Two years later he published *The Coming of the Saucers,* a book on which he collaborated with Arnold.

Arnold, by the way, was a great admirer of Charles Fort. Like so many Forteans who seem unable to comprehend that the Fortean Society was a joke, Arnold was inclined to take seriously every published UFO story, no matter how outlandish, including tales of little men seen coming out of saucers. "I realize it's the 'data of the damned,' " he told a newspaper in 1950, quoting one of Fort's famous phrases. "Who's to determine what is and isn't real?" he asked.

It would be foolish to suppose that UFOmania would never have gathered steam without Palmer's aid; yet no one can deny that he played an enormous role, now almost forgotten, in tirelessly promoting the craze. Here are some of the pulps he started, ostensibly to publish SF but primarily devoted to beating the drums for UFOs and other aspects of the paranormal scene: *Other Worlds, Imagination, Universe, Hidden Worlds, Mystic, Search, Forum,* and *Space World*. When *Other Worlds* folded he changed the title of *Universe* to *Other Worlds*. It was later changed again to *Flying Saucers from Other Worlds* and finally shortened to *Flying Saucers*. No one knows how many pseudonyms Palmer used in writing for these publications.

Palmer's first mistake was pushing his Shaver hoax to absurd extremes. Then he made a second, more serious blunder. He decided to tie UFOs into his beloved underground caverns. So far as I can determine, his first article to do this was "Flying Saucers from the Earth," in the December 1959 issue of *Flying Saucers*. From then on, articles began to appear with increasing frequency, most of them written by Palmer, contending that the earth is hollow, with enormous openings at both poles. UFOs were spacecraft built inside the earth and sent through the polar holes for reasons that were never too clear. (Palmer was seldom consistent in his flimflams.) From 1960 until his death 17 years later, Palmer seemed obsessed by the hollow-earth theory, though there is not a scintilla of evidence he ever believed it. Indeed, he added almost nothing to the old hollow-earth theories (you'll find a history of them in my book *Fads and Fallacies*) except the Shaver mythology of subsurface creatures. But the idea of a hollow earth was new to most of his young readers, and Palmer was careful never to admit even to friends (were his wife and children exceptions?) that it was another calculated scheme to boost magazine sales.

The most ridiculous artifact in this mad history was the June 1970 cover of *Flying Saucers*—a NASA photograph that Palmer called "the most remarkable photo ever made." It was a composite picture of the earth, seen by a satellite above the North Pole, that seemed to show a huge black hole surrounding the pole. Palmer knew perfectly well that the hole was nothing more than the region where sunlight could not penetrate at the time the photos were taken, but of course he didn't tell his readers that. "We do not see any ice fields in the large circular area directly at the geographic pole," he wrote. "Instead, we see—The Hole!"

Mariner photos had also disclosed, Palmer assured his readers, a similar opening at the north pole of Mars. Mercury too was hollow. Palmer printed numerous letters from readers who raised objections, some of them written by Palmer himself. You have only to read his clever responses to get the picture—a strange little man, chuckling to himself as he wrote, somehow getting enormous kicks out of hornswoggling people bigger than he was.

Most histories of UFOlogy either do not mention Palmer or give him only a passing glance. One exception is Robert Sheaffer's splendid book *The UFO Verdict: Examining the Evidence,* published by Prometheus Books in 1981 and recently reissued in paperback. It is the source for what I have written above about Palmer's exploitation of the NASA photograph. The only leading UFOlogist who didn't scoff at Palmer's holey-polar theory was Brinsley LePoer Trench, a member of the British House of Lords and founder of the influential *Saucer Review.* Trench liked the hollow-earth theory so much that he wrote an entire book about it: *Secret of the Ages: UFOs from Inside the Earth* (Pinnacle, 1977).

A book titled *The Hollow Earth,* by Dr. Raymond Bernard (he claimed a Ph.D. from New York University) was first printed in 1963 by a New York house called Fieldcrest Publications, and later reprinted by several other firms. Because Bernard frequently quotes Palmer, calling him "America's greatest authority on flying saucers," and because his hollow-earth book was heavily advertised in *Fate,* it has been rumored that Bernard and Palmer were one and the same. Not so. According to several informants, Bernard's real name was Walter Siegmeister, a German crank who at one time ran a health-food store in Brooklyn and who wrote many worthless books and pamphlets on health, sex, and occult topics. I am told he died in Brazil, but I have been unable to confirm this or to learn any more about him.

Now that almost 40 years have gone by without finding a single nut or bolt from a flying saucer, leading UFO buffs have switched to the safe, untestable view that UFOs are ghostlike things from some higher plane of reality, perhaps illusions created in our minds by alien superbeings. Ken Arnold himself moved with the psi flow. In an interview in *UFO Review* (November 1982) he recalled many UFO sightings since 1947, including one craft that kept changing in such a way that it led him to think it was a living creature, possibly a link between our life-forms and those of a spirit world. He repeated his claim that invisible entities from UFOs once entered his home. "I was aware of their presence," he stated on an earlier occasion, "because I could see my rugs and furniture sink down under their weight. . . ."

Arnold belonged to a large class of what are known in UFO circles as "repeaters." These are people who, contrary to all laws of statistics, keep seeing the same kinds of UFOs. In a *Seattle Times* interview (June 26, 1983), shortly before his death in January 1984, Arnold speaks of seven occasions since 1947 on which he saw UFOs, always in clusters and always traveling at fantastic speeds. Who can have confidence in such repeated claims?

The September 1957 issue of *Fate* carried an amusing ad. Arnold was selling a product called "Turn-ers," guaranteed to cure dandruff, restore hair color, and "make your scalp pink and clean as a baby's." A testimonial by Palmer says it not only banished his dandruff in one week but turned his father's snow-white hair back to the color it was when his dad was 30.

Ray and Marjorie spent their later years on a large farm near Amherst, Wisconsin, where they brought up two daughters and a son. For a time, Shaver and his wife lived on a nearby farm. It was in 1977, while the Palmers were visiting a daughter in Tallahassee, Florida, that Ray died after a series of strokes. Marjorie still lives in Amherst, where she heads Amherst Press. The firm publishes books about parascience and the occult, including two basic references on Palmer's life, *The Secret World* (1975) by Palmer and Shaver, and James Wentworth's *Giants in the Earth* (1973). Marjorie continued Ray's magazine *Search* until 1981, when she sold it to another publisher.

The Secret World is one of Palmer's masterpieces of hokum. Although his is the only name on the cover, only the first third of this large hardcover volume is by him. It is an autobiographical account of his early life, filled with startling anecdotes that may or may not be true. He claims, for example, that he remembers seeing Halley's Comet through a window as a baby while being held in his grandmother's arms, although he learned later that, when he was born, in August 1910, the comet had passed beyond the range of being visible to unaided eyes.

Palmer devotes many pages to his discovery of *Oahspe,* a book he heavily promoted as a revelation that reinforces Shaver's claims. "The book proved itself," he writes. "To me, it could not be a fake. It had to be authentic—because it proved the key to all the vast amount of material I had collected in my lifetime, and especially . . . the Shaver Mystery. *Oahspe* proved Shaver, and Shaver proved *Oahspe.*"

For readers unfamiliar with the wild history of spiritualism, *Oahspe* was written by Dr. John Ballou Newbrough, a New York City dentist and psychic. He claimed he could paint pictures in total darkness, using both hands at once, that he could remote view and read any book in any library, and that while under a spirit's control he could lift a ton of weight. *Oahspe,* subtitled *A Kosmon Bible in the Words of Jehovah and His Angel Ambassadors,* was published in Boston in 1882. According to its author, it was dictated by angels who manipulated his hands while he sat at his typewriter. One morning he looked out the window and "beheld the line of light that rested on my hands, extending heavenward like a telegraph wire towards the sky. Over my head were three pairs of hands, fully materialized; behind me stood another angel with her hands on my shoulders. My looking did not disturb the scene, my hands kept right on printing . . . printing. For fifty weeks this continued. . . . The peculiar drawings in *Oahspe* were made with pencil in the same way."

For an excellent summary of the strange doctrines in this 800-page Bible—they are funnier than the doctrines in the *Book of Mormon* and almost as funny as those in the Unification Church's Bible, written by the Reverend Sun Moon—see the entry on *Oahspe* in the *Hastings Encyclopedia of Religion and Ethics.* Followers of the new religion call themselves "faithists." They were strict vegetarians and pacifists, and hated all forms of capitalism. In 1894 a sect of faithists actually established a colony called "Shalam" in New Mexico. The sect later shifted to California, where for a time they published a periodical, *The Faithist Messenger.*

Where can you obtain a copy of this great revelation? Why, all you have to do is send $19.95 to Amherst Press. Here is how their catalogue describes this modest work:

A history of the higher and lower heavens and of the Earth for the past 24,000 years; also a brief history of the preceding 55,000 years. An explanation of all the world's religions; the cosmogony of the universe; the creation of the planets, of man; new commandments applicable to the present day; the unseen worlds. Written in 1881, *Oahspe's* science is today being confirmed by space satellites, new archaeological discoveries and many other sources. Perhaps the most remarkable and important book in the world today!

Move over Bible! Move over Velikovsky! *Oahspe* is here! If Ray Palmer for one moment believed the crap in this crazy volume then the man was a moron, which of course he wasn't.

The last two-thirds of *The Secret World* carries Shaver's byline. He describes in detail, with many color pictures, how you can obtain "rock books" by slicing a stone in half. The cross-section is then photographed and magnified. If you study it carefully, turning the photo this way and that, you'll see vague shapes of objects, animals, and people—like the shapes you see in clouds. It was Shaver's contention that before the Atlans and Titans left the earth they recorded the life-forms on our planet, before Noah's Flood, by fabricating these rocks. Shaver sliced thousands of stones to get such pictures. The book reproduces some of Shaver's paintings, many erotic, that he had based on rock books.

James Wentworth's *Giants in the Earth* is a history of the Shaver hoax. I have no idea how much of it should be trusted, and I have been unsuccessful in learning anything about the author—not even if his name is a pseudonym.

Less than two months before his death, Ray attended the First International UFO Congress in Chicago, June 1977—a conference sponsored by *Fate*. Ken Arnold was on hand to give the keynote address. Both men participated in a symposium that you'll find in the hilarious *Proceedings of the First International UFO Congress* (Warner Books, 1980), edited by Palmer's old sidekick, Curtis Fuller.

Calling himself "basically a science-fiction writer," Palmer reminded his audience that airships were common in fiction long before a single plane had been successfully flown. Was it possible, he asked, that Jules Verne's stories about airships were based on reports that had come his way from persons who had seen UFOs? Palmer closed his remarks with an unusual admission. "It's a basic weakness that we like to fool ourselves. We go out and catch a big fish. It's always a big fish, and the bigger it is the more it gets away."

Perhaps we have here the key to Palmer's declining years, when he faded away from both SF and UFO landscapes. Flying saucers from inside the earth was just too whopping a fish story. Palmer did his best to defend this fish that got away, but only a few kooks on the lunatic fringes of UFOlogy could believe him.

Afterword

The following response to my article on Ray Palmer was published in *Free Inquiry,* Spring 1988.

> Martin Gardner's article contains numerous inaccuracies, and I feel it would be helpful to set the record straight for the benefit of those interested in the history of Ray Palmer, Richard Shaver, and the "Shaver Mystery."
>
> I was a member of Ray Palmer's so-called stable of writers between 1943 and 1950 as well as one of the inner circle who bowled and played poker and gin rummy with him. My memory of events is not all that it might be after some 40 years. Ray's wife, Marjorie Palmer (whom Gardner never contacted while he was doing whatever passed for research for his article) supplied details where my recollection failed.
>
> Let's take Gardner's errors in order of commission:
>
> 1. Whereas Gardner claims Palmer is "forgotten," Marjorie says,"ten years after his death, I receive many letters, telephone calls, and visitors from all over the world, almost every week."
>
> 2. The "A" in Raymond A. Palmer stood for Alfred—not nothing, as Gardner would have us believe.
>
> 3. Palmer was nearly five feet tall, not four. He was injured by a truck at age seven. Later, as an adult, he fell off a church roof while doing sheet-metal work.
>
> 4. Howard Browne was not "editor-in-chief of all Ziff-Davis pulps for six years." Only Palmer held that title for such a length of time. Browne was managing editor under Ray and did not become editor until Ray left in 1950. Browne held the post for less than a year before leaving Ziff-Davis for a screenplay-writing job in Hollywood.
>
> 5. Marjorie characterizes as "baloney" Gardner's allegation that "Palmer's nose began to sniff the burning fuse of the coming occult explosion." Ray once wrote he had noted that sales increased by a couple of thousand whenever a story-title with "Atlantis" or "Lemuria" appeared on the cover of *Amazing Stories.* This hardly indicated to Palmer (or anyone else) that "millions" of young readers "were hungering for far-out science." Ray did follow up on this clue to reader interest, however, when he gave the title "I Remember Lemuria" to the first Shaver Mystery (SM) story. Sales of *Amazing* prior to SM were about 65,000—quite high as far as the sales of science-fiction magazines usually went (40,000 to 50,000 was the norm, and this because fans tended to buy most of the science-fiction magazines being published).

At the height of interest in the SM, sales increased to over 95,000. The "occult" readership thus amounted to less than 30,000 (a long way short of "millions," it need hardly be said), and even then that figure no doubt includes readers attracted simply by the excitement that the SM was generating.

6. Marjorie insists that Palmer never deliberately conducted a "monstrous swindle" in connection with SM. He never once indicated—even to her—that he promoted the SM solely for the sake of circulation or profit. Privately as well as publicly he was quite serious about it. For my part I recall how the members of Ray's inner circle often asked one another, "Do you think Ray really believes that Shaver stuff?" He certainly seemed to.

7. Marjorie states that Ray edited but did not rewrite all of Shaver's stories—only the very first one, because it was submitted as a letter rather than a story. Shaver did not "feed Palmer raw data for eight years while [Shaver was] in a mental hospital." He was working as an overhead-crane operator in a Briggs auto-body plant in Detroit when he began corresponding with Ray about what Ray came to call the "Shaver Mystery." In 1968, long after the termination of SM in *Amazing Stories,* Shaver revealed in an interview that he had spent eight years in a mental hospital. That he "escaped" from there appears to have been Shaver's melodramatic way of stating the unexciting truth: He was often given leave to visit home, and on the last one he did not return. No effort seems to have been made to enforce his return.

8. Gardner to the contrary, Palmer and Shaver remained on good terms after the mental-hospital disclosure. Shaver firmly maintained his original position on SM, while Ray explored alternative theories in his magazines; but, despite such differences of opinion, the two men respected each other and continued to exchange letters practically up to Shaver's death in 1975. Marjorie insists that Ray and Shaver never had any sort of partnership and never "cooked up" any debates "to keep the SM alive."

9. Because of strong protests from organizations of conservative science-fiction fans, the Ziff-Davis management ordered Palmer to cease publishing material on the SM, but it did not "ask Palmer to go." He remained with Ziff-Davis until the company prepared to move its offices to New York City, whereupon Palmer, who did not wish to move, resigned.

10. Gardner states that Curt and Mary Fuller of *Fate* "have almost as little belief in what they publish as Palmer did" and gives as an example a remark by Mary that "The Bermuda Triangle is for the birds." In fact, *Fate* published "The Bermuda Triangle and Other Hoaxes" by Larry Kusche in its October 1975 issue. At that time Mary wrote Lloyd's of London to inquire about its insurance rates and claims for the area called the "Bermuda Triangle." Lloyd's reply, stating that it could "find no evidence to support the claim that the 'Bermuda Triangle' has more losses than elsewhere," was published along with Kusche's article. The Fullers, whom I have known and worked with for four decades, have always been open about what they do and do not believe.

11. The name Gardner gives as "Robert T. Webster" is inaccurate. It is "Robert N. Webster," a house name used not only by Palmer but by others

during *Fate's* early years.

12. Gardner lists *Imagination* among the magazines edited by Palmer. In fact, *Imagination* was published and edited by William L. Hamling, who was a close friend of Ray and an assistant editor of the Ziff-Davis pulp magazines between 1944 and 1950.

Chester S. Geier
Chicago, Ill.

My reply followed:

Chester Geier, a Ziff-Davis editor and prolific writer of pulp science-fiction, was Ray Palmer's top booster of the Shaver hoax. He organized the Shaver Mystery Club, and for its fans he edited the *Shaver Mystery Magazine*. It is unthinkable that either he or Palmer saw the hoax as anything but a flimflam to boost the circulation of *Amazing Stories*. I will comment briefly on Geier's dubious points.

1. "Forgotten" is a vague word. No doubt Marjorie Palmer and some older SF buffs have not forgotten Ray, but it is hard to find younger fans who know who he was.

2. Charles Brown, in his Palmer obit (*Locus,* September 1987) said the "A" stood for Arthur. In an effort to verify this, I asked Jerome Clark, a *Fate* editor. He replied that his boss, Curtis Fuller, told him the "A" stood only for "the first letter in the alphabet." Fuller added that the "B" in Raymond B. Palmer (Palmer's son) stood for the alphabet's second letter. I'll accept "Alfred" when I see a copy of Ray's birth certificate.

3. I don't know Palmer's exact height, but it was surely closer to four feet than five. The *Science Fiction Encyclopedia* (Peter Nicholls, ed.) says he was "four feet tall." Brown's obit calls him a "four foot tall hunchback." An accompanying photo shows Palmer standing with a group that includes Geier. If Palmer were five feet it would give Geier a height of more than eight. Palmer gave conflicting accounts of how he had been injured. Geier buys the truck version. Howard Browne, in an article on Palmer cited below, says Ray told him he had been hit by a Milwaukee streetcar.

4. When Palmer left Ziff-Davis in 1949, Browne became chief editor of the firm's Fiction Group, a post held until he returned to Hollywood in 1956. See Browne's article and the entries on Browne and his successor at Ziff, Paul Fairman, in the *Science Fiction Encyclopedia.*

5. I stand by my statement that Palmer sniffed the coming occult explosion long before other SF editors. My "millions of young readers" obviously refers to readers in general, not just *Amazing* subscribers. Recent surveys show that about half of all college students now believe in astrology and the paranormal.

6. Ray may never have told his wife that the Shaver flap was a swindle, but no one who worked for Ziff at the time, or who knew Palmer, thought otherwise. Browne, in his article on Palmer, "A Profit without Honor"(*Amazing,*

May 1984) calls it a deliberate effort to capture the "lunatic fringe." Yes, it would turn off some readers, Palmer admitted to Browne, but it would "bring in more than we lose." Brown responded with a slogan: "There is no God but Palmer, and Shaver is his Profit."

7. In a 1961 piece in *Hidden Worlds* (quoted in the entry on Shaver in the *Visual Encyclopedia of Science Fiction,* by Brian Ash), Palmer confessed that "a great deal of the actual writing of the stories produced under Mr. Shaver's name has been mine." He added that what he usually did was rewrite Shaver's basic plots. According to Browne, Palmer "rewrote extensively" the Shaver documents. Details about Shaver's stay in a mental hospital are scanty and conflicting.

8. "What is less known," says the *Visual Encyclopedia of Science Fiction,* "is the animosity between Palmer and Shaver themselves." This is evident in the angry letters from Shaver that Palmer published, unless of course the animosity was cooked up to keep the deros hoax alive.

9. It is often hard to know whether a person resigned or was fired. "Palmer left Ziff-Davis in 1949 under strange circumstances"—this is how Browne puts it in his obit. "Some claimed that the publisher had decided to kill the Shaver material, and fired Palmer, while others claim that Palmer wanted to start his own magazine catering more to psychic phenomena." Browne favors the second conjecture. My information favors the first.

10. True, *Fate* now and then prints a token skeptical piece, such as Kusche's article on the Bermuda Triangle, but earlier issues ran more positive pieces about the triangle.

11. Geier is right on this one. The "T" was my typo. I have several letters from Robert N. Webster.

12. The *Science Fiction Encyclopedia* states that Palmer "began a companion magazine, *Imagination,* in 1950," and later sold it to Hamling. A recent editor of *Amazing* told me that Palmer edited the first two issues.

I give Geier's letter an overal accuracy score of D+.

31 | Prime-Time Preachers

It is too early, it seems to me, to send the firemen home. The fire is still burning on many a far-flung hill, and it may begin to roar again at any moment. . . . Heave an egg out of a Pullman window and you will hit a Fundamentalist almost anywhere in the United States today. They swarm in the country towns. . . . They are thick in the mean streets behind the gasworks. They are everywhere where learning is too heavy a burden for mortal minds. . . .

H.L. Mencken, *Prejudices,* vol. 5.

When Mencken suggested that fundamentalism might blaze once more, who took him seriously? Clarence Darrow had made William Jennings Bryan look like the country bumpkin he was. Outside the Bible Belt, many mainline churches were promoting the "social gospel" as they tumbled down the hill of liberal theology toward secular humanism. Remember that hullabaloo over the proposition "God is dead"? Then a few decades ago, to the amazement of intellectuals, hardline fundamentalism began to roar again.

Sociologists are still trying to figure it out. There is no evidence of a large-scale religious revival sweeping the nation, but within Protestantism there has been an unmistakable decline in liberal theology and an upsurge of fundamentalist dogma. While the congregations of mainline churches dwindle, especially with respect to the young, the old-time gospel churches are bursting at the seams. Scores of fundamentalist magazines, seldom seen in public libraries, have circulations larger than the liberal *Christian Century*. Fundamentalist books, published by sectarian houses and distributed through Christian bookstores, never make the *New York Times* best-seller lists even though their sales often far exceed those of most books on those lists.

Polls taken during the last decade all agree that the United States is one of the most deeply religious nations in the world. Over 95 percent of its population say they believe in a personal God and life after death. Only about 25 percent now believe in hell, a remarkable decline, but 25

A shorter version of this essay originally appeared in the *New York Review of Books,* August 13, 1987, and is reprinted with permission.

percent means a lot of souls who are worried. Many who have abandoned Christianity are still drifting East into reincarnation and the New Age of psychic wonders, but growing numbers of those who remain Christian want more from their ministers than hazy doctrines and dull sermons about beauty and ethics. They want to be told about heaven. They want to sing and shout about the Blood of Jesus that washes away all sins.

This growth of fundamentalism was a time bomb for the Democrats that exploded in 1984. An estimated eight million white evangelicals switched allegiance that year from Democrat to Republican. The South's Bible Belt, once solidly Democratic, shifted heavily toward Republican. In June 1987 the Southern Baptists, our country's largest Protestant denomination, voted itself firmly under the control of fundamentalist leaders. In 1980, its white clergy were 28 percent Republican. In 1984 (see James Guth's "Political Converts: Partisan Realignment Among Southern Baptists," in *Election Politics,* Winter 1985-1986) the percentage rose to 43, with the steepest rise among young ministers.

Jimmy Carter was elected president in 1976 partly because born-again Protestants, black and white, perceived him as one of them. They abandoned him in 1980 partly because they thought Ronald Reagan was even more born-again. Raised by a devout fundamentalist mother, Reagan has often spoken about how she "planted a great faith in me." Later we shall consider his remarks about the Second Coming. It is always hard, of course, to know when Reagan is expressing actual beliefs, or just skillfully choosing words to win votes, and the same ambiguity surrounds his appointments of ultraconservative Christians to high posts. James Watt, for example, wasn't joking when, as secretary of the interior, he told environmentalists not to worry because Jesus would soon be here.

Whatever the president's inner convictions, and however his popularity may be diminishing, evangelical Christians continue to see the Republican Party as the bastion of conservative Christian values. Democrats are perceived as too tolerant of sexual (especially homosexual) freedoms, pornography, abortion, Marxism, liberalism, secular humanism (as reflected in the teaching of evolution and the forbidding of prayer in public schools), and women's rights. "Wives, submit yourselves unto your own husbands, as unto the Lord," wrote Saint Paul. "For the husband is the head of the wife, even as Christ is the head of the church" (Ephesians 5:22-23). Every time the Democrats promote ERA they lose evangelical votes.

The religious programs on radio and television are now almost wholly dominated by fundamentalist preaching. It obviously meets the needs of believers in ways that mainline preaching cannot, but there is another aspect that is economic. The FCC's free-market policies sell air time to the highest bidders, and the highest are the Bible thumpers. They are the only preachers so fired by the Holy Ghost that they are not ashamed to engage in the perpetual, blatant money hustling so necessary to stay on prime time.

Why do so many poor people send them money? Surveys show that there are about five million hard-core donors, most of them women from 50 to 75, with 71 as the peak age for giving. Many live alone on Social Security, some in nursing homes. Many are too disabled for churchgoing. Lonely, neglected, they see the electronic evangelist as their pastor. A widow's mite dropped in an offering plate is anonymous, but the smallest donation to a television preacher brings a warm letter of thanks that makes the giver feel that he or she is a true partner in a great soul-winning enterprise.

Of the country's top six television preachers—Oral Roberts, Jim Bakker, Jimmy Swaggart, Pat Robertson, Jerry Falwell,[1] and Robert Schuller[2]—all but the last two are Pentecostals. (Southern Baptist William Franklin "Billy" Graham, though still the most admired fundamentalist preacher, has no regular television program.) But what is a Pentecostal? Before examining the wild careers of the first four, some definitions will be useful.

Evangelicals are born-again Protestants whose views can vary from fundamentalist to liberal. Fundamentalists are evangelicals who regard the Bible as free of all error. Pentecostals are fundamentalists who think the gifts of Pentecost (Acts 2) were given for all time. On the Pentecost (Greek for *fifty*), a Jewish feast day that took place 50 days after Passover, the Holy Ghost descended on Jesus' disciples, taking the form of tongues of fire; the disciples began to "speak with other tongues, as the Spirit gave them utterance. . . . Now when this was noised abroad, the multitude came together, and were confounded, because that every man heard them speak in his own language."

To lead a full Christian life, most Pentecostals believe, a born-again person must undergo a second miracle, the Baptism of the Holy Spirit. This confers upon the baptized the ability to speak the Unknown Tongue, a prayer language understood only by God and the angels. Saint Paul, in First Corinthians, writes at length about the practice, warning against its misuse but thanking God that he speaks in tongues "more than ye all."

Tongue speaking, or glossolalia,[3] almost vanished after the apostolic age except for a brief revival by Montanus in the second century. Saint Augustine set the pattern for the Catholic church and the Reformers by asserting that God withdrew the gift after it served its purpose. This was also the view of Thomas Aquinas. There is no evidence that Luther or Calvin spoke in tongues. The practice was revived in the seventeenth and eighteenth centuries by the French Protestant Camisards, the *convulsionnaires* of the Roman Catholic Jansenists, and the early Methodists. It was soon flourishing among the Quakers, Shakers, Irvingites, Mormons, and other fringe sects. After 1900 a variety of churches sprang up in the United States, on fire with tongues and faith healing, to become the denominations now called Pentecostal. Today there are about 35 of them. They are the fastest growing segment of Christianity, not only here but throughout the world.

Charismatics, sometimes called "neo-Pentecostals," are evangelicals, not necessarily fundamentalist, who accept the gifts of faith-healing and tongues. The term applies of course to the old or "classical" Pentecostals, but also to Catholics, Episcopalians, and members of mainline Protestant churches where there has been since 1960 an astonishing inrush of Pentecostal fervor.

Non-Christian glossolalia is a problem for charismatics. Ancient sooth-sayers, and devotees of Greek and Roman mystery cults, often gurgled meaningless sentences. In the *Aeneid* (Book 6) Virgil describes tongues speaking by a Roman sibyl. Some Moslem sects and primitive cultures practice glossolalia. In *The Great Dictator,* Charlie Chaplin's Hitler gives a rousing speech in German doubletalk. None of this, charismatics maintain, is the real thing. Non-Pentecostal fundamentalists think the babbling of their Pentecostal brothers isn't the real thing either, and may even be inspired by Satan.

Roberts, Bakker, Swaggart, and Robertson all speak in tongues, as do their wives and most of their children, but no one has stressed the gift more than Oral Roberts, the oldest and best-known Pentecostal preacher of the four.[4] He and his wife, Evelyn, pray in tongues daily, though you'll seldom hear them do this on camera. Pentecostal televangelists discovered early in the game that glossolalia frightens too many viewers.

"Ye ked ee aky shangda" was how *Time* reported a phrase spoken at the first international assembly of charismatics at Kansas City in 1977, but you can put down your own nonsense syllables and they'll sound as authentic as anyone's glossolalia. Linguists who have studied tongues speak-ing find the tongues have nothing in common except the sounds and rhythms of a natural language. Visit any Pentecostal church and you're likely to see someone stand up and babble the prayer language, often followed by a person with the "gift of interpretation" who will explain what has been said. Sometimes you'll see and hear an entire congregation kneel and babble in tongues.

Oral Roberts was born in 1918 on a farm near Ada, Oklahoma, of Pentecostal parents, both part-Indian.[5] At 17 he collapsed on a high school basketball court, bleeding through his nose. Local doctors told him his lungs were in the "final stages" of tuberculosis. Home in bed, watching his father's face miraculously become the face of Jesus, Oral was reborn.

Soon thereafter, when a traveling evangelist touched his head, there was a blinding flash of light, and Oral leaped to his feet shouting "I am healed!" *My Story* (1961), one of Oral's numerous autobiographies, reproduces medical documents proving that a few months later his lungs were perfect, but there is no shred of evidence that he ever had TB. There is only his memory of what some country doctors told him.

Oral's healing also cured a bad stammer. Before the year ended, the teenager was ordained by the Pentecostal Holiness Church, but it was not until after a decade of pastoring in dreary hamlets that Oral discovered he had a supernatural, electricitylike energy in his right arm. He didn't need to touch a person directly for God to use this energy for healing. A "point of contact" could be made if the sufferer touched the radio or television screen that carried Oral's voice or image. His rise to fame was swift, and his books swarm with lurid accounts of hundreds of miracle cures. The blind see, the deaf hear, the dumb speak, the lame abandon crutches. A missing hip socket materializes. A large goiter vanishes instantly. Demons are exorcised.[6] There are, of course, no prior medical evaluations, no later follow-ups. Oral never mentions those who expired a few days after a miraculous healing. There was one widely publicized occasion in 1959 when a woman died soon after throwing away her insulin.

In the second volume of *The Holy Spirit in the Now* (1974), Oral writes about a crusade in Fresno, California, during which "a little baby died." The mother tossed its "stiffening" body to Brother Roberts. "I held that baby in my arms. I felt the Holy Spirit coming through my body, coming into my hands, and I touched that little baby." The baby began to breathe. "I stood there thinking about God. God, how could I ever limit You again?"

Stichomancy is an ancient art of divination. One opens a sacred book at random, then reads. The Greeks consulted Homer. Moslems consult the Koran. Pentecostals, like medieval Christians, love to consult the Bible. In 1947, when Oral flipped his Bible open, his eyes fell on 3 John: 2. "Beloved, I wish above all things that thou mayest prosper and be in health." The passage hit Oral like a thunderbolt. God doesn't want anyone to be poor!

Soon Oral was proclaiming his famous doctrine of seed-faith. Don't wait for something good to happen before you give to the Lord. Give money, especially to Brother Roberts, and God will multiply it back many times over.[7] Hundreds of other evangelists have adopted this seed-faith doctrine (calling it by other names), as well as Oral's ingenious methods of obtaining seed. Roberts's monthly letters to his millions of "prayer partners" are often accompanied by token gifts designed to involve the partner in a physical ritual that will encourage giving. Here are three typical items Oral has sent to his partners:

A prayer cloth with a print of Oral's magic right hand. Put your hand on the imprint, send money, and await your blessing.

A tiny bag of cement. Send it back, with a donation, so Oral can mix it with cement from others to symbolize cooperative faith in a building project.

A tiny sack of cornmeal. Pray over it and return it with cash. "I am going to have Evelyn mix the cornmeal . . . and bake for me God's representative of the body of Christ."⁸

Oral folded his circus-size healing tent when God told him to start preaching on radio and television. In the early sixties the Lord said to him, "Build Me a university." After ORU (Oral Roberts University) was completed in Tulsa, God told Oral to build beside it a City of Faith— a towering hospital that would combine prayer with medicine. Tulsa doctors opposed it on the sensible grounds that the city didn't need another hospital, but of course Oral had to obey the Lord. It was when he desperately required money to complete the edifice that he had his most spectacular vision:

> I felt an overwhelming holy presence all around me. When I opened my eyes, there He stood . . . some 900 feet tall, looking at me. . . . He stood a full 300 feet taller than the 600 foot tall City of Faith. There I was face to face with Jesus Christ, the Son of the Living God. I have only seen Jesus once before, but here I was face to face with the King of Kings. He stared at me without saying a word; Oh! I will never forget those eyes! And then, He reached down, put his Hands under the City of Faith, lifted it, and said to me, "See how easy it is for Me to lift it!"

The funds poured in—more than $5 million. Posters around Tulsa showed the City of Faith behind a warning sign: "Begin 900-foot Jesus Crossing." A few years later Oral collected another $5 million for a research center after announcing that his doctors were on the verge of a major cancer discovery.

Oral saw Jesus a third time in 1984 while recovering from surgery at the City of Faith. After the Lord left, Oral reported in his magazine *Abundant Life,* he spotted an angel in the corner of the room "so tall his head touched the ceiling." A full-page ad followed, offering a seven-inch angel figure in return for donations.

Roberts's empire started to crumble in 1985. Hospital patients were few, expenses were skyrocketing, and new electronic preachers were carving up the cash flow. Oral's television ratings dipped below those of Jimmy Swaggart and Robert Schuller. Oral closed his dental school. He gave his law school to Pat Robertson.

The next year Oral took an enormous public-relations risk. He said God told him he would be called home if he failed to raise $8 million by a certain date. A few weeks before the deadline, Oral revealed that during the night Satan had sneaked into his bedroom and tried to strangle him. Evelyn rushed in and persuaded the fiend to leave. Tulsa bumper stickers urged, "Send Oral to Heaven in 87."[9] Brother Roberts climbed his Prayer Tower to fast and pray. A few days later his life was spared by a $1.3 million check from a Florida dog-track owner.

Oral's handsome singing son Richard, who now has his own daily television show and conducts healing crusades around the world, is being groomed to take over the Roberts conglomerate.[10] Richard's first wife, Patti, who used to warble hymns with him on his father's show, has written in her book, *Ashes to Gold* (Word Books, 1983), about her distress in watching Richard turn into a clone of Oral, and the shameless way that she and Richard rationalized their jet-set ways of life. The Bible says a workman is worthy of his hire, Richard would remind her, and if an ox treads the grain it has a right to eat it. How about "The Lord is my shepherd, I shall not *want*"?[11]

There is a horror story in Patti's book. Before she and Richard left on their honeymoon, Oral summoned them to his study and began to weep. He had a dream, he said, in which God told him that if Patti and Richard ever left his ministry they would be killed in a plane crash.[12] After years of faking the feelings of a loving wife on television, Patti tells us, she divorced Richard, remarried, and is now living contentedly near Nashville. In 1977, the year Patti left the Roberts organization, Oral's own daughter Rebecca was killed in a plane crash.[13]

As soon as Brother Roberts came down from his Prayer Tower he had another revelation. God told him to build a $14-million healing center. Construction work has begun, and he and Richard are now pleading for funds to complete it. Last May, God told Oral to raise $1 billion, his largest request ever, as an endowment for ORU.[14]

Oral blundered again last June when he told a conference of charismatics at ORU that he had often raised the bodies of persons who died during a service. "I had to stop and go back in the crowd and raise the dead person so I could go ahead with the service." There are "dozens and dozens and dozens of documented instances," his son Richard added, of people resurrected by ministers. Oral also revealed that God has told him he will die or be raptured (see Note 22) before the Second Coming, but that he will return with Jesus to help rule the new earth, presumably from a throne in Tulsa. "Watch what happens to ORU when I get back," he said.

I grew up in Tulsa and have been a bemused Oral-watcher for many years. Friends there like to say, "Oral may be a charlatan, but he's *our* charlatan." True, his fundraising tactics are deceptive, and he often stretches the truth, but Oral is not a charlatan. He genuinely believes, I am convinced, that everything he says and does is part of God's plan for him to heal and save as many souls as possible before Jesus returns. Insecure feelings about his early poverty and lack of education mix with an awesome ego. Oral will never consider that when he hears the voice of God he is listening to himself, that when he builds a bigger monument it is a monument to himself. His visions are too childish to be fabrications. As his financial woes proliferate, his God-told-me's become more bizarre and self-destructive.

Richard Roberts is trying hard. Last July he sent his partners a tiny plastic bag of "anointed water" from the River of Life, an artificial stream that flows under the huge bronze praying hands near the City of Faith. Richard and his father had blessed the water by placing their palms on the river and praying. The water was then put in 50-gallon drums and sent to a factory for packaging.[15] Poor Richard is trapped. He couldn't leave even if he wanted to. The old man would disinherit him and die of a broken heart.

Jim and Tammy Bakker, top bananas in the still unrolling PTL burlesque show, met when they were students at a Bible college in Minneapolis. (PTL is supposed to stand for Praise the Lord and People That Love. Pass the Loot, Pay the Lady, and Pass the Lady are recent interpretations.) James Orson Bakker had gone there from Muskegon, Michigan, where his father was a machinist. Tammy Faye LaValley came from International Falls, Minnesota. Her Pentecostal mother had fought constantly with her unsaved father. After a divorce, the mother (with custody of Tammy and her younger brother) remarried and had six more children. They all lived in a ramshackle house with no bathtub and a privy in back. The family never went to doctors, relying instead on God's healing powers. When Tammy's dog Chi Chi died, she prayed in the Unknown Tongue and begged Jesus to raise Chi Chi from the dead. But God knew what was best, and after a few days Chi Chi had to be buried.

The Bible college forbade student marriages, so when Jim and Tammy took the vows, during their first year, they had to leave. Jim had no further education, but the Assemblies of God ordained him anyway. In 1965 he joined Pat Robertson's newly started Christian Broadcasting Network (CBN), now the largest cable network in the nation. For a while he and Tammy had a Christian puppet show, then Jim founded and hosted CBN's

"700 Club." (The name came from an early telethon that sought 700 pledges.)

In her autobiography, *I Gotta Be Me* (New Leaf Press, 1978),[16] Tammy is candid about her love-hate feeling for Pat. She loved him, but when "he would do certain things. . . . I built up a terrible, terrible resentment." Every time she and Jim consulted God's Word it fell open on Ezekiel 12:1-6, where God tells the prophet to take all his "stuff" and leave a "rebellious house." Jim and Tammy packed up their stuff and left, taking along their most valuable possession—trade secrets of the "700 Club." Tammy writes in her autobiography that she was devastated when Satan saw to it that their beloved puppets and all the tapes of their show were destroyed to prevent reruns.

Jim and Tammy first tried to get the PTL Club under way in California in collaboration with Pentecostal evangelist Paul Crouch and his wife, Jan, but the plan fell through when the two couples began to quarrel. In her autobiography Tammy tells of a vision she had during this turmoil. There were angels in robes, wearing helmets and carrying swords. Jesus stood "tall and straight with a helmet on his head and a sword in his hand. He wore the most beautiful white gown. Over the gown he had a beautiful blue sash that came down and covered his shoulders and fell to the floor. He spoke to me in an audible voice. 'Even as you stand here, My angels and I are going forth to do battle for you.' . . . That vision gave us the courage to live through the next three months."

Jim and Tammy finally got the "PTL Club" rolling in Charlotte, North Carolina. Modeled on Johnny Carson's "Tonight Show," PTL soon became the nation's most widely watched Christian talk show and vaudeville act, featuring chats with such famous born-again guests as Dale Evans, Pat Boone, and Charles Colson. Jim and Tammy frequently cried on camera, especially when they talked about how poor they were. Tammy's mascara dripped from her huge false eyelashes until she started using waterproof clown makeup.

In their autobiographies, Jim and Tammy weep on almost every page. Tammy doesn't just cry. She likes to write "I cried and cried" and "I sobbed and sobbed." In her book *Run to the Roar: The Way to Overcome Fear,* coauthored by Cliff Dudley with a foreword by Efrem Zimbalist, Jr. (New Leaf Press, 1980, p. 70), she "sobbed and sobbed and sobbed." When things are not going well, Jim often lies on the floor and sobs.

Jim's out-of-print autobiography *Move That Mountain!* (New Leaf, 1979) was written with Robert Paul Lamb, who also coauthored the autobiography of Bakker's enemy, Jimmy Swaggart. Jim and Tammy collaborated on *How We Lost Weight and Kept It Off!* (New Leaf, 1979). The book's foreword is by Pentecostals Pat and Shirley Boone. I haven't read this book, so I don't know whether Jim and Tammy wept or not when they lost weight.

The 60 blue telephones of Jim's telethons, which he ran about 200 times a year, were monitored by operators who took down pledges, reports of miracle cures, and prayer requests. Ailments were checked on alphabetized lists (arthritis to ulcers), then a computer would mail out responses. It's hard to believe, but millions of people actually think that when they get a letter with their name on top, signed in ink, the evangelist has written to them personally. The tens of thousands of letters that go daily to every prominent television evangelist are, of course, mechanically opened, sorted by the kinds of requests, then answered by computers with appropriate form letters. It's not dishonest, but then it's not exactly honest either, since the evangelist implies that he reads every letter. Oral Roberts once asked his partners to send photos of themselves so he could see what they looked like when he prayed for them. Can you imagine Brother Roberts studying each face in a million snapshots?

With the money that poured into PTL, Bakker built Heritage USA, his spectacular Jim-and-Tammy-Land theme park south of Charlotte.[17] We all know what happened to it, and to the weepy little minister with the Howdy Doody grin. Most PTL partners seem to be willing to forgive him for his fling with Jessica Hahn, but not for buying her silence with $265,000 stolen from their donations to the Lord, or for a style of life that made Oral and Richard look almost as poor as Jesus.

Unlike the Baker, when confronted by a Boojum in Lewis Carroll's *Hunting of the Snark,* the Bakkers are not likely to "softly and suddenly" disappear. They have hired the flamboyant attorney Melvin Belli to help them regain PTL ("like asking the fox back into the hen house," said Jerry Falwell), and a group of loyal PTL'ers have formed a BBB Club (Bring Back the Bakkers). The plan is for Bakker fans to put contributions in escrow, to be released only when Falwell turns the ministry back to Jim and Tammy. "Farewell Falwell," the loyalists like to chant. Meanwhile, the Bakkers have announced, from their home in Gatlinburg, Tennessee, that they hope to start another television ministry soon. We can all look forward to this new vaudeville act, and to court battles that may be even more bizarre than the Iran hearings.

Ollie North, by the way, is a charismatic and, according to the *New York Times* (July 11, 1987, p. 16), is claimed as a "friend of some years" by Pat Robertson, whom he asked to pray for him just before his secret trip to Iran. Although raised a Roman Catholic, Colonel North attends the Church of the Apostles, a charismatic Episcopal church in Fairfax, Virginia. A severe backache, he has often said, was once instantly healed when a charismatic friend prayed for him.

Oral Roberts's reaction to Brother Jim's downfall was another blunder. The Lord told him, he said, that the Devil was attacking a "young prophet of God" through an "unholy trio of forces." One of the trio was Jimmy Lee Swaggart, an Assemblies of God minister who for months had been trying to convince his denomination's elders that the Bakkers were a "cancer that needed to be excised from the body of Christ."

Swaggart, it has been noted, is as aptly named as Oral. Not since Billy Sunday has a soul saver done more swaggering about the podium, waving the Good Book, flailing his arms, perspiring, shouting, and telling a tearful audience, with hurtin' in his voice, that they will all go straight to perdition if they don't get right with Jesus. Between exhortations he pummels a piano, bouncing his right leg to his band's pounding Nashville beat, and belting out hymns that often make him cry. "King of Honky-Tonk Heaven," *Newsweek* called him.

Jimmy grew up in Ferriday, Louisiana, with his first cousin Jerry Lee Lewis, the rock singer who has been on such a sinful slide into booze, hard drugs, and seven miserable marriages. After Jimmy was baptized by the Holy Ghost at the age of nine, he reveals in his autobiography, *To Cross a River* (Jimmy Swaggart Ministries, 1984), he spoke almost nothing for days except the Unknown Tongue. He and cousin Jerry dropped out of high school to sing together professionally, but soon went their separate ways.

Jimmy's autobiography, like those of Roberts, Bakker, and Robertson, is filled with miraculous healings, bouts with Satan, Bible consulting, weeping, glossolalia, and the power of the Blood. On one occasion, Jesus healed Jimmy's "battered, blue Plymouth . . . held together with bailing wire" and about to expire from sticky valves. "Prayer was my only weapon," Jimmy writes. "If God could heal my sick body, surely He could repair my sick car." Jimmy took some anointing oil from his pocket and poured it over the car's silver ornament. When he started the car, it ran "like a new Singer sewing machine." Jimmy shouted, "Thank you, Jesus!" The valves were perfect when he sold the car a few months later.

Jimmy began preaching in the late fifties, when God told him he could also cut records of gospel songs. His success as both singer and televangelist has been extraordinary. With funds from donations and sales of recordings, he has built the imposing Jimmy Swaggart Ministries on 270 acres in Baton Rouge. The 12 buildings of this complex include a Jimmy Swaggart Bible College, a printing plant, and television and recording studios. Jimmy's income tops $140 million a year. Not even the IRS knows exactly where the money goes. He and his attractive wife, Frances, live in a $1.5-million house. Son Donnie is nearby in a $726,000 house. A desk for Frances (some 20 of Jimmy's relatives are on his payroll) cost $11,000.

As with all fundamentalists, Swaggart's ignorance of science is monumental. Most fundamentalists believe the universe was created about 10,000 years ago, but Jimmy knows better. The universe is indeed as old as astronomers say, but there is an enormous time gap between the first and second verses of Genesis. Before Adam, the earth was the locale of a prior creation over which Lucifer and his angels reigned before they rebelled and became demons. God destroyed this creation and tried again. Adam, Eve, and all the beasts we know were made in six days just as Genesis says. Other fundamentalists think the dinosaurs, too big to go on Noah's Ark, perished in the Flood. The old "gap theory" has them flourishing only in pre-Adamic times.[18]

Pentecostal preachers have come a long way from the days of Reverend Gerald L. K. Smith, when they could thunder against blacks, Jews, and Catholics. Like almost all of today's Pentecostal ministers, Swaggart professes nothing but great admiration for blacks, but Jews and Catholics are something else. In 1984 he displayed a picture of a Nazi death camp and implied that six million Jews would not have been exterminated had they accepted Jesus as Savior. "Don't ever bargain with Christ," Jimmy once said. "He's a Jew." As for Catholicism, it's a "false cult," and Catholics are "poor, pitiful individuals who think they have enriched themselves spiritually by kissing the Pope's ring." Saint Augustine's evil doctrines "caused millions to be lost." Mother Theresa, he assures us, is on her way to hell. "None of the things [she] does will add one thing toward her salvation."[19]

We come now to Marion Gordon (Pat) Robertson, the best educated of all electronic Pentecostal preachers. He seems modest enough, and well informed when he talks quietly about economics and politics, then suddenly, still smiling, he says something idiotic. Pat is the son of a U.S. senator from Virginia, a Phi Beta Kappa graduate of Washington and Lee, a former Marine officer and Golden Gloves boxer, and a graduate of Yale Law School. His autobiography, *Shout it from the Housetops* (Bridge, 1972), tells how he and his wife, Dede, had been sophisticated New York swingers before Pat was converted during a lunch in Philadelphia with a Dutch minister.

In no time at all Pat was opening his Bible at random for divine guidance, listening to the voice of God, and telling Satan to vamoose. After attending several fundamentalist schools he was finally ordained a Southern Baptist, though essentially he's a neo-Pentecostal. His baptism by the Holy Spirit occurred when his son had a fever. Pat prayed, the fever broke, and while Pat was praising Jesus his speech became garbled. Out poured the Unknown Tongue, sounding (he writes) like an African dialect. When Dede later received the baptism, her glossolalia sounded French.

There was a time when Pat, taking seriously Jesus' advice to the rich young man, actually sold all his possessions and gave the money to the poor. It was not until after years of living in rat-infested apartments that this spectacular seed-sowing began to work. God first instructed him to buy a defunct radio station. Later he acquired a television station and hired Jim Bakker. Now his Christian Broadcasting Network (CBN) has its headquarters on 685 acres in Virginia Beach, in a complex of colonial-style buildings that include CBN University and a Georgian mansion in which Pat and Dede live rent-free. They also have a country house in Hot Springs, Virginia. Selling all your goods seems to be a one-time thing.

Like Brother Bakker and Richard Roberts, Pat practices the shotgun technique of healing—much simpler than the laying on of hands. God gives him a "word of knowledge" about the afflictions of unnamed people. With millions of viewers he is sure to score many lucky hits. Those who are hit report their miracle cures and make generous donations. If an interviewer likes the way they talk, they may be invited to appear on the show to give stirring testimonies.

Dick Dabney, in a fascinating article about Robertson in *Harper's* (August 1980), quotes this chilling sample of Pat's healing technique:

> There is a woman in Kansas City who has sinus. The Lord is drying that up right now. Thank you, Jesus. There is a man with a financial need—I think a hundred thousand dollars. That need is being met right now, and within three days, the money will be supplied through the miraculous power of the Holy Spirit. Thank you, Jesus! There is a woman in Cincinnati with cancer of the lymph nodes. I don't know whether it's been diagnosed yet, but you haven't been feeling well, and the Lord is dissolving that cancer right *now!* There is a lady in Saskatchewan in a wheelchair—curvature of the spine. The Lord is straightening that out right now, and you can stand up and walk! Just claim it and it's yours. Stand up and walk. Thank you, Jesus! Amen, and amen!

Dabney reports an occasion on which Pat's sidekick, the tall, handsome, silver-haired black Ben Kinchlow, dashed up to Pat to tell him a lady had just phoned to say she had decided to "go all the way" and give the "700 Club" all the money she was spending for cancer medicine—$120 a month. She had previously been giving half of her limited income to the club. "Three days later," said Ben, "—get this!—from an entirely unexpected source she got a check for three thousand dollars!"

"Praise God!" exclaimed Brother Robertson. "Let's give God a hand!" While the studio audience applauded, Pat added, "And I won't be surprised if God doesn't do something about that cancer, too."[20]

Pat's sin of pride, the pride of willful ignorance, has grown with CBN. His powers now rival Saint Peter's. In China he once preached in English and his listeners, he says, all heard him in their native dialects, just like on the day of Pentecost (see Note 3). A woman in California listened to Pat say that someone had broken an ankle and God was healing it. Her ankle was instantly okay. The awkward fact is she had been watching a rerun—Pat actually spoke his lines *before* the woman broke her ankle. Healing future accidents, Pat writes, happens often in his ministry.

On at least three occasions the prayers of Pat and his associates have saved CBN headquarters from damage by a killer hurricane. In *Beyond Reason* (William Morrow, 1984), he tells how they diverted hurricane Betsy from Virginia Beach. Two years later they did it again with another violent storm. "Since that time," Pat wrote in 1984, "not one single hurricane has returned to the region." Unfortunately, hurricane Gloria threatened the town in 1985, but it, too, politely moved away after Pat said, "In the name of Jesus I command you to stop."

Pat's autobiography (written with Jamie Buckingham, foreword by Pat Boone) is filled with funny anecdotes, but none funnier than the time Satan "appeared" to him and tried to persuade him that back in his college days he had committed the unpardonable sin by telling a blasphemous joke. Pat finally was able to banish the Devil, but "It took days to completely recover." When Pat first started CBN his devout mother telephoned to say she had a vision from God in which she saw bank notes floating down from heaven into Pat's hands. When CBN University opened in 1979, Ed Meese was the principal speaker.

Some things Pat doesn't write about are in Gerard Straub's eye-opening book *Salvation for Sale* (Prometheus, rev. ed. 1988). Straub was producer of the "700 Club" until he became disenchanted and was fired over his affair with an employee. He tells of an occasion in 1980 when Pat was about to be interviewed by Tom Brokaw. NBC carelessly left a copy of questions Tom was going to ask Pat on a desk, and Straub managed to swipe it. Pat was delighted. He studied the questions, formulated careful replies, and gave a brilliant performance. Not once did he consider this unethical. Next day, during a prayer meeting, he proudly told his staff how Brother Gerry had boldly invaded the enemy camp and snatched the document.

Although Straub is no longer a fundamentalist, when he started working for Pat he was a devout Pentecostal and a skilled tongue speaker. He now believes that anyone can learn to glossolate, and, like bicycle riding, once you learn you never lose the knack. He noticed that Pat never varied the way he spoke in tongues—the same words kept coming up but in different order. "If God really were the giver of this gift," Straub writes, "he would have done better." Straub is convinced that for many the gift is little more than an act. "I believe the result—not the aim—of tongues is to create a closed community, a cult."

Straub's wildest revelation concerns a 1979 CBN plan known as GSP (God's Secret Project). It was nothing less than to televise the Second Coming. Pat is convinced that recent events involving Israel prove that Jesus is about to return. Not only that, but CBN's ministry is hastening that glorious event by carrying the gospel "into all the world" (Mark 16:15), something that couldn't be done before the electronic age.

When Straub listened to a tape he had made of a conversation with his boss about televising the Parousia, he couldn't believe he had once taken the plan seriously:

> The greatest show on earth was in our hands. I wondered where we would put the cameras. Jerusalem was the obvious place. We even discussed how Jesus' radiance might be too bright for the cameras and how we would have to make adjustments for that problem. Can you imagine telling Jesus, "Hey, Lord, please tone down your luminosity; we're having a problem with contrast. You're causing the picture to flare". . . . The tape indicated that I had some doubts about the Second Coming and Rapture stuff, but my love and concern for these men made the plan seem not odd. . . . Clinically, this would be called paranoid-schizophrenia with delusions of grandeur. . . But at CBN it was normal.

Still, I find it easier to believe than a story Pat himself relates in *Beyond Reason*. One Sunday, after services, when he was assistant pastor of a church in Mount Vernon, New York, a 12-year-old girl ran out of the entrance into the street and was killed by a car. Next day, Pat and his congregation prayed that the child would rise from the dead. The girl's body, lying in an open casket, had been embalmed.

Here then is a man who wants to be president and has the support of Jimmy Swaggart and millions of other Pentecostals. He believes that God, hearing his prayer, can revivify a corpse. Did not Jesus call Lazarus from the grave after his body (as Martha said) "stinketh"? Did he not turn water into wine? It would be no great thing—after all, a miracle is a miracle—for Jesus to resurrect the poor girl and turn her embalming fluid into blood of the right blood type.

Pat sees nothing unusual or funny about this incident. "She did not rise," he concludes solemnly, "and we buried her on Tuesday."

Earlier we considered some of the national political implications of the fundamentalist revival. Although Robertson has no chance of getting the Republican nomination for president, the loyalty of his followers may exert a strong influence on whom the Republicans choose. Perhaps even more disturbing are the subtle pressures on foreign policy that flow from the universal belief of fundamentalists that the Second Coming is near at hand. "I firmly expect to be alive when Jesus Christ comes back to earth," Robertson writes in his *Answers to 200 of Life's Most Probing Questions* (Thomas Nelson, 1984).[21] Here is how he outlines the grim scenario.

The Bible's prophecies about the Second Coming began to be fulfilled with the establishment of Israel. The Jews are still God's chosen people, and before Jesus returns they will convert in large numbers to Christianity. Robertson's passionate support of Israel, like that of Falwell and most other fundamentalists, rests on biblical prophecy and nothing more. Robertson's television station in Lebanon, the "Voice of Hope," blasts out a steady stream of anti-Arab rhetoric.

Before Jesus returns the world will experience a Great Tribulation, a time of economic and political chaos. Satan's counterfeit Jesus, the Antichrist, will take over—"the most hideous example," writes Pat, "of dictatorial power the world has ever known." No one will be able to buy or sell without the Number of the Beast, 666, stamped on a hand or forehead. Robertson urges the stockpiling of food for the terrible times just ahead. He wrote the foreword to Jim McKeever's *The Almighty and the Dollar* (Omega, 1980), a survivalist book that tells believers how to take advantage of the coming financial panic.

The Battle of Armageddon, almost surely a nuclear holocaust, will engulf the planet. Only the arrival of Christ will restore peace. The faithful will be "raptured"—caught up in the air to meet the Savior—and for the next thousand years, the Millennium, Jesus will rule the earth.[22] Why does he tarry? So the electronic ministry can reach as many sinners as possible before it is too late. It is not mere fantasy to contemplate the possibility of a Pentecostal in the Oval Office, who accepts the above scenario, who hears and obeys direct orders from Jehovah, and whose finger is on the nuclear button.

There is a more plausible possibility. As the flames of fundamentalism leap higher, there will be a growing subliminal longing among believers for provoking Armageddon. The war is inevitable, so let's get it over with, and maybe we shall be among those who escape death by being levitated above the clouds. As go public sentiments, so talk our politicians. You'll find Reagan's pronouncements about Armageddon collected in Grace Halsell's frightening *Prophecy and Politics: Militant Evangelists on the Road to Nuclear War* (Lawrence Hill, 1986). "We may be the generation that sees Armageddon," the president said in 1980 on Bakker's PTL show. "Jerry, I sometimes believe we're heading very fast for Armageddon," he told his friend Falwell in 1981. Here are some remarks Reagan made at a 1971 dinner:

> Everything is falling into place. It can't be too long now. Ezekiel says that fire and brimstone will be rained upon the enemies of God's people. That must mean that they'll be destroyed by nuclear weapons. They exist now, and they never did in the past.
>
> Ezekiel tells us that Gog, the nation that will lead all of the other powers of darkness against Israel, will come out of the north. Biblical scholars have been saying for generatons that Gog must be Russia. What other powerful nation is to the north of Israel? None. But it didn't seem to make sense before the Russian revolution, when Russia was a Christian country. Now it does, now that Russia has become communistic and atheistic, now that Russia has set itself against God. Now it fits the description of Gog perfectly.

Was Reagan voicing his own beliefs or just shrewdly currying fundamentalist favor? In any case, let us all pray that if the presidential nominees of 1988 feel compelled to make similar noises, none of them will believe what they are saying.

Notes

1. Jerry Falwell founded Thomas Road Baptist Church in Lynchburg, Virginia, the right-wing Moral Majority (now called the Liberty Federation), and Liberty University. His "Old Time Gospel Hour" televises his Sunday sermons over some 350 stations. A noncharismatic, Falwell takes a dim view of tongues speaking and faith healing. Jesus advised going into a closet to pray, but Falwell allowed *People* magazine (June 15, 1987) to photograph him kneeling at the foot of his bed, his praying hands above a Bible, while a poodle on the bed listens intently.

2. Robert Schuller is a noncharismatic minister of the Reformed Church in America, with misty doctrinal views as hard to pin down as those of his mentor Norman Vincent Peale. Instead of Peale's positive thinking, Schuller calls it "possibility thinking," but it's the same thing. Avoid negative thoughts, trust God, and you'll be healthy, happy, and make lots of money. Like Peale, he has written dozens of breezy books peppered with such snappy slogans as "Turn your scars into stars" and "It takes guts to leave the ruts." His mammoth Crystal Cathedral, in Garden Grove, California, has 10,000 windows of mirror glass. It is filled with flowers, fountains, chirping canaries, and the world's largest pipe organ. There is a vast drive-in theater where worshippers can "Come as you are in a family car" to enjoy the services on a jumbo television screen.

Schuller once sent his contributors a letter saying "I am here!" along with a photo of himself in front of the Great Wall of China. The letter was dictated before the trip. For the picture, he stood in front of an enlarged photo of the Wall. When Ted Koppel, on "Nightline," asked Schuller what he thought of Oral Roberts's death threat, Schuller responded with a speech about the power of positive thinking. It was, commented Koppel, the longest, most elegant evasion he had ever heard.

Schuller doesn't like to beg for money. He will offer free gifts, such as a tiny crystal cross, in return for the recipient's "positive support" of his ministry. Such low-key requests bring in about $35 million a year.

3. Glossolalia should be distinguished from heteroglossolalia and xenoglossolalia. The second chapter of Acts has been interpreted by Bible scholars in two ways. If the disciples spoke in languages they did not know but that were understood by listeners, the phenomenon is xenoglossolalia, or the Gift of Tongues, to distinguish it from talking in an Unknown Tongue. Since apostolic times many claims have been made about saints speaking natural languages they did not know. The most notable instances are said to have occurred in the sixteenth century when the Spanish Jesuit missionary Saint Francis Xavier preached to the heathen. Persons who claim under hypnosis to recall a previous incarnation and speak a language they profess never to have learned provide other examples of xenoglossolalia.

Another interpretation of what happened on the day of Pentecost is that the disciples spoke their own language but listeners *heard* the preaching in their native tongues. This is called heteroglossolalia. As mentioned earlier, Pat Robertson claims to have been given this gift when he preached in China.

4. Oral's opinions about glossolalia are detailed in his three-volume work *The Holy Spirit in the Now* (1974), and in an earlier book *The Baptism with the Holy Spirit and the Value of Speaking in Tongues Today* (1964). Although Oral began to speak in what he calls the "prayer language of the Spirit" soon after his Baptism by the Spirit, he did not realize its importance until much later when he was walking in an open field and suddenly began to glossolate. After he finished, he was startled to hear himself continuing in English. It was God interpreting what he had just said in the unintelligible language. Since then Oral has urged everyone, immediately after praying in tongues, to ask God for an interpretation.

The early Pentecostals—rural, poor, uneducated—also practiced the gift of being unharmed by serpent venom and other poisons (Mark 16:18). This gift is downplayed by today's Pentecostals, and some states even have laws against snake-handling and poison-drinking. Oral's view is that when Mark speaks of "serpents" he really means "enemies," and that poison won't kill you only if you drink it by accident. (See *The Baptism with the Holy Spirit,* Chapter 2.)

5. Among several biographies of Oral Roberts, the most recent, most accurate, and best documented is *Oral Roberts: An American Life* (Indiana University Press, 1985), an objective, impressive study by David Harrell, Jr., a historian at the University of Alabama. The strongest critical attacks are in two out-of-print books: James Morris's *The Preachers* (St. Martin's, 1973) and Jerry Sholes's *Give Me That Prime-Time Religion* (Hawthorn, 1979).

6. How does Oral recognize possession by demons? "First I feel God's presence, usually through my hand, then I catch the breath of a person—it will have a stench as of a body that has been decayed. Then I notice the eyes. They're—they're like snake eyes." During one of Oral's wild exorcisms in Brazil, he tells us, a demon levitated a woman in midair, "horizontally between me and the audience."

The first quotation is from John Kobler's interview, "Oral Roberts: King of the Faith Healers," *American Magazine* (May 1956). Similar statements can be found in many of Oral's books. His account of the levitated Brazilian woman is in the second volume of *The Holy Spirit in the Now,* page 70.

7. For a while Oral actually promised to refund a donation if the giver didn't get it back in some miraculous way by the end of a year, but he soon wisely dropped the offer. On the doctrine of seed-faith see his *Miracles of Seed-Faith* (Oral Roberts Evangelistic Association, 1970). *God's Formula for Success and Prosperity,* another of more than 50 books by Oral, is mainly about persons who gave seed money to Oral, then got much more back from unexpected sources.

8. Among the many other free gifts offered by Oral to his partners was a "little alabaster box" holding a "precious vial" of anointing oil that he had blessed. When one of his associates suggested he save time by praying "symbolically" over just a few cartons, Oral was indigant. "If I did that, then the ones I prayed over would be the only ones that actually would work." Nobody in the room, Jerry Sholes reports in his book about Oral, snickered. On another occasion Oral offered a tiny piece of an old rug from his prayer room—a rug

he had worn out by 16 years of trampling and kneeling.

Oral once sent his partners a letter with a blue outline of his magic right hand. "Put the drawing . . . on any part of you that's hurting. Place it in your billfold to help in financial need." After that, write your needs on the drawing and mail it back with some money. "I will literally lay my right hand on exactly what you want and begin to pray for GOD'S MIRACULOUS ANSWER TO YOUR NEEDS."

Less imaginative freebies included gold-filled pins that said "Jesus heals," wafers for a simultaneous communion at 2:00 P.M. on a certain day, a coin from Israel, a jigsaw puzzle of Oral on a horse. Sometimes Oral offered more expensive gifts for sale: a coffee mug with "Expect a Miracle" on it, an album of his son's gospel songs, and his big *Commentary on the Bible* with the partner's name in gold on the cover.

No one has learned better from Oral how to mooch money from followers than Reverend Ike, Manhattan's handsome black minister. Ike long ago dropped all pretense of saving sinners to concentrate on giving them "green power," the power of money. I quote from a letter he sent to his partners on January 3, 1984:

> In this letter you will find a . . . blessed red "token string." Take that . . . string in your hand and hold it while you read this letter. My eyes are filled with tears of joy as I write. . . . I was working and praying for you this morning in my Prayer Tower, and I felt in my heart that you needed some special prayer work done. . . .
>
> As I prayed, the Holy Spirit led me to see the special things you need. . . . Put this special blessed red "token string" in your window. . . . Leave it in the window overnight. Then mail it back to me with a faith donation. The spirit of the Good Lord has spoken that I must put this same blessed red "token string" in my Prayer Tower after you have mailed the red "token string" and donation back to me. And then you will receive the new blessings of health, happiness, love, success, prosperity and More Money—according to your faith.
>
> Don't keep this blessed red "token string" in your home longer than overnight (Joshua 2:12,18). Get it out of your home tomorrow not later than 8:37 P.M. Then believe and expect miracles. . . . Rush this blessed red "token string" back to me by tomorrow, along with a faith donation of $27 or more. . . .

9. The bumper sticker was a play on the words of Oral's many earlier slogans. "Miracles from Heaven in 77" was his motto for the year in which he started building the City of Faith. The following year it was "God Won't be Late in 78," which was followed by "Miracles Will Be Mine in 79."

10. In his autobiography, *He's the God of a Second Chance!* (Oral Roberts Evangelistic Association, 1985), Richard tells how his healing ministry started in 1980, a few months after his second marriage. At the close of a preaching service, God suddenly gave him the "word of knowledge" (another gift of Pentecost; see 1 Corinthians 12:8), and he blurted out "Lord, heal that man's toe." Later he received a letter from a man who had been in the audience. He said he had felt his broken toe pop, and when he got home the toe was as good as new. Before the year ended, Richard was healing the deaf, blind, and lame.

Oral still generates low comedy, but somehow Richard's polished performances—smiling, self-assured, oozing with sincerity—are more sad than funny. Tune in on his morning cable hour and you'll see him close his eyes as he gets the "word of knowledge." ("It's like a pop or a ring . . . in my ears," he explained to a reporter in 1981). The periodicals of Roberts's ministry now bristle with details about Richard's miraculous cures. Like his father, he claims that through his preaching God has instantly healed cataracts. A cataract is the clouding of an eye lens. There has never been a case of such a lens becoming unclouded. This would be comparable to a fried egg uncooking itself. It is easy to understand why Oral has found it difficult to keep competent doctors on the staff of his City of Faith.

11. Richard and Oral golf at Tulsa's most expensive country club. They drive luxury cars, wear costly clothes, and own palatial homes in Tulsa and California. The closet in Richard's Tulsa house is 432 square feet. Nobody attacked conspicuous waste more stridently than Jesus, not to mention his use of whips to drive money changers from the temple,

but rich Christians have always found marvelous ways to evade the Savior's unambiguous remarks. I recall a cartoon by Art Young that showed a minister at a blackboard explaining to his wealthy congregation how to put a camel through a needle's eye. First you run the beast through a meat grinder.

12. On Phil Donahue's television show, April 28, 1987, Patti begged Phil not to read this passage from her book, but he read it anyway.

13. In 1982 God or Fate (or Satan?) struck again. Roberts's oldest son Ronald, the best educated of his four children—he spoke five languages and almost got a doctorate from that heathen university, Stanford—shot himself through the heart. Ronnie had doubts about his father's theology and had refused to work at ORU because Oral insisted he shave his beard and stop smoking. He was running an antique store in Tulsa at the time of his suicide and for many years had been hooked on drugs and alcohol.

14. In 1985, in *Charisma Magazine,* Oral said God had told him never to seek an endowment for ORU because big endowments cause a university to lose its faith. Apparently God changed his mind. Oral hasn't said how long it will take to raise the billion, or what will happen to him if he doesn't get it.

15. Richard's letter, sent along with about a million bags of anointed water, advised his partners to "cut open your bag . . . and anoint something that is symbolic of your need. Anoint your billfold if you have a financial need; anoint your body if you have a physical need. Anoint yourself right over your heart if you have a spiritual need."

John Erling, a Tulsa radio-show host, became suspicious. Did the anointed water really come from the River of Life? He had samples analyzed and was told that the acid content of the water in the river differed from that of the water in the bags. When he reported this on his radio show, Richard was furious. He told the press that purifying chemicals had been added to the river after he and his father blessed it and that this explained the difference in acidity. (See the *Tulsa World,* June 11 and 12, 1987, and the *Tulsa Tribune,* June 11.)

One of Richard's earlier gifts to his partners was a small bag of stones with these instructions: "Take the bag of stones I have sent you that represent your wall of problems crumbling before you and walk on them just as the Israelites walked over the crumbled wall of Jericho. . . . As you walk over these stones as a point of contact and return them to me, God is going to use this seemingly foolish way to bring the answers to your life."

16. Tammy's autobiography was written with Cliff Dudley, former manager of Consolidated Foods Corporation, and later Sales Director of Moody Press. He has coauthored numerous books by Pentecostals, and now heads New Leaf Press, in Green Forest, Arizona. The book has a foreword by Gary Paxton, a now-forgotten country and rock singer. It was Tammy's fondness for Gary that forced her jealous husband, so he claims, to lust for other women. Does Tammy have a moustache? "No," Gary answers in his playful foreword. "The moustache she wears sometimes is definitely phony. . . . We all love you. Yours in Christ, Gary Paxton."

17. For a faith donation of a thousand dollars PTL partners were promised three nights a year free in Heritage's Grand Hotel. No smoking or drinking, but one can enjoy such diversions as visiting Billy Graham's boyhood home (Jim had it moved to Heritage USA), getting healed in the Upper Room, attending communion, and watching baptisms. You can also enjoy such sports as tennis, horseback riding, camping, and a waterpark with a 52-foot water slide. Shops along a cobblestoned Main Street carry Pentecostal literature, dolls that sing "Jesus loves me," and Tammy's own line of cosmetics and panty hose. You can watch an Easter Passion Play with a crucifixion that has plenty of stage blood and a Jesus whose robes glow under black light as He ascends to Heaven in a puff of smoke.

18. The gap theory of creation was popularized early in the century by the notes on Genesis in the *Scofield Reference Bible* (1909), still a favorite annotated Bible among fundamentalists of all varieties. For Swaggart's defense of the theory, see his *The Pre-Adamic Creation and Evolution,* on cassette tapes available from the Jimmy Swaggart Ministries, and his booklet *The Pre-Adamic Creation and Evolution* (1986).

Jimmy's self-admiration is so enormous that, although he never finished high school, he considers himself an expert on science and Bible criticism. Moreover, any Christian (all Catholics, for instance) who disagrees with his own special blend of primitive Biblicism is in Jimmy's egocentric eyes under the influence of the Arch Fiend.

19. Jimmy Swaggart's main attack on Catholicism is his hardcover book *Catholicism and Christianity* (Jimmy Swaggart Ministries, 1986). "To be brutally frank," he writes (p. 16), "I am sure there must be *some* priests *some*where who do have some Bible knowledge, but I have never met one personally. . . . Sadly, it would do little good if they were given Bible training, simply because *most priests are not saved*!" (his italics).

In Jimmy's grim theology very, very few people are saved, not even Catholics. "The whole world is going to hell with hundreds of millions dying without Christ," he wrote in his monthly periodical *The Evangelist* (August 1987). "Still, we spend hundreds of millions on waterslides, resort hotels, time-share apartments, and nonproductive 'entertainment.' . . . Look at the Catholic church. They are engaged in almost every charitable activity known to man—while they simultaneously lead hundreds of millions to hell. They want the public to admire them (and this is fostered by Satan) for their good works. And all the while they proclaim doctrines that are in complete opposition to the Word of God."

Jimmy knows, of course, precisely what God's Word is. Like Oral Roberts, he can say, "I know that I know that I know that I know." What about fundamentalists who do not believe in today's tongues speaking? If they are born again, Jimmy allows they are saved, but (he adds in the same issue of his magazine cited above) "our differences are great, and the chasm is wide, and there is very little room for fellowship. Love, yes; friendship, no."

Although much of the issue is devoted to attacking the PTL for its "immorality, greed, avarice, hyprocisy, and more," Jimmy's attitude toward noncharismatic fundamentalism is typical of his Pentecostal brethren. It explains why so many PTL partners opposed Falwell's control of the ministry.

20. In 1986 the *Chicago Tribune* ran a cartoon showing the ever-smiling Pat, arm upraised, saying ". . . and, Lord, there is a massive case of hemorrhoids that you are healing *now!*" In the next panel a lightning bolt strikes the lectern with a "Voomp!" No sign of Pat.

21. There is not an original idea in this appalling volume. To give some notion of how quaint and dated Pat's fundamentalist views are, consider his answer to that hoary conundrum, "Where did Cain get his wife?" Cain obviously married a sister, Pat writes, "otherwise, there would have been no way for mankind to replenish the earth." Permit me to pass on a better answer. In those days, the Bible tells us, people lived for hundreds of years. If Cain had waited only a few generations he would have had thousands of distant relatives to pick from.

Initially, there would have been incest, but Genesis 4:16-17 says that Cain went to the land of Nod, where he found a wife and built a city. As Saint Augustine reasons in "The City of God" (Book 15): "Who then can doubt that during the lifetime of one man the human race might be so multiplied that there would be a population to build and occupy not one but several cities." See chapter 18 of my *Magic Numbers of Dr. Matrix* (Prometheus, 1985), where Dr. Matrix estimates the population at the time of Abel's murder to be about half a million.

22. The word *rapture* is not in the Bible. Most fundamentalists believe that before the Second Coming, when Jesus arrives visibly on Earth to reign during the Millennium, there will be a prior invisible coming during which the saints (true believers) will be instantly caught up in the air to be with Jesus. Presumably terrible car and airplane crashes will occur when born-again drivers and pilots suddenly vanish.

Almost all fundamentalists today are "premillennialists" who believe the rapture and Second Coming will precede the Millennium. A minority of "postmillennialists" expect Jesus to return in glory *after* the Millennium. Will the rapture occur before or after the Great Tribulation of seven years? On this question premillennialists divide into three groups. The largest, the "pretribulationists," expect the rapture any time now, before the tribulation. This includes Roberts, Swaggart, and Falwell. In his *Drama of the End Time* (1961), Oral's fullest account of how he interprets Biblical prophecy about the Second Coming, he writes:

If it is true that the Bride must go through the Tribulation, I pray, let me not live till Jesus comes. Let me die before the Rapture. Then I shall, by death, escape the Tribulation and have part in the First Resurrection. Let me die now, if the storm of the Tribulation is about to break! If the saints must go through the Tribulation, then the only way that the Lord of glory has of delivering His people, will be by death. God forbid.

But thank God, the saints are *not* going to have to go through the Tribulation but are scheduled to go up before it begins!

"Midtribulationists" put the rapture in the middle of the tribulation, and "post-tribulationists," after. The Seventh-Day Adventists are posters. Pat Robertson shares their time schedule. Unlike the Adventists, however, he believes that before the tribulation there will be a great revival of faith all over the world, and possibly the election of a U.S. president who has been baptized by the Holy Spirit. In a Dallas speech in 1984 Pat actually said:

What's coming next? . . . I want you to think of a world (with) . . . a school system . . . where humanism isn't taught anymore and people sincerely believe in the living God . . . a world in which there are no more abortions . . . juvenile delinquency is virtually unknown . . . the prisons are virtually empty . . . there's dignity because people love the Lord Jesus Christ.

And I want you to imagine a society where the church members have taken dominion over the forces of the world, where Satan's power is bound by the people of God, and where there is no more disease and where there's no more demon possession. . . .

We're going to see a society where the people are living Godly, moral lives, and where the people of God . . . will have so much that they will lend to others but they will not have to borrow . . . and the people of God are going to be the most honored people in society . . . no drug addiction . . . pornographers no longer have any access to the public whatsoever . . . there's a Spirit-filled President in the White House, the men in the Senate and the House of Representatives are Spirit-filled and worship Jesus, and the Judges do the same. . . .

You say, that's a description of the Millennium when Jesus comes back . . . (but) these things . . . can take place now in this time . . . and they are going to because I am persuaded that we are standing on the brink of the greatest spiritual revival the world has ever known! . . . hundreds of millions of people are coming into the kingdom . . . in the next several years.

. . . we've got to understand the nature of prosperity and prepare for what God's going to do . . . God is going to put us in positions of leadership and responsibility and we've . . . got to think that way . . . you mark my words, in the next year, two years . . . the next three or four, we're going to see things happen that will absolutely boggle our minds! Praise God!

I quote from Jimmy Swaggart's magazine *The Evangelist* (September 1986). Although Swaggart has endorsed Robertson's bid for the presidency, he strongly disagrees with Pat's expectation of a great religious upwelling before the tribulation. Note that Pat's time frame of one to four years after 1984 ends in 1988, the year Pat hopes to become president. Such an event truly boggles the mind.

All three groups—pre-, mid-, and post-tribulationists—expect the tribulation to be almost upon us, with the excellent possibility that they or their offspring will be raptured. "I don't think my children will live their full lives out," Falwell has declared, and it is said that he is proud of not owning a burial plot. "In my opinion, there is no way we can make it to the year 2000," he declared in a 1983 broadcast on "Nuclear War and the Second Coming of Christ," adding, "I really believe Jesus is coming first."

Such hopes surely contribute to the indifference of Falwell and others on the fundamentalist political right toward the nation's rising national debt. Why worry if we and/or our children will soon be taken into the clouds to be with the Lord forever?

Afterword

In September 1987, Oral Roberts sent out a special pamphlet titled: "The Media Have Had Their Say. Now the Truth." It is his reply to what he calls the lies of the media. God did not, he says, tell him, "If you don't raise eight million dollars, I'll kill you." What God actually said was that if he (Oral) didn't raise eight million for his overseas healing teams, he would call him home.

Oral denies he said he had raised people from the dead. It is God, through him, who does the work. He retells the story of the dead baby brought to life and how a thousand people stood up to accept Christ after witnessing this miracle. He reminds his readers that Jesus commanded his disciples to "heal the sick, cleanse the lepers, raise the dead. . . ." (Matthew 10:8). "What I have claimed is that the resurrection power of Jesus Christ has flowed through the human vessel of Oral Roberts at times in my crusade services, and at such times I have seen the dead raised in my ministry." He is glad the media picked up on what he said because "all over the world now people are talking about God raising the dead. I praise God that they are!"

As for his homes, the investment on his Tulsa house was $150,000 in 1960, but it is not *his* house. It belongs to ORU, and he is "required" to live there as the president. The only property he and his wife own is their $285,000 house in Southern California. They get a combined salary from ORU of $98,000 a year. Richard and his wife have a combined annual salary of $96,000. It is not their choice to live in large homes, Oral says, but necessary because of their positions. "As for our personal choice, both Richard and I would live in a smaller house . . . but that would not serve the best interest of the ministry at this time."

"To be perfectly frank with you," Oral writes, "the PTL scandal has hit us like a freight train. Financially I underestimated its effect on us. . . . Our income is down at least a third."

When the adultery revelation came out, Oral says, he went to Jim and Tammy's home to pray for them. Jim knelt on the floor "and I've never seen a man weep more uncontrollably." When he later heard about Jim's excessive salary, he phoned to ask if it was true. "Yes," said Jim. "But, Oral, I earned it." Oral replied by telling Jim he earned more in one year than he (Oral) had received in the past 20 years. Oral says he has publicly apologized to the Assemblies of God and to Jimmy Swaggart for unkind remarks he made before he knew the awful truth about Jim and Tammy's income. Oral forgot to say his previous false judgments had been preceded by the statement that they came directly from God. Evidently either God can give Oral false information or Oral can think he is hearing God when he isn't.

32 | L. Ron Hubbard

For 35 years I believed that L. Ron Hubbard, founder of Scientology, was no more than a writer of mediocre fiction who, lusting for power and money, became one of the world's most successful mountebanks. Russell Miller's admirable, meticulously documented biography, *Bare-Faced Messiah: The True Story of L. Ron Hubbard* (Henry Holt, 1988), has persuaded me otherwise. Hubbard was a deeply disturbed man—a pathological liar who steadily deteriorated from a charming rogue into a paranoid egomaniac "unable to distinguish," as Miller puts it, "between fact and his own fantastic fiction."

Almost everything Ron ever said about himself was false. He was never a swashbuckling explorer or distinguished naval officer. Although he claimed to be a physicist, his knowledge of science was negligible. His father, a lieutenant-commander in the United States Navy, had hoped his son would pursue a similar career, but near-sightedness kept Ron out of Annapolis. His only education was in the engineering school of George Washington University, where he dropped out after two years of dismal grades.

During the ten years preceding the Second World War, Ron became one of the nation's most industrious contributors to western, mystery, and adventure pulp fiction. His four years in the wartime Navy are summed up in a fitness report saying he "lacked essential qualities of leadership . . . not considered qualified for command or promotion." The closest he came to combat was while in command of a submarine chaser. On its shakedown cruise Hubbard mistook a magnetic deposit for submarines, and his battle against the nonexistent enemy cost him his command. Assigned to a ship on its way to a war zone, he at once applied for and obtained transfer to a school at Princeton. "Far from being a hero," Miller concludes, Hubbard was a "malingering coward who had done his best to avoid seeing action."

Ron's record as husband, father and bigamist was even more deplorable.

This review appeared in *Nature,* vol. 331, January 14, 1988, and is reprinted with permission.

He deserted his first wife, Polly Grubb, and their two children to marry Sara Northrop. They met in the "temple" of Jack Parsons, an addlepated California chemical-propulsion expert who secretly practiced black magic. A firm believer in witchcraft, Parsons had become a devoted disciple of England's "Beast 666," the notorious satanist Aleister Crowley. Hubbard, Parsons informed his "Blessed Father," was a kindred spirit eager to assist in blasphemous rituals. Ron left the temple with Parsons's young mistress, Sara. A few years later, Parsons blew himself to Hades by accidentally dropping a vial of nitroglycerin. His mother, hearing the news, killed herself with sleeping pills.

Hubbard's bigamous marriage to Sara, which produced a daughter, Alexis, lasted five years. Polly, of course, divorced him. In Sara's later divorce action he was said to be "hopelessly insane." In 1952, at age 41, Hubbard married Mary Sue Whipp, 19, by whom he had four more offspring. When their son Quentin committed suicide, Hubbard's only reaction was one of fury.

It was while Ron was hacking out science fiction that he conceived of dianetics. In this hilarious parody of psychoanalysis, ills are said to spring from "engrams" recorded on an embryo's brain by what it overhears even before it develops ears. After engrams have been erased by "auditing," one becomes a "clear," with perfect memory and robust health. The new science was released to the world in a rousing article by Hubbard in *Astounding Science Fiction,* quickly followed by his book *Dianetics.* The ludicrous therapy exploded into a national craze.

Hubbard discovered that a crude lie detector he called an E-meter was a valuable auditing tool. With its aid, "preclears" were soon recalling not only birth traumas but previous lives. Ron saw at once that by combining dianetics with reincarnation he could fabricate an exotic "religion" capable of raking in millions of tax-free dollars. The Church of Scientology began with recruitment of naive youngsters who really believed Ron had found a "bridge" to transcendent realities that would transform the world. The bridge grew more baroque as dozens of new books by Ron improved the "tech" (auditing technology) and elaborated the mythology.

Hubbard began to annoy the FBI with wild reports of Communist persecution. The Bureau considered him psychotic. On the estate of the Maharajah of Jaipur in Sussex, which Hubbard had purchased, he conducted plant research to "reform the world's food supply." E-meters convinced him that tomatoes scream when sliced. Mary Sue learned she had once been D. H. Lawrence. Ron revealed he had written *The Prince* but "that son-of-a-bitch Machiavelli stole it from me." During an incarnation on another planet, Hubbard said, he had managed a factory that made steel humanoids.

Hubbard, researching the emotions of tomatoes.

Harassed by real and fancied enemies, Hubbard sought escape by buying three ships. From his flagship *Apollo,* resplendent in officer's uniform, he became the naval commander his father had wanted him to be. Pubescent girls in miniskirts and high-heeled boots transmitted the "Commodore's" orders, lit his cigarettes, washed his hair, dressed and undressed him. Hubbard's temper tantrums, abusive language and dictatorial behavior grew more perverse. A young woman aboard shot herself to death.

For years Hubbard's Sea Org, as he called his fleet, wandered around the eastern Atlantic, its Commodore convinced that Nazis and Reds were chasing him. Crude, slapstick efforts were made to take over Rhodesia and Morocco. A proof that Hubbard—now fat, flabby-faced and impotent, with hair to his shoulders and rotting teeth—had come to believe his mythology is that his crew wasted months searching for treasures he recalled having buried in earlier incarnations.

Operation Snow White was Hubbard's secret plan to infiltrate federal offices and steal material related to his church. The plan was carried out by loyal scientologists firmly convinced they were obeying higher laws. In 1977 FBI agents broke into two of Hubbard's headquarters and carted off 48,149 documents. Mary Sue and eight others were convicted, fined and incarcerated.

Ron escaped punishment because no one could find him. For a while he hid out in a Nevada desert where, with no previous experience, he struggled to make fantasy films. The Church was ordered to allocate "unlimited funds" for a campaign to get their leader a Nobel prize. Mary Sue was released after a year in prison, a pathetic woman who to this day, perhaps out of fear, will not talk about the man who abandoned her.

Hubbard seems to have spent most of his hidden years churning out more science fiction. St. Martin's published his 800-page *Battlefield Earth*. Ten even more worthless novels have since been issued by the Church and lavishly advertised. After promoting himself to Admiral, his red hair now white, Hubbard apparently died in Creston, California, on January 24, 1986. He had been living in a motor home parked on a ranch he had recently bought.

This is only the barest sketch of the sordid details in Miller's incredible account. An even more savaging life of Hubbard, by his oldest son in collaboration with Bent Corydon, another scientologist who "blew the Org," has just been published in the United States. *L. Ron Hubbard: Messiah or Madman* (Lyle Stuart, 1987) is carelessly written, poorly organized and documented, with neither bibliography nor index. It does, however, have a useful glossary of Scientology's major neologisms and a chilling chapter on the cult's heartless efforts to destroy Paulette Cooper for writing *The Scandal of Scientology*.

I finished the two books with double amazement. How could a man this crazy have lived to 74 without being committed? How could a science-fiction cult, with such preposterous doctrines and evil morals, continue to flourish? Idiotic religions, I suppose, like old soldiers, never die, and centuries can pass before they finally fade.

Afterword

My review could have been ten times as long. Here are some remarks I had to leave out because of space limitations.

Hubbard claimed to have grown up on the huge cattle ranch of a wealthy grandfather. Fact: his grandfather was a small-town veterinarian.

Hubbard claimed to have been crippled and blinded in World War II. Fact: the war's end found Hubbard in a naval hospital with a long catalogue of complaints, but doctors could find nothing but symptoms. There was not a single war wound. Ron was laying the groundwork for a persistent effort to obtain a high disability pension. The four medals he received from the Navy were of the sort given to everyone in the service. A proof of Ron's later paranoia is that he would petition the Navy for 17 medals he never received but believed he was entitled to.

One of Jack Parson's most insane schemes, during the period that Hubbard assisted him in black magic, was to fulfill one of Aleister Crowley's prophecies by creating a "moonchild." Ron intoned the infernal incantations while Parsons inserted his "wand" into a naked "scarlet woman" who presumably would give birth to the moonchild. Crowley, dying from heroin addiction in England, wrote that he considered this ritual an "idiocy" performed by two "louts."

When Alexis, as a grown woman, tried to visit her father, Hubbard refused to see her. He sent a messenger instead to tell her that Parsons was her real father and that he (Hubbard) had never married Sara but only took her in out of pity because she was pregnant. All lies.

As Scientology began its reptilian creep around the world, it met its strongest resistance in Australia. In 1965 an Australian Board of Inquiry issued a report calling Hubbard a "paranoid schizophrenic" with delusions of grandeur, a compulsion to neologize, and the behavior of a dictator. "Scientology is evil . . . its adherents sadly deluded and often mentally ill. . . . Scientology is a delusional belief system. . . . Its founder, with the merest smattering of knowledge of the various sciences, has built upon the scintilla of his learning a crazy and dangerous edifice."

The Church issued a 48-page reply titled *Kangaroo Court*—a vicious attack on Australians. Ron turned the other cheek. "Well, Australia is young," he said. "In 1943, as the senior naval officer in Northern Australia . . . I helped save them from the Japanese. For the sake of Scientologists there, I will go on helping them."

Of all Hubbard's crazy books, his *History of Man* (1952) is the craziest. It argues that every human body is inhabited by an immortal soul called a "thetan" and a genetic entity (GE) living in the middle of the body. GEs go back to the beginning of life on Earth, but thetans entered our bodies only about 35,000 years ago.

Thetans transfer from body to body. The aim of Scientology is to restore to a person the original powers of his thetan; to raise him to the level of "operating thetan" (OT). Neither Buddha nor Jesus ever rose that high. According to Ron they were only "a shade above clear."

Some engrams trace back to clams and the conflict between their efforts to open and close. Preclears were asked to repeatedly open and shut finger and thumb while visualizing a clam opening and closing. One must be careful not to overdo this exercise, Hubbard warned, or one could develop severe jaw pains. He recalled a preclear who couldn't open his mouth for days. The inability to weep is an engram hangup from a mollusk called the Weeper or Boohoo. When thetans leave a body they report to an "implant station" for a new assignment. Most such stations are on Mars, but there is one right here in the Pyrenees.

It would be hard to invent a more infantile mythology. Evidently Hubbard's idiotic fantasies were designed to appeal to such brilliant Scientology converts as John Travolta (the actor), Sonny Bono (Cher's former husband), that eminent parapsychologist Harold Puthoff, formerly with SRI International, and his top superpsychic Ingo Swann (OT).

33 | Psychic Astronomy

Over the centuries thousands of religious cult leaders, seers, psychics, and spirit mediums have favored the public with exotic revelations about astronomy, especially about life on other planets. A huge volume would be needed to survey these revelations, and a bibliography of books alone would run to hundreds of titles. Herewith a small sampling of the more outrageous examples.

Emanuel Swedenborg (1688-1772), called by Conan Doyle the "first and greatest of modern mediums," began his career in Sweden as a distinguished scientist. In his middle years he began to experience trances, during which he talked endlessly with Jesus, angels, devils, and departed human souls—Moses, Saint Paul, Luther, Calvin, popes and kings, and many others. So convinced was he that the Lord had chosen him to be the Bible's infallible interpreter that he dated the Second Coming as having occurred in 1757, the year his vision of the Last Judgment marked the end of the Christian dispensation and the beginning of what he called the New Jerusalem.

The Church of the New Jerusalem, based on Swedenborg's voluminous Latin writings, emerged in England after his death. Among the thousands of people who admired him were such literary lights as Baudelaire, Goethe, Emerson, Strindberg, Balzac, Blake, and the elder Henry James, father of William. (Of Henry's book *The Secret of Swedenborg,* one critic complained that James had *kept* it.) The young Immanuel Kant was so impressed by Swedenborg's alleged remote vision of a great fire in Stockholm that he wrote a treatise about it. The American parapsychologist Joseph B. Rhine called Swedenborg "the pioneer in the work I am doing."

In a small book, *The Earths in the Universe,* Swedenborg described the inhabitants of all the Sun's planets—except, of course, the then-unknown Uranus, Neptune, and Pluto—as well as those of their moons and of planets in other solar systems. These visions are many cuts below tenth-rate science fiction. All Swedenborg's extraterrestrials are monotonously humanoid.

This was originally published in *Free Inquiry,* Winter 1987/88. Reprinted with permission.

Most of them worship Jesus, who occasionally visits them.

Mercurians see the Sun as huge, but their climate is moderate. The women are small, beautiful, and wear linen caps. The men dress in tight-fitting blue raiment. They have good memories and a vast knowledge of astronomy. Their oxen and cows are like ours, only smaller. Venusians are divided into two races, one "mild and humane," the other a race of cruel, stupid giants. Martians speak in "sonorous" tones, live on fruit, and wear clothes made from the bark of trees. The lower parts of their faces have a black skin color.

Jovians are kind and gentle, living on fertile lands where there are many wild horses. Although grouped into nations, warfare is unknown. Those in warm climates go naked except for loincloths. Their tents and low wooden houses have sides decorated with stars on blue backgrounds. When they eat they sit on the leaves of fig trees with their legs crossed. Curiously, they do not walk erect but "creep along" by using their hands.

Saturnians are "upright, modest" people who live on fruits and seeds. Their planet's rings appear in the sky as "white as snow." Moon people are about the size of our seven-year-olds. Their voices, which sound like "thunder," are produced by expelling air from their abdomens.

In America the leading precursor of the spiritualist movement, which began with the toe-rappings of the Fox sisters, was Andrew Jackson Davis (1826-1910), known as the Seer of Poughkeepsie (New York). He began his crazy career as a passionate Swedenborgian. When Davis was 20 the spirit of Swedenborg allegedly dictated to him, while he was in hypnotic trances, the most famous of his more than 30 books: *Principles of Nature, Her Divine Revelation, and A Voice to Mankind* (1847). My copy is a twelfth printing that runs to 756 pages. The book had more than 30 editions; a later tome, *The Great Harmonia,* is said to have had 40. Conan Doyle considered *Principles of Nature* "one of the most profound and original books of philosophy ever produced." He believed it came from the same "divine source" as the "valour of Joan of Arc, the sanctity of a Theresa . . . [and] the supernatural powers of Daniel Home."

Many familiar ploys of later psychic charlatans were pioneered by Davis. He earned large sums of money by clairvoyantly peering into people's bodies, diagnosing their ailments, and prescribing strange remedies. He performed what magicians call "eyeless vision"—having his eyes covered and reading documents handed to him. Doyle, who devotes a chapter to the Poughkeepsie Seer in his *History of Spiritualism,* was impressed by Davis's prophecies of horseless carriages, airplanes, typewriters, and the growth of spiritualism. Doyle makes much of the fact that Davis was uneducated and read almost nothing, though there is ample evidence that he was a voracious reader of books on philosophy, science, and religion. He founded and edited magazines, spewed forth a steady stream of articles, tracts, and pamphlets, lectured widely, and was more admired by his contemporaries than is any psychic today. But when he died in 1910, at the age of 84, he was running a small bookshop in Boston and his popularity was on the wane.

Davis's visions disclosed that all our planets are inhabited except Uranus, Neptune, and an unnamed ninth planet that occultists later identified as Pluto. The closer a planet is to the sun, the younger its age and the more gross and imperfect its inhabitants. Davis probably got this notion from Swedenborg, though it is also defended by Kant in a 1755 work on cosmology—"a view to be praised for its terrestrial modesty," comments Bertrand Russell in his *History of Western Philosophy,* "but not supported by any scientific grounds." Kant believed, as did Swedenborg, that there are other galaxies like our Milky Way, with planets that also teem with life.

Mercurians, Davis declared, have a "powerful retentive memory," but their ferocious animal nature generates perpetual warfare. "At this moment," he continues, "one of those destructive battles is about being consummated." Bodies of the Mercurians are completely covered with hair, giving them an appearance that "would be to us no more pleasing than that of an orangutan." Two barren deserts, covering almost all the planet's surface, are surrounded by boiling water. Severe winds blowing over the hot water cause great destruction.

Most of Venus, Davis reveals, is covered with water, and its atmosphere is "nearly like that which encompasses the earth." Astronomers then knew little about the rotation of Venus. Davis gives it a period of 23½ hours. It is now known to be 243 days, but let's not waste time on dull errors. Venusians on one side of the planet are kind, but their reasoning powers are weak. On the other side of Venus the inhabitants are giant savages— Davis here follows Swedenborg—who practice torture and cannibalism, sometimes devouring their own children.

Seven pages are devoted to the Martians—small humanoids with blue eyes and yellow faces. Davis confirms Swedenborg's revelation that the lower parts of their faces are dark in color. They are kind folk of high morals, who communicate by facial expressions. "When one conceives a thought . . . he casts his beaming eyes upon the eyes of another; and his sentiments instantly become known."

Of the asteroids that circle the Sun between the orbits of Earth and Mars, Davis writes only about the four then known: Ceres, Pallas, Juno, and Vesta. All bear only plant life, "although an era is now approaching that will call into existence a class of zoophytes." Eventually the four will coalesce into a single planet.

Davis's vision of Jupiter closely parallels Swedenborg's. The Jovians are larger and more beautiful than we are, and much more intelligent. "They do not walk erect, but assume an inclined position, frequently using their hands and arms in walking." Their upper lips are unusually prominent. The giant planet is free of diseases, but the Jovian life span is only about 30 years. Their nations are united in peaceful brotherhood.

The geography of Saturn is "very beautiful," Davis writes, "it being divided into two-thirds water and one-third earth." Its inhabitants represent the highest stage of development in our solar system—even more intelligent, beautiful, and good than the Jovians. Their heads are "very high and long," with brains composed of cortical glands, "each of which attracts and repels, performing systolic and diastolic motions" like those of our heart. I spare the reader Davis's dull descriptions of the lower forms of Saturn's animal life.

Hundreds of psychics and mediums in the nineteenth and early twentieth centuries followed Swedenborg and Davis in their visions of life on the moon and the planets. They drew maps. They sketched pictures of the aliens and their dwellings, their flora and fauna. A few even spoke their languages. These great revelations were uniformly and singularly un-imaginative, as vapid as descriptions of heaven regularly channeled by the dead through the throats and hands of mediums.

Thomas Lake Harris (1823-1906) was born in England, his parents settling in upstate New York when he was five. As a youth of 20 he became an enthusiastic disciple of the Poughkeepsie Seer, but the pair soon had a violent falling-out. Harris founded his own colony of believers, first near Wassaic, New York, later moving to nearby Amenia, then to Brockton, Pennsylvania, and finally to Santa Rosa, California. Harris was in constant communication with good and evil inhabitants of planets in our solar system and elsewhere, as well as with earthly fairies whom he preferred to call "fays." His astronomical revelations were recorded in books of mediocre verse, starting with his *Epic of the Starry Heavens,* which he claimed was dictated to him during a trance. Doyle, in a chapter on Harris in his *Edge of the Unknown,* thinks Harris's poetry is of "high order," even reminding him of Blake and Shelley!

As is so often the case with weird religious cults, there was considerable free love in the colony where Harris was top guru to a motley group of wealthy women and befuddled men. Harris believed that everybody is bisexual, including all the angels and even God. He considered himself united to a spirit called "Lady Lily." Lilistan was Harris's name for heaven. Doyle found his prose books incomprehensible and disliked the way Harris attacked the rising spiritualist movement as satanic in origin. He said he couldn't decide whether Harris was a "megalomaniac ranter endowed with considerable worldly cunning, or one who really had a breath of the divine afflatus."

Laurence Oliphant, a distinguished British diplomat and writer, and his beloved mother, Lady Oliphant, were Harris's most notable converts. Both joined his colony, and for a dozen years obeyed the guru's every whim. Laurence was forced to perform such menial tasks as cleaning stables and selling strawberries at railway stations. After he and his mother became disenchanted, he sued Harris for the return of property he had given the community, and Harris in turn tried to get Oliphant committed to a mental hospital.

Harris claimed to have achieved the seventh and final stage of breath control. This, he said just before his death at age 83, made him young again. Unable to believe their leader truly dead, his followers waited several months before reporting his departure for Lilistan.

Hélène Smith was a young French medium whose spirit controls included Victor Hugo and the eighteenth-century Italian impostor Alessandro Cagliostro. Queen Marie Antoinette was one of her many incarnations. Hélène levitated tables and materialized flowers, fruit, shells filled with wet sand, vases, Chinese money, and other objects. Only a hopeless paranormalist could suppose that these miracles were anything but conscious fraud. She is best known, however, for her frequent out-of-body trips to Mars. Not only did she (or Martians speaking through her) describe the Martians and their culture in boring detail, but she wrote and spoke fluently a bizarre Martian language.

Hélène's Martians were three feet tall, with heads twice as wide as they were high. Both sexes dressed in trousers. Théodore Flournoy, a Swiss psychologist, investigated Hélène's claims, and wrote a book about them, *From India to the Planet Mars* (1900). He concluded that her Martian language was a form of French glossolalia, and that her visits to Mars revealed nothing except what was inside her head.

In the United States Miss Smith had a rival in a medium who was the wife of preacher William Cleveland, but who used the pseudonym Mrs. Smead. About 1900 she began to channel messages from inhabitants of Mars and Jupiter. She sketched maps of the surfaces of both planets, including the famous Martian canals then widely promoted by astronomer Percival Lowell. She drew pictures of Martians, their houses, ships, airplanes, and so on, and began to speak the Martian tongue. The Martian word for man was *mare,* for woman *kare.* Sample sentence: *Moken irin trinen minin aru ti maren inine tine,* which means "Flowers bloom there, many of the great men plant them." According to Mrs. Smead, Jupiter is where Earth's babies go when they die. James Hervey Hyslop, professor of philosophy and psychology at Columbia University and one of the nation's leading spiritualists, authenticated Mrs. Smead's great psychic abilities.

America's most famous "direct voice" medium—a medium through whom discarnates speak in their own natural intonations—was George Valiantine, of Williamsport, Pennsylvania. Hundreds of different voices, in many languages, came through his lips as his controls varied. One control was Confucius. I mention Valiantine because a discarnate named Dr. Barnett fed him the usual dreary information about humanoids on Mars. Valiantine wrote numerous books. His devoted followers were typically undismayed whenever he was caught in fraud. After one séance, when a floating trumpet was found to be warm on the sides and moist at the mouthpiece, Valiantine explained that spirits who spoke through it had to materialize both warm hands and wet lips. A thumbprint of Conan Doyle that Valiantine produced in a séance was discovered to be a print of the medium's right big toe. Supposed fingerprints of other discarnates came from his left big toe, his fingers, and his elbow. Valiantine sobbed when confronted with these facts, though he denied any cheating and said he couldn't understand what had happened. According to Doyle, Valiantine had "exceptional psychic powers."

Among religious leaders who explored planets by way of clairvoyance or out-of-body travels, the most famous was Mrs. Ellen G. White, inspired prophetess of Seventh-Day Adventism. In her younger days she repeatedly went into trance states during which, her followers maintained, she completely stopped breathing. On the basis of her lurid visions, which she said came directly from God, she filled dozens of books with exotic details about biblical events—details missing from the Bible—as well as about doctrines peculiar to the Adventist movement. She also appeared before local church congregations to give what today would be called "psychic readings" about problems facing church members.

One day in 1846, when Ellen was 19, she went into her usual trance and made a quick tour of the solar system. She gave glowing descriptions of Jupiter and its four large moons, Saturn with seven moons, and Uranus with six. She failed to mention Neptune or Pluto, at that time unknown. Ellen insisted she knew nothing about astronomy. Church elder Joseph Bates, an amateur astronomer present during the trance, murmured "This is of the Lord," and instantly abandoned his doubts that Ellen's visions were from on high. Unfortunately, a few years later telescopes spotted additional Jovian and Saturnian moons. The count now stands at 17 or more for Jupiter, and at least 22 for Saturn. Uranus was found to have only four moons, correcting an earlier faulty report of six. A fifth, however, was discovered in 1949, and a dozen or so more were found by Voyager 2 in 1986.

In 1849 Mrs. White wrote: "The Lord has given me a view of other worlds. Wings were given me, and an angel attended me from the city to a place that was bright and glorious. The grass of the place was living green, and the birds there warbled a sweet song. The inhabitants of the place were of all sizes, they were noble, majestic, and lovely. . . . Then I was taken to a world which had seven moons. There I saw good old Enoch, who had been translated."

Was Mrs. White referring to her 1846 vision of Saturn? Seventh-Day Adventist minister J. L. Loughborough, in his *Rise and Progress of the Seventh Day Adventists* (1892), quotes from a letter written by a woman who was present at the 1846 trance:

> Sister White was in very feeble health, and while prayers were offered in her behalf, the Spirit of God rested upon us. We soon noticed that she was insensible to earthly things. This was her first view of the planetary world. After counting aloud the moons of Jupiter, and soon after those of Saturn, she gave a beautiful description of the rings of the latter. She then said, "The inhabitants are a tall, majestic people, so unlike the inhabitants of earth. Sin has never entered here." It was evident from Brother Bates's smiling face that his past doubts in regard to the source of her visions were fast leaving him. We all knew that Captain Bates was a great lover of astronomy, as he would often locate many of the heavenly bodies for our instruction. When Sister White replied to his questions, after the vision, saying that she had never studied or otherwise received knowledge in this direction, he was filled with joy and happiness. He praised God, and expressed his belief that this vision concerning the planets was given that he might never doubt again.

In 1905, when pastor Loughborough revised his book for a new edition, an eighth moon of Saturn had been found. It is hard to believe, but the word *seven* in the above passage was changed to *eight*. Adventists later claimed this was a printer's error! Incidentally, Mrs. White's allegedly God-inspired books are now known to swarm with long passages shamelessly plagiarized from earlier writers. (See *The White Lie,* by ex-Adventist minister Walter T. Rea, 1982, a book with such explosive disclosures that hundreds of Adventist ministers have since abandoned the church. See also Rea's article in *Free Inquiry,* Fall 1984.)

In 1848 Mrs. White had one of her most dramatic visions of the Second Coming. She saw the Holy City of Jerusalem emerge from an open space in the nebula of Orion. Here is how she spoke of the vision in *Early Writings:*

> December 16, 1848, the Lord gave me a view of the shaking of the powers of the heavens. I saw that when the Lord said "heaven," in giving the signs

recorded by Matthew, Mark, and Luke, He meant heaven, and when He said "earth" He meant earth. The powers of heaven are the sun, moon, and stars. They rule in the heavens. The powers of earth are those that rule on the earth. The powers of heaven will be shaken at the voice of God. Then the sun, moon, and stars will be moved out of their places. They will not pass away, but be shaken by the voice of God.

Dark, heavy clouds came up, and clashed against each other. The atmosphere parted and rolled back; then we could look up through the open space in Orion, whence came the voice of God. The holy city will come down through that open space. I saw that the powers of earth are now being shaken, and that events come in order. War, and rumors of war, sword, famine, and pestilence are first to shake the powers of earth, then the voice of God will shake the sun, moon, and stars, and this earth also. I saw that the shaking of the powers in Europe is not, as some teach, the shaking of the powers of heaven, but it is the shaking of the angry nations.

The beautiful nebula of Orion, which appears to the unaided eye as a bright star in Orion's sword, is a cloud of extremely low-density luminous gas that has long fascinated astronomers and poets. Here is Merlin speaking in Tennyson's *Merlin and Vivien:*

> A single misty star
> Which is the second in a line of stars
> That seem a sword beneath a belt of three,
> I never gazed upon it but I dreamt
> Of some vast charm concluded in that star
> To make fame nothing.

Near the nebula's center is a small dark patch that seems surrounded by four stars at the corners of a trapezium. In his book *Astronomy and the Bible* (published by the Adventist church in 1919), Lucas A. Reed devotes his last three chapters to the "vast charm" of this nebula. It is nothing less, says Reed, than the entrance to God's dwelling place. He sees the nebula as shaped like a funnel, wide end toward us, the dark patch marking an open space that leads directly to God's throne. With the familiar combination of assurance and ignorance so characteristic of fundamentalists, Reed writes:

We believe, then, that without question, beyond or through this inapproachable light of Orion lie, somewhere, heaven and the throne of God. Mrs. White, without astronomical knowledge, told something about Orion that no astronomer of that time had yet measured up to. Now, without knowing a thing about her statement, and probably not caring to know, they tell us facts which bear out her statement about an "open space in Orion."

Astronomers still haven't measured up to this claim, and I cannot say how many Adventists today take it seriously. Most of them, I suspect, have never heard it made. Nor do I know how many now take seriously their church's early belief that millions of transparent hailstones are circling Earth, held there in reserve until the last days of Judgment when they will fall as one of the seven last plagues described in the Apocalypse.

You might suppose that in this enlightened age of science no educated person would take psychic astronomy seriously. Alas, our age is far from enlightened. Probably a larger fraction of intelligent people believe in astrology today than did in thirteenth-century Europe. Parapsychologists tell us that remote viewing (clairvoyance) is independent of distance. If so, it is entirely reasonable to suppose that modern psychics can remote-view another planet as easily as they can a distant spot on Earth.

In 1973, when those two indomitable paraphysicists Harold Puthoff and Russell Targ were at Stanford Research Institute, they supervised a psychic probe of Jupiter. Two psychics were involved: the Manhattan Scientologist Ingo Swann, one of the most successful subjects of earlier remote-viewing experiments by Puthoff and Targ; and Harold Sherman, an elderly psychic who runs the ESP Research Associates Foundation in Little Rock, Arkansas. Sherman's *ESP Manual* tells how to forsee the future, enter higher dimensions, communicate with the dead, and record spirit voices. His book *The Dead Are Alive* was praised by Norman Vincent Peale (in a letter that Sherman quotes in his *Fate* magazine advertisements) as "a masterpiece . . . [perhaps] the greatest of all your great books. I hope it will be widely read."

Sherman professes to have seen UFOs in the presence of hundreds of witnesses. "There has to be an intelligence behind them far surpassing our own," he told *Psychic Magazine* in an interview in 1973, "and they must have a purpose in visiting us in greater and greater numbers at this truly momentous time in our troubled earth history." Sherman believes he had precognitive knowledge of UFOs as early as 1946 and 1947, when he wrote two science-fiction yarns for *Amazing Stories:* "The Green Man" and "The Green Man Returns," which told of an extraterrestrial with enormous psi powers who visits Earth in a spaceship. The stories may have given rise to the popular view of "little green men" from other worlds. You can buy a book containing the two stories from Sherman. Here is how he advertises it in *Fate:*

Who knows—in keeping with world-famous Sherman's amazing psychic vision—the peoples of Earth may be on the eve of an actual visitation of Space Beings in a fleet of UFO's! So, why not prepare yourself for this possible future happening by reading about the coming of the Green Men, their appearance to be signalled by the sighting of a Great Light, to herald the bringing to earth of a New Plan of Living designed to bring Peace to Mankind!

Like all contemporary seers, Sherman has a miserable record as a prophet. Consider what he said (in the same interview) about the approach of the comet Kohoutek:

The spectacular advent of Comet Kohoutek is bound to have an immense effect upon man's mind. This issue of your publication is scheduled to be in the hands of your readers at the time that the comet is blazing in our skies.

I predict many will be struck with fear to the point of panic; others will regard this heavenly display as the most spiritual experience of a lifetime, and will look for new metaphysical and religious meanings. I also feel that the physical effects of the comet's passing may influence weather conditions on earth and lead to eventual meteoric showers and other astronomic happenings.

I do not, however, think the comet's appearance is by divine decree. Rather, I may have sensed an event such as this coming toward us in time, its arrival synchronized with a most critical time on earth, which could certainly be now.

Back to the Stanford Research Institute farce. On April 27, 1973, Sherman was at his house near Mountain Home, Arkansas, and Ingo Swann was at SRI in Menlo Park, California. Each simultaneously projected his astral body toward Jupiter in an attempt to preview the results of Pioneer 10, scheduled to fly by the giant planet in December. Each wrote down what he "saw." Swann then culled what the two reports had in common and submitted the results to P and T.

"I was asked to examine the accuracy of their account," Carl Sagan wrote in his book *Other Worlds* (1975). "If their reports had been submitted in my elementary astronomy course, they would have received grades of D. Their reports were not better than what can be extracted from the worst popularizations of planetary astronomy; they were filled with the most obvious misunderstandings both about Jupiter and about Pioneer 10."

Sagan continues:

As just one example, Pioneer 10 was reported shaped like a bullet—perhaps the average man's most naive picture of an interplanetary spacecraft. In fact, interplanetary spacecraft are not streamlined because they do not enter planetary atmospheres. They may have, and Pioneer 10 does have, all sorts of odd and convenient shapes because there is negligible atmospheric resistance in the medium through which they travel.

So far as I know, the results of this puerile probe have not been published, and P and T have had little to say about it. Undaunted, P and T sent the same two psychics to Mercury on March 11, 1974, in advance of the probe by Mariner 10 later that month. This time Swann was at his New York City apartment while Sherman was again in Arkansas. Swann wrote that his astral body was up into space in a few minutes, speeding toward the Sun. Sherman did not describe his own blast-off, though he spoke later of flying around Mercury to get good close-up looks.

The two psychics scored one lucky hit. They reported a magnetic field around Mercury; astronomers had not anticipated this because of the little planet's slow spin. But this success was balanced by huge blunders. Sherman described Mercury's surface as quivering like jelly, with "enormously hot energy bubbles of gigantic size and there seems to be depths or craters from which exude whitish yellow and green vapors." He also saw a "jagged mountain landscape" with "great black bands" that formed an immense "loop-like figure eight some hundreds of miles in width and length."

Although Mercury has an extremely thin atmosphere, there are no clouds. Ingo saw lots of clouds that "come and go very fast and they form, sort of, on the day side of the planet." He also saw primitive life forms: ". . . lichens, sort of water life which attaches to the rocks. . . ." Unfortunately, the Mariner probe showed no water, no clouds, no green vapors, no mountain ranges, no bubbles, no black figure eight, no quivering jelly—only a desolate crater-pocked surface similar to the moon's.

In 1976 Swann and Sherman collaborated on a visit to Mars, but I have been unable to locate information about that voyage. That same year they also remote-viewed a canoe trip by Canadian explorer Dale Graff down the Coppermine River north of the Arctic Circle. Each day Swann and Sherman mailed their impressions to P and T at SRI, and Sherman claimed dramatic success. But, if P and T have published the results of this out-of-body probe, I am unaware of it.

Sherman and Swann did not see any humanoids on Jupiter or Mercury (and presumably none on Mars). Does this mean that today's occultists are less naive than those of the past? I think not. When Davis had his remote visions, little was known about conditions on the planets, and the possibility that they were inhabited could not be ruled out. Even as late as the early years of the flying-saucer mania it was believed that the aliens came from Venus or Mars. Today, new information makes it extremely unlikely that life of any sort exists in the solar system except on Earth, and possibly on Saturn's largest moon, Titan. The aliens have been moved outward to planets orbiting other suns, or up to "higher dimensional planes." Allowing for scientific progress, the astronomical visions of Sherman and

Swann are no less flatulent than the visions of Davis.

Sagan has summed up the results of psychic astronomy crisply in *Other Worlds:*

> There is no evidence that any mystic has done better in guessing the nature of the planets than he could do without his mystical powers but with the ability to read the better elementary astronomy books.

Name Index